A cookbook dedicated to the
Great California Lifestyle

The Great California Lifestyle COOKBOOK

Co-Authors: Elvira Wilkinson, Claudia O'Brien, Margaret Howard, Lawry's Consumer Services Managers

Editor: Sandra Petrov

Photography: Wm. R. Eastabrook/Photography

Layout and Cover Design: Mike Nelson, Mariposa Press

The Great California Lifestyle Cookbook

© Copyright 1981

Published by Lawry's Foods, Inc., 570 West Avenue 26, Los Angeles, Ca. 90065

Printed by Mariposa Press, 2100 Meridian Park Boulevard, Concord, Ca. 94520

Cover Photo: Lawry's California Center, Los Angeles

Outdoor Photography at Lawry's California Center in Los Angeles

Printed in U.S.A.

LIBRARY OF CONGRESS CATALOG CARD NO.: 81-81207
ISBN 0-960634-0-9

TABLE OF CONTENTS

Let Us Introduce Ourselves 2

Presentation...make what you cook look terrific 4

Party Starters...appetizers galore 8

Special Occasion Dishes...featuring entrees, side dishes
    and desserts 28

Lawry's All-Time Favorites...our special collection 42

Mexican Specialties...featuring unusual dishes 56

Salads and More Salads...for all occasions 76

California's Vegetable Bounty...includes light soups 98

Outdoor Cooking and Indoors Too...recipes for the grill
    or the oven 110

Easy Recipes for Young People and Beginning Cooks...
    a starter collection of simple recipes 122

Snacks and Light Meals...cheese and egg dishes,
    sandwiches and hearty soups 134

Just the Two of You...specially created recipes 150

Prepare Ahead Dishes...simplify your life 166

Eating to Feel Great and Look Good...the rewards are yours 180

A Winning Combination...Lawry's products and your microwave . . 181

LET US INTRODUCE OURSELVES....

We are proud of and enthusiastic about our company, its products and our California heritage and decided to share that enthusiasm with you in a cookbook about food and California living.

This book reflects the California lifestyle, which we know possesses a quality all its own. Just exactly what comprises this quality is difficult to put into words (even Californians have differences of opinion), but here are some of our thoughts.

California is the "last frontier," a state composed of people who left their homes and came West seeking adventure, a new experience or a different and more satisfying way of life. They were drawn to California, a place where they would be uninhibited by tradition and where new things were happening.

Lawry's co-founders were among these pioneers. They left the Midwest, as so many have done before and since, and established a new life in California where they and their associated co-workers found an atmosphere conducive to their innovative, entrepreneurial ideas—first in the restaurant business and later in the food industry.

It's this "atmosphere" that draws people like a magnet. California, a relatively young state, is a cosmopolitan mixture of people from all nationalities, all walks of life and all parts of the country and world. In fact, such a large percentage of California's population has emigrated that to be a "native" is rather prestigious indeed!

No commentary on California would be complete without mention of our attractive climate, wonderfully sunny and mild most of the year. And for change of scenery, the beach, mountains and desert are all within easy driving distance.

And speaking of driving, drive we do! It simply comes with the territory. Our involvement with our automobile is undoubtedly why the concept of the drive-in restaurant, now so much a part of our experience, was a California and a Lawry's restaurant innovation.

We have adapted our lifestyle to the wonderful climate and profusion of outdoor beauty. We moved from inside to outside, to a more casual way of life. We tend to be just a bit more colorful and quite a bit less conservative in our attitudes and ways of doing things. Our state's bountiful agricultural resources have influenced our cooking and eating habits, while stimulating creativity and experimentation.

As a company, Lawry's has absorbed this spirit of innovation and used it to try new and different food concepts. For example, we put spice blends in glass jars back when spices were traditionally packaged in tins. We created a product called Spaghetti Sauce Mix and began a whole new concept of cooking with dry seasoning blends in foil envelopes. Lawry's also was first to introduce Taco Seasoning Mix and to make Taco Shells available nationally, making Mexican cooking easy to enjoy at home.

Our involvement with food and dining made it natural to expand this interest to include the wonderful wines of California. In our restaurants* we introduced Americans to carafe table wine service and helped popularize the enjoyment of wine with meals. We pioneered, too, the idea of serving only a single entree and introduced salad as a prominent part of the meal rather than as an afterthought.

Since Californians want to do things in different ways, this sometimes takes us from the sublime to the ridiculous and we are the first to admit it. Restaurants built to look like hot dogs, doughnuts, teacups and even footwear—the latter constructed to recall "the old woman who lived in the shoe"—are part of the "show biz" experience so common to the Coast. But in daring to be different, Californians have come to expect the new and creative in everyday life!

Though this is a place where people came to break with the past, traditions have not been put aside just for the sake of something new. Lawry's California Center, our corporate headquarters, blends tradition and contemporary ideas. The architecture is early California, the site an historical Mexican rancho and the concept, conceived and developed by Lawry's president, a modern version of the hospitality Californians have always been proud to call their own. Lawry's California Center is an experience for visitors from all over the world. It is what one would expect to enjoy in California—beautifully lush gardens and outdoor dining. Added to this are unusual shops featuring the finest of California wines and gifts—all within a 14 acre garden oasis.

What comes as a great surprise to many are the railroad tracks running alongside pretty flowers in the garden and the sudden recognition that, amidst all this beauty, exists an honest-to-goodness factory. Here, thousands come to tour our test kitchens, research laboratories and manufacturing facilities. They see our products being made and learn that they are manufactured, too, at other facilities in the United States, in Canada and around the world. Most people react to Lawry's California Center as though it is their own personal discovery...and we're glad they do!

And so, in this atmosphere, **The Great California Lifestyle Cookbook** was created. This is more than a book of great recipes. Chapters are geared to today's lifestyles, with hints, photos and tips galore, plus serving suggestions to enhance the enjoyment of food. Since we feel that the presentation of food

*A group of restaurants owned and operated by Lawry's Restaurants, Inc.

2

is so important, we devoted a whole chapter on how to make what you cook look terrific.

The recipes include those created by our staff of home economists, some developed in our restaurants and others that originated with a co-worker or friend. Under serving suggestions, recipe titles in *italics* mean that the recipe may be found elsewhere in the book. Just check the index.

All of these recipes have been consumer tested and all reflect Lawry's recipe philosophy—readily available ingredients, moderate cost, easy preparation and a "perceivable difference." At Lawry's we use the latter phrase to describe the extra effort and that element of creativity that gives a recipe, a product or any company activity a special quality.

We designed this book to be enjoyable to read as well as use. We hope you find it so.

The Editors

PRESENTATION
Make What You Cook Look Terrific

Food, beautifully prepared and presented, is artistry. Coordinating colors, shapes and textures calls upon resources often reserved for decorating a room or planning a wardrobe. These same skills are drawn upon, along with culinary know-how, to make your food pleasing to both the eye and the palate.

Very often, in daily cooking, time is too limited for involved planning and attention to every detail. And yet, with just a little extra effort, everyday fare can be presented as attractively as special occasion dishes.

That "extra effort" is a habit well worth cultivating. We all know people who make everything they touch a work of art. We can pass it off by saying, "Oh, well, they're artistic (or creative) or they have more time or money than I do." Maybe so, but while some talent is "natural," anyone can perfect the art of presentation. As we said in the chapter "Easy Recipes for Young and Beginning Cooks," practice is essential. With practice, you can train and develop your eye for color and texture. For example, a simple garnish can make all the difference; a dish, plate, placemat, napkin or tablecloth of just the right color enhances a dish, turning it from ordinary to special.

If you think you can't afford to buy all those "just right" accessories, few can! That's why this chapter is included—to show how, by using what you have on hand and by adding to your current inventory with some carefully planned purchases, you can turn your good cooking into a feast for the eyes.

Use crinkle cutter to make attractive melon slices and wedges.

Score radish in V-shaped sections and remove. Or, with tip of paring knife, cut oval or flower-shaped petals around outside. Place in ice water to open.

The Food

Let's talk first about the food itself which requires love, attention and careful selection.

- Select foods with an eye toward nutrition, color and texture.
- Always use top quality, fresh ingredients. They taste better and look better, too.
- Learn to care for foods properly (washing, handling, storage) to maximize their freshness.

Just as in decorating, think in terms of colors, shapes, textures and sizes when planning a dish or meal. For example, when preparing vegetables for a salad, make sure that they are not all cut the same size, unless it is specified in the recipe. Cobb Salad is one where everything is very finely chopped. Chop some ingredients fine and some coarse. Cubes and julienne shapes add interest and are easy to handle and eat.

Learn to arrange ingredients attractively. A salad can be artistically arranged and tossed at the table, so that everyone can see the beautiful arrangement. The Cartwheel Salad is a good example.

Vegetables, when accompanying an entree, should not be an afterthought. If you're featuring meat sliced in strips, serve round vegetables (peas, carrot chunks, zucchini slices) for shape variation. If the meat is in large pieces, the vegetable choices are greater and could include a vegetable casserole dish. Remember, consider color contrasts too.

Rice or noodles are often served as accompaniments. Snipped parsley, chopped nuts or pimiento add color and texture to these foods which might otherwise be quite uninteresting.

Dip edge of lemon wedge in Lawry's Seasoned Pepper, paprika or finely chopped parsley.

Cut ends of celery in thin strips about 1-inch long. Place in ice water to open and curl.

Dip grapes in beaten egg white and then in super-fine sugar. Shake off excess.

Score cucumber skin, lengthwise, with tines of table fork; slice.

Cut slices of jicama, carrot or turnip with fancy cutter (or use knife and hand-cut design). Secure cut centers with short piece of toothpick.

Cut to center of lime or lemon slice, twist and arrange, with cherry, on toothpick or piece of green onion top.

The Garnish

Garnishes may be as simple or as elaborate as you care to make them. Intricacy, however, requires practice and skill, and perhaps more time than you would care to devote. Simple garnishes are often the most effective anyway.

Select one or two of the ingredients contained in the dish for the garnish. For example, if a recipe uses sliced ripe olives, garnish with whole ripe olives and perhaps another more colorful vegetable like cherry tomatoes or tomato wedges.

Note the variety of garnish ideas illustrated in this chapter and throughout the book.

Setting the Stage

Your kitchen and eating area are the stage. The kitchen should be well organized and carefully planned so that you can be efficient but relaxed while preparing food. Organize your equipment so that it is stored near where it is to be used. Why not store frequently used utensils in crocks or pitchers on the counter or near the stove for accessibility? Spend a day rearranging your kitchen. Store items infrequently used in an out-of-the-way cupboard, give them away, or have a garage sale. We all have excess baggage in the kitchen.

- Invest in good knives and keep them sharp. You don't need many— a paring knife, slicing knife, serrated and a French chopping knife will do nicely. You may want to add a boning knife at some point.
- Have a good solid chopping block or board.
- Adequate lighting in your kitchen is a must, especially over the work area.
- Keep all appliances in top working order.

Everyone's taste differs, so there are no set rules in terms of color schemes or arrangements. You spend a considerable amount of time in the kitchen area, and it should be decorated and arranged to work for you. The eating area, be it in the kitchen or in a dining room, should be a pleasant setting where you and your family can relax and enjoy themselves.

Serving Pieces

While you may wish to stay with a matched set of dishes, serving pieces that complement, rather than match, are usually more interesting and offer greater flexibility

Begin a collection of various bowls, dishes and platters of all sizes. Look for specials and sales. If there is a pottery or dinnerware outlet in your area, so much the better. The prices are good and the selection vast. Antique shops can be good sources for platters, often found there in larger sizes than in standard dinnerware sets.

Be imaginative in your use of serving containers. Such pieces can often serve double duty. A colorful enameled or copper colander makes a handsome holder for vegetable relishes or an equally effective vegetable centerpiece. Turn it upside-down over a cabbage or styrofoam ball, place decoratively cut vegetables on long bamboo skewers and insert through colander holes into the center object. A small bowl of dip often fits nicely on top of the upside-down colander. Use a large, flat-topped candleholder (the type for large, fat candles) as a serving piece for a cheese ball or spread.

Remove pulp and membrane from 1/2 of lemon slice, leaving peel. Curl peel to make design.

Cut strawberry into 3 slices, almost cutting to stem but leaving slices attached. Spread slices to separate.

Score mushroom, at an angle, with tip of sharp knife. Lift out cut sections.

Place strips of carrot, celery, jicama or zucchini through pitted ripe olive.

With a knife, cut small V-shaped sections around edge of lime or lemon slice.

Use crinkle cutter to make this interesting design.

Cut both ends of green onion in thin strips about 1-inch long. Place in ice water to curl.

Cut pickle into 3 slices, almost cutting to end but leaving slices attached. Spread slices to separate.

Skewer an olive, carrot strip and pickle slice on toothpick.

A variety of fruits and vegetables (hollowed-out) make great containers. Green or red bell peppers are perfect for dips or cheese spreads. Eggplants, tomatoes or melons may also be used. Watermelon, used for serving punch or salads, is not a new idea but is one well worth remembering. Pumpkins make wonderful soup tureens. Don't throw these edible containers away; they often can be used as an ingredient.

The Table

California table setting is casual, often with elegant touches. Mood settings, such as Mexican, Oriental or Indian, are fun and imaginative. Often a theme is accomplished with accessories and color rather than complete sets of dishes. A centerpiece can also set the mood. Use inexpensive fabric for tablecloths and napkins—the tablecloth doesn't even have to be hemmed.

Candlelight is flattering to everyone. Candles set a relaxed mood, add subtle fragrance if lightly scented and add color. Arrange in groupings, using different heights and sizes of candles and candleholders. Don't forget votive candles for a special effect, and use lots of them to be dramatic. They're great indoors and outdoors too. If you have a swimming pool, votive candles floating in aluminum foil pans are spectacular. Float large flowers for color and added beauty.

Flower and green plants are a lovely way to decorate a table. Don't be intimidated by "formal" flower arranging. Arranging flowers in natural, informal ways is easy and fun. Don't limit yourself to traditional vases. Use baskets, pitchers, carafes, jars, crocks—anything that works.

Use these ideas to stimulate your thinking and creativity. You will enjoy the rewards of your efforts and find a new outlet for your own individuality.

PARTY STARTERS

The very idea of a party is joyful and brings images of friends and conviviality. Party starters, those wonderful tempting tidbits known as appetizers, hors d'oeuvres or nibbles, can be the most creative kind of cooking. Because many party starter recipes are for little tidbits, they can be artistically prepared, arranged, garnished and presented in a festive manner.

When served prior to a meal, limit appetizers to just a few and keep them light. Crisp raw vegetables (crudités) and a simple dip, for example, are refreshing and enjoyed by everyone. If serving spreads and cheese, provide unusual crackers and breads as accompaniments. Above all, keep appetizers simple and concentrate your energy on the meal. Make it the star!

When the appetizers are the central focus, splurge! Plan a selection that incorporates both hot and cold foods. Arrange the menu so those foods to be served "right from the oven" can be done with ease and a minimum of fuss. Choose foods that can be prepared ahead and frozen or refrigerated. Invest in or borrow appropriate serving pieces. As always when planning a menu, think in terms of shapes, colors, textures and tastes. And think through every detail in advance, right down to serving dishes, utensils, garnishes and traffic flow so there will be no last minute fluster.

Learn the art of garnishing and display in order to make an attractive table. (See "Presentation" chapter.) Establish a reputation for one or two special appetizers. More importantly, establish a reputation for relaxed parties where everything flows, where there is an interesting mixture of people and personalities and where people have fun. And where you have fun too!

Great parties don't just happen. The most successful hosts and hostesses are those who have spent time planning and organizing every detail. A good host or hostess is attentive to the guests at the party. That's why the food and beverages must be so carefully planned that mad dashes to the kitchen are kept to a minimum.

This party starter collection includes many of Lawry's favorites as well as tried and true recipes from individuals known for their great parties. May all of yours be great!

Mexican Blintzes
Guacamole con Cilantro
Eric's Orange Sunrise Special

Mexican Blintzes

A popular favorite served at Lawry's California Center.

1 dozen flour tortillas, 6-inches in diameter
2 pounds Monterey Jack cheese, cut in 3 x 1 x 1/4-inch slices
1/4 cup diced green chiles OR 1 can (4 oz.) whole green chiles, cut in strips
Toothpicks
Salad oil for deep frying
Guacamole con Cilantro

Heat tortillas until warm; place 1 slice of cheese in center. Spread 1/2 teaspoon green chiles or chile strip on cheese. Fold over ends and roll up; secure with toothpick. Repeat with each tortilla. Deep fry blintzes at 400°F., a few at a time, until golden. Drain on paper towels and remove toothpicks. Cut in half crosswise and stand on end to prevent cheese from running out. Serve with Guacamole con Cilantro for dipping. Makes 24 Mexican Blintzes.

Hints:
Prepare and fry early in the day and reheat before serving. Or, assemble, cover with a damp cloth and aluminum foil. Fry just before serving. To serve as an entree, leave whole.

Guacamole con Cilantro

Cilantro, also called Chinese parsley, is fresh coriander. It adds a wonderful distinctive flavor to this favorite Lawry's recipe for Guacamole.

2 medium-size ripe avocados, peeled
1 tablespoon lemon juice
2 medium tomatoes, peeled and finely chopped
1 cup finely chopped onion
1 1/2 teaspoons Lawry's Seasoned Salt
1/2 teaspoon Lawry's Seasoned Pepper
1 tablespoon chopped cilantro

Mash avocados with a fork. Add lemon juice and blend. Add remaining ingredients and combine thoroughly. Makes 3 cups.

Hints:
Dip can be made slightly ahead of time and covered tightly. It will not keep long before it begins to discolor. Best to make only the quantity needed.

Karen's Roquefort Appetizer Bread

Serve this for rave reviews!

1/2 cup Roquefort OR blue cheese dressing
1/4 cup grated Parmesan cheese
4 slices pre-sliced sourdough French bread
Diced green chiles
Parmesan cheese

Combine Roquefort dressing and 1/4 cup Parmesan; mix well. Spread about 2 tablespoons of mixture on each bread slice; top with green chiles. Sprinkle with additional Parmesan cheese. Bake in 450°F. oven 10 to 15 minutes until lightly browned around edges. Cut in "finger" slices and serve hot. Makes about 2 dozen.

Hints:
Use a Roquefort or blue cheese dressing with fairly small chunks of cheese or break up chunks during mixing. This recipe is easily doubled or tripled—just use the above proportions.

Mexican Cheese Ball

A colorful cheese ball to serve on any party occasion. Pack any leftover into a small container and serve with crackers for a snack. A great gift idea, too.

2 ounces roasted and peeled green chiles (1/2 of a 4 oz. can)
1 pound sharp Cheddar cheese
1 jar (2 oz.) pimiento, drained
1 tablespoon tarragon vinegar
1 tablespoon finely chopped parsley
1 teaspoon Lawry's Minced Onion with Green Onion Flakes
3/4 teaspoon tarragon leaves
1/4 teaspoon Lawry's Garlic Powder with Parsley
1/4 teaspoon Lawry's Seasoned Salt
1/4 teaspoon sugar
1 drop green food coloring
4 anchovy fillets, finely minced (optional)
1/2 cup mayonnaise
1/4 cup softened butter

Rinse seeds from chiles. Grind chiles, Cheddar cheese and pimiento, using medium blade on food grinder. Blend vinegar, seasonings, sugar, food coloring and anchovies. Add mayonnaise and butter to chiles, cheese and pimiento. Beat with electric mixer until thoroughly combined. Lightly butter a small mixing bowl. Pack cheese mixture into bowl. Cover and refrigerate until firm. Unmold about 1/2 hour before serving. Makes about 3 cups cheese mixture.

Hints:
Keeps several days in refrigerator. For easier removal from the bowl, line it with plastic wrap, leaving plenty of excess on the ends to cover the mixture once it's packed into the bowl. To remove, pull ends of wrap to loosen and it will slip out easily. Smooth creases on cheese with spatula.

Pastacies

Keep a supply of these delectables in the freezer. Good for snacks, too.

1/2 pound lean ground chuck or round
1 cup chopped fresh mushrooms
1 cup chopped ripe olives
1/4 cup water
1 package (1 1/4 oz.) Lawry's Taco Seasoning Mix
2 packages (10 oz. each) frozen patty shells, thawed
1 egg white, beaten

Combine ground beef, mushrooms, olives, water and Taco Seasoning Mix in a bowl; mix well. Overlap the thawed patty shells and roll into a very thin rectangle. Cut the pastry in 2-inch squares. Place a teaspoon of the meat mixture in center of the square; moisten edges. Fold one edge over to form a triangle and pinch edges together. Brush with egg white. Place on ungreased cookie sheet. Bake in 375°F. oven 15 to 20 minutes or until golden brown. Makes about 4 dozen.

Hints:
To serve as an entree, cut pastry in 4-inch squares and add more filling.

Antipasto on a Skewer

Hints:
Smaller versions may be made by using toothpicks instead of skewers.

1 package Lawry's Italian Salad Dressing Mix, prepared according to package directions
1/2 teaspoon dry mustard
1/2 teaspoon leaf oregano, crushed
8 ounces Mozzarella cheese, sliced in 1/4 x 1/4 x 2-inch strips
4 ounces thinly sliced salami (12 slices)
24 cherry tomatoes
24 pitted olives, black, green or pimiento-stuffed
12 small mushrooms, washed, stems removed
1 package (10 oz.) frozen artichoke hearts, cooked according to package directions
12 (6-inch) bamboo skewers

Pour prepared dressing in 13 x 9 x 2-inch baking dish. Add mustard and oregano; mix well. Wrap each cheese strip in 1 slice salami. Thread meat and vegetables on skewers. Place skewers in dressing and marinate in refrigerator 24 hours, turning several times. Makes 12 skewers.

Bagna Cauda

Hints:
Pronounced "bahn-ya kow-dah."

A traditional, very "garlicky" Italian dip. Serve with plenty of red wine.

2 cans (2 oz. each) anchovy fillets, drained and minced
1 cup butter
1/2 cup olive oil
2 tablespoons Lawry's Garlic Spread Concentrate
Crisp raw vegetables
French bread slices

Combine all ingredients except vegetables and bread. Heat 10 minutes; do not boil or brown. Keep warm in fondue pot or chafing dish. To serve, dip vegetables into mixture, using a slice of French bread to catch drippings. Makes about 2 cups dip.

Chili Apple Dip

Hints:
May be served hot, without the cream cheese, as a meat accompaniment.

A lively flavor combination.

1 tablespoon chopped green bell pepper
1/3 cup sugar
1/3 cup wine vinegar
1/3 to 1/2 cup chili sauce
1 package Lawry's Chili Seasoning Mix
1 apple, finely chopped
1 package (8 oz.) cream cheese, softened

Combine all ingredients, except cream cheese, in a saucepan. Bring to a boil, reduce heat and simmer, covered, 30 minutes. Stir occasionally. Whip cream cheese until fluffy. For a mild dip add 1/3 cup chili mixture; for a more flavorful dip, add 1/2 cup chili mixture. Serve with corn chips or fresh vegetables.

Jiffy Pâté

Serve with thinly sliced rye bread or pumpernickel.

1/2 pound liverwurst
1 package (3 oz.) cream cheese
2 tablespoons mayonnaise
2 tablespoons Lawry's Garlic Spread Concentrate
1/3 cup light cream
1 tablespoon dry sherry
1/4 teaspoon Lawry's Seasoned Salt
1/4 teaspoon Lawry's Seasoned Pepper

Cream together liverwurst, cream cheese, mayonnaise and Garlic Spread. Beat in remaining ingredients. Chill overnight to blend flavors. Makes about 3 cups.

Hints:
Use any leftover for a sandwich filling.

Pollo Pâté

A delightfully easy pâté variation.

3 cups minced cooked chicken (about 3/4 pound)
1 package Lawry's Chicken Taco Seasoning Mix
1 cup water
2 packages (8 oz. each) cream cheese, softened
Minced parsley and pimiento strips, to garnish

Combine chicken, Chicken Taco Seasoning Mix and water in skillet. Bring to a boil, reduce heat and simmer, uncovered, 10 to 12 minutes or until liquid is absorbed; cool thoroughly. Blend chicken mixture with cream cheese. Line a 3-cup mold or bowl with plastic wrap. Pack chicken/cheese mixture into mold. Cover and refrigerate several hours. Turn mold out on serving dish and garnish with minced parsley and pimiento strips. Serve with crackers. Makes 3 cups.

Hints:
Leave plenty of plastic wrap to cover ends of mixture after it's packed in the mold or bowl.

Tuna Tartar Pâté

Easy and delicious.

1 cup large curd cottage cheese
1/4 teaspoon hot pepper sauce
1 tablespoon milk OR light cream
1 package Lawry's Tartar Sauce Mix
1 can (7 oz.) water-packed tuna, drained and flaked

Puree cottage cheese, hot pepper sauce and milk in blender or food processor until smooth. Add Tartar Sauce Mix; process until well blended. Remove to small bowl. Fold in flaked tuna. Pack into small fancy mold or small bowl. Chill at least 3 hours. Unmold, serve with crackers, tortilla chips or melba toast rounds. Makes 2 cups.

Hints:
Add 2 tablespoons chopped green bell pepper, chopped celery and/or chopped pimiento for extra color.

Zucchini Fingers

Hints:
Coat zucchini and refrigerate. Bake just before serving.

Similar to French-fried zucchini but easier to make and just as tasty.

1/2 cup dry unseasoned bread crumbs
3 tablespoons grated Parmesan cheese
2 medium zucchini, cut in 1 x 4-inch strips
1/2 cup Lawry's San Francisco Dressing

Combine bread crumbs with Parmesan cheese. Dip zucchini strips in San Francisco Dressing; then coat with bread crumb mixture. Place on baking sheet and bake in 375°F. oven about 20 minutes or until crisp and golden.

Picante Taco Dip

Hints:
This dip freezes well.

A hearty appetizer, good as a snack or light supper dish.

1 pound ground beef
1 package (1 1/4 oz.) Lawry's Taco Seasoning Mix
1 can (10 1/2 oz.) jalapeño bean dip
1 can (10 oz.) tomatoes, cut up
2 tablespoons diced green chiles
3 tablespoons corn meal
1/2 cup water

Garnishes:
Grated Cheddar cheese
Chopped green onion, including tops
Diced green chiles
Sliced ripe olives
Dairy sour cream
Tortilla chips

Brown ground beef until crumbly; drain fat. Add Taco Seasoning Mix and stir until thoroughly blended. Add bean dip, tomatoes and chiles; blend well. Add corn meal and water; blend well. Bring to a boil, reduce heat and simmer, uncovered, 20 minutes, stirring often. Pour into shallow serving dish and garnish as desired. Arrange tortilla chips around edges and use for dipping. Serve hot. Makes 6 to 8 appetizer servings.

Cheese 'n Bean Dip

1 can (20 1/2 oz.) refried beans
2/3 cup grated Cheddar cheese
1/2 cup chopped onions
1/2 cup Lawry's Chunky Taco Sauce

Combine all ingredients; heat. Serve with tortilla chips. Makes about 4 cups.

California Olive Dip

A mild and tasty dip.

1 can (4 oz.) chopped ripe olives
1 tablespoon Lawry's Minced Onion with Green Onion Flakes
3/4 teaspoon Lawry's Seasoned Salt
1 pint dairy sour cream

Blend all ingredients thoroughly. Cover and refrigerate for at least 2 hours. Makes about 2 1/4 cups.

Lemon Pepper Dip

Hints:
In addition to carrots and celery, try zucchini, green pepper, jicama, broccoli, cauliflower and green onions.

This refreshing dip is a favorite on any occasion.

1 pint dairy sour cream
4 teaspoons Lawry's Lemon Pepper Seasoning

Blend ingredients and refrigerate 1 to 2 hours before serving. Serve with assorted raw vegetables. Makes 1 pint dip.

Clam Dip

1 package (3 oz.) cream cheese, softened
1 cup dairy sour cream
1 can (6 1/2 oz.) minced clams
1/2 teaspoon Lawry's Seasoned Salt
Dash Lawry's Seasoned Pepper
2 teaspoons lemon juice
1 1/2 teaspoons Worcestershire sauce

Blend cream cheese and sour cream. Drain clams and reserve 1 tablespoon clam juice. Add to sour cream mixture. Add remaining ingredients and blend well. Makes 1 1/2 cups.

Lemon Pepper Dip
California Olive Dip
Clam Dip

Delectable Eggplant Dip

Also known as Eggplant Caviar.

1 large eggplant
1/4 cup salad oil
1/4 cup olive oil
1 large onion, finely chopped
1 green bell pepper, finely chopped
1/4 teaspoon Lawry's Garlic Powder with Parsley
2 medium tomatoes, peeled and chopped
2 tablespoons dry sherry
1 1/2 to 2 teaspoons Lawry's Seasoned Salt
1/4 teaspoon Lawry's Seasoned Pepper

Bake eggplant in 400°F. oven about 1 hour or until soft. Remove skin; chop pulp. Heat salad and olive oil. Sauté onion and green pepper. Add Garlic Powder with Parsley, eggplant, tomatoes, sherry, Seasoned Salt and Seasoned Pepper. Bring to a boil, reduce heat and simmer, uncovered, until thickened, about 15 minutes. Stir occasionally. Chill thoroughly. Serve with corn or tortilla chips. Makes about 4 cups.

Hints:
This dip may also be served as a hot or cold relish with meats.

K.T.'s Hot Pepper Cocktail Jelly

This is a colorful and unusual jelly that makes a great appetizer spread and a nice hostess gift.

2 cups chopped green bell peppers
1/2 cup chopped yellow chile peppers OR green serrano chile peppers
1 cup white vinegar
1/4 teaspoon onion juice
4 cups sugar
1/2 cup strained fresh lemon juice
1 bottle (6 oz.) pectin
Green food coloring

Combine green peppers, chile peppers and vinegar in blender; blend until smooth. Pour into saucepan. Add onion juice, sugar and lemon juice. Bring to a boil and stir until sugar dissolves; boil, uncovered, 5 minutes. Remove from heat, add pectin and blend well. Add green food coloring to obtain desired color. Pour into sterilized jars to about 1/4-inch from top. Top jelly with paraffin or simply use screw-on lid. If refrigerated, the jelly will keep indefinitely. There is no need to "can" according to canning procedures. Jelly may not "gel" immediately but will when refrigerated. Makes 4 cups.

Note: For hotter jelly, do not remove seeds in chile peppers before blending.

Hints:
Use Flour Tortilla Dippers for all kinds of spreads and dips. If flour tortillas are not available, serve with melba toast rounds. Jelly is also an excellent accompaniment for meats.

Flour Tortilla Dippers:
Butter flour tortillas, stack and cut in bite-size pieces. Arrange, in single layer, on cookie sheet. Bake in 350°F. oven 15 minutes or until crisp and golden.

To Serve:
Arrange Flour Tortilla Dippers around a bar of softened cream cheese on a platter. Either spoon jelly over cream cheese or serve in separate dish. Guests help themselves by spreading the tortilla with cream cheese and topping with jelly.

Cool as a Cucumber Dip

Cool as a Cucumber Dip

Low in calories and so refreshing.

1 cup plain yogurt
1 cup dairy sour cream
1 cup seeded and grated cucumber, drained
1 teaspoon lemon juice
1/3 teaspoon Lawry's Garlic Powder with Parsley
1 teaspoon Lawry's Seasoned Salt
1/2 teaspoon Lawry's Lemon Pepper Seasoning

Combine all ingredients and chill at least two hours. Serve with crisp fresh vegetables. Makes 2 cups.

Mexican Fondue

Hints:
Be sure to use processed cheese. It melts easily and doesn't separate while standing.

This is always a hit.

2 pounds processed American OR Cheddar cheese, cubed
2 cans (7 oz. each) green chile salsa
1 can (4 oz.) diced green chiles
1 package (1 1/4 oz.) Lawry's Taco Seasoning Mix
1 long loaf sourdough French bread, cubed OR corn chips

Melt cheese in double boiler or fondue pot. Add chile salsa, diced chiles and Taco Seasoning Mix to melted cheese. Let flavors blend at least 1/2 hour before serving. Serve hot with bread cubes or corn chips.

Herbed Mushroom Appetizers

This crustless quiche may be enjoyed as an appetizer or as a brunch or light supper dish.

10 eggs
2 cups cottage cheese
1/2 cup flour
1 teaspoon baking powder
1/2 teaspoon Lawry's Seasoned Salt
1 pound Swiss cheese, grated
1 can (8 oz.) sliced mushrooms, drained
1/2 cup butter, melted
1 tablespoon Lawry's Pinch of Herbs

Preheat oven to 400°F. In a large bowl, beat eggs, cottage cheese, flour, baking powder and Seasoned Salt. Stir in cheese, mushrooms, butter and Pinch of Herbs. Pour in a 13 × 9 × 2-inch glass baking dish. Bake, uncovered, 15 minutes at 400°F.; reduce heat to 350°F. and continue to bake for 35 to 40 minutes. Cut in bite-size squares. Serve hot or cold. Makes about 100 pieces.

Hints:
Use 1 package (9 oz.) frozen artichoke hearts, thawed and quartered or 1 can (4 oz.) diced green chiles in place of mushrooms.

Stuffed Mushrooms

Hints:

Make early in the day and refrigerate until time to bake. To clean mushrooms, wash quickly under running water; do not soak. Wipe with paper towels. Wash just before using or only several hours in advance.

A variety of fillings for beautiful fresh mushrooms.

24 whole large mushrooms, about 1 pound

Wash mushrooms. Remove and finely chop stems to use in one of the fillings listed below. Reserve caps for stuffing.

Garlic Flavor

1 1/2 to 2 tablespoons Lawry's Garlic Spread Concentrate
2 tablespoons butter or margarine
Finely chopped mushroom stems
1 teaspoon Lawry's Seasoned Salt
1/4 teaspoon Lawry's Seasoned Pepper
2 cups fresh bread crumbs
2 tablespoons dry sherry

Melt together Garlic Spread Concentrate and butter; brush mushroom caps with garlic-butter. Sauté mushroom stems in remaining garlic-butter until tender. Add remaining ingredients; sauté an additional 2 minutes, mixing thoroughly. Spoon stuffing into each mushroom cap; place on a baking sheet. Bake in 400°F. oven 10 minutes.

Herb Flavor

1/4 cup dry white wine
1 cup chicken bouillon
1/4 cup finely chopped onion
Finely chopped mushroom stems
2 tablespoons butter
1/2 cup fine dry bread crumbs
1/2 teaspoon Lawry's Pinch of Herbs
Melted butter

Combine wine and bouillon. Sauté onion and mushroom stems in butter until tender. Remove from heat; add liquid, bread crumbs and Pinch of Herbs. Mix thoroughly. Brush mushroom caps with butter and fill. Bake in 400°F. oven 10 to 12 minutes.

Bacon Chicken

Finely chopped mushroom stems
2 tablespoons butter
1 package Lawry's Bacon Salad Dressing Mix
1 tablespoon light cream
1 can (4 3/4 oz.) chicken spread
1/2 cup fresh bread crumbs
Melted butter
Parmesan cheese, optional

Sauté mushroom stems in butter until tender. Add remaining ingredients except cheese and blend thoroughly. Brush mushroom caps with butter, fill and sprinkle with Parmesan cheese, if desired. Bake in 400°F. oven 10 minutes.

California Marinated Mushrooms

1 pound medium-size fresh mushrooms
1 tablespoon Lawry's Garlic Salt
1/4 cup dry red wine
1/2 cup salad oil

Wash mushrooms and remove stems. Combine remaining ingredients. Pour over mushrooms and marinate several hours or overnight in refrigerator. Stir occasionally. Serve on cocktail picks. Makes 20 to 25 mushroom appetizers.

Hints:
For marinade, you may also use your favorite Lawry's oil and vinegar salad dressing.

Marg's Square Meatball Appetizers

A speedy way to make meatballs.

1 pound ground beef
1/2 package Lawry's Meat Loaf Seasoning Mix
1/2 cup water OR vegetable liquid
Sliced ripe olives OR pimiento-stuffed green olives
Cocktail onions
Cheese cubes
Pickle slices

Combine ground beef, Meat Loaf Seasoning Mix and water; mix well. On a jelly-roll pan, shape meat mixture into 8 x 6 x 1/2-inch rectangle. Mark in 1-inch squares. Top each square with choice of olive, onion, cheese or pickle slice. Bake in 400°F. oven 15 minutes. Cut in squares and serve with frilled toothpicks. Makes 4 dozen.

Hints:
Mark meat in squares and freeze. Do not freeze garnishes.

Hot Crabmeat Appetizer

Serve with assorted crisp vegetables, chips or crackers.

1 package (8 oz.) cream cheese, softened
1/2 teaspoon cream-style horseradish
1 tablespoon Lawry's Minced Onion with Green Onion Flakes
1 tablespoon milk OR cream
1/4 teaspoon Lawry's Seasoned Salt
1 can (6 1/2 oz.) crabmeat, drained

Combine all ingredients; mix well. Chill at least 4 hours to blend flavors. Place in ovenproof serving dish. Bake, uncovered, in 375°F. oven 15 minutes. Serve hot or cold. Makes about 1 cup.

Hints:
If left at room temperature too long, these become limp and difficult to handle.

1 head butter lettuce
1 can (4 1/2 oz.) deviled ham
1 tablespoon minced green onion
Dash Lawry's Seasoned Pepper

Tear large outer lettuce leaves in pieces about 4 x 2-inches; crisp in bowl of ice water. Blend ham, green onion and Seasoned Pepper. Pat lettuce dry; spread ham mixture on lettuce leaves. Roll up, place seam side down on serving platter and chill at least 1 hour before serving. Makes 12 appetizers.

Lettuce Roll-Ups

Taco Crescents

Hints:
These freeze well. Reheat in microwave or in 300°F. oven until warm.

A great snack, too.

3/4 pound ground beef
1/2 cup minced onion
1 package (1 1/4 oz.) Lawry's Taco Seasoning Mix
1 can (2 1/4 oz.) minced ripe olives, drained
2 eggs, well beaten
2 packages (8 oz. each) refrigerated crescent dinner rolls
1 cup grated Cheddar cheese
Lawry's Chunky Taco Sauce

Brown meat and onions; drain. Add Taco Seasoning Mix and mix thoroughly; add olives. Set aside. When cool, mix in eggs. Remove rolls from package; separate into triangles. Place some Cheddar cheese on each, then spread with about 1 1/2 tablespoons of meat mixture. Roll up and shape into crescents; place on baking sheet. Bake in 375°F. oven 15 minutes or until golden. Serve with Chunky Taco Sauce for dipping. Makes 16 crescents.

Nachos con Guacamole

Nachos are a favorite California party food.

4 cups tortilla chips
2 cups grated Cheddar cheese
2 medium-size avocados, peeled
1 tablespoon lemon juice
2 medium tomatoes, peeled and finely chopped
1 cup finely chopped onion
1 1/2 teaspoons Lawry's Seasoned Salt
1/2 teaspoon Lawry's Seasoned Pepper
1 tablespoon chopped cilantro, optional
Grated Romano cheese

In a shallow oven-proof dish, spread a layer of tortilla chips (overlapping). Cover chips with grated cheese. Bake in 400°F. oven about 5 minutes or until cheese melts. Meanwhile, to make guacamole, mash avocados with a fork. Add lemon juice; blend well. Add remaining ingredients, except Romano cheese, and combine thoroughly. Mound guacamole in center of heated chips and sprinkle grated Romano cheese over top. Serve immediately. Makes 6 to 8 appetizer servings.

Hints:
Use Lawry's Taco Shells, broken in pieces, for tortilla chips. Be creative with Nachos. Top with chopped green onion, diced green chiles, sliced ripe olives, chopped tomatoes and/or Lawry's Chunky Taco Sauce.

Tallegio

A fried cheese Italian appetizer that is truly wonderful.

1 pound Mozzarella cheese
1 cup fine dry bread crumbs
2 tablespoons Lawry's Pinch of Herbs
1/2 cup flour
2 eggs, beaten
Salad oil for deep frying
1 package Lawry's Extra Rich & Thick Spaghetti Sauce Mix, prepared
    according to package directions

Slice cheese into 1/4 x 1/4 x 4-inch sticks. Mix together bread crumbs and Pinch of Herbs. Roll cheese sticks in flour, dip in eggs, then coat with seasoned bread crumbs. Repeat 2 or 3 times until well coated; refrigerate between dippings. Fry in 2-inches of oil at 400°F. until golden. Drain on paper towels. Serve with Spaghetti Sauce for dipping. Makes about 5 dozen.

Hints:
Refrigerating the cheese sticks between dippings (in the crumb mixture) helps the crumbs to stick and results in a crisp exterior when fried.

Mabel's Curried Almonds

Hints:

Find a source selling nuts in bulk. They're often less expensive and fresher.

These are non-stop nibblers.

2 cups whole blanched almonds
1 tablespoon butter
2 teaspoons Lawry's Seasoned Salt
3/4 teaspoon curry powder

Spread nuts in shallow baking pan; dot with butter. Bake in 350°F. oven 15 to 20 minutes or until golden; stir during baking to coat nuts with butter. Blend Seasoned Salt and curry powder in mortar and pestle; sprinkle over nuts and stir. Return to oven and bake 5 minutes. Spread on paper towels to cool. Makes 2 cups.

Crispy Potato Skins

Hints:

Use Lawry's Garlic Salt or Pinch of Herbs for flavor variation. Top skins with grated Parmesan cheese before baking, if desired. Use potato skins from Sally's Baked Potato Casserole (see page 102).

Serve alone or with a bowl of dairy sour cream for dipping.

Skins from 5 baked potatoes, cut in half
Lawry's Seasoned Salt
Lawry's Seasoned Pepper
Melted butter

Cut each potato skin half into fourths. Place on cookie sheet; sprinkle with Seasoned Salt and Seasoned Pepper. Drizzle with melted butter. Bake in 350°F. oven until crisp, about 7 to 10 minutes. Makes 40.

Mexican Meatballs

Hints:

Freeze before or after baking. Cut down on the green chiles for a milder version.

1 package (1 1/4 oz.) Lawry's Taco Seasoning Mix
1/3 cup water
1/3 cup diced green chiles
1 pound ground beef
Lawry's Chunky Taco Sauce, optional

Combine Taco Seasoning Mix and water. Add green chiles and ground beef; mix well. Form in 1-inch meatballs. Bake on ungreased jelly-roll pan in 350°F. oven 20 minutes. Serve alone or with Chunky Taco Sauce for dipping. Makes 40 meatballs.

Cheese 'n Bean Dip
Boursin Cheese Spreads

Herb Cheese Spread

This herb cheese spread mellows and will keep well about 2 to 3 weeks if covered tightly.

3 ounces cream cheese
2 teaspoons Lawry's Pinch of Herbs
1 teaspoon dry mustard
1/4 cup sherry wine
1/4 cup salad oil
1 pound grated Monterey Jack OR Cheddar cheese

Combine cream cheese, Pinch of Herbs and mustard. Add sherry and salad oil and blend well. Fold in grated cheese. Pack mixture into small bowl, cover and refrigerate several hours. Makes about 3 cups.

Hints:
If using Cheddar cheese, add 1 to 2 tablespoons more sherry for a creamy, spreadable consistency.

Hints:

For optimum spreading consistency, let spread stand at room temperature at least 1/2 hour before serving.

These are wonderful hostess and holiday gifts.

11 ounces cream cheese
1/3 cup dairy sour cream OR 2 tablespoons light cream

Cream together and season with any one of the following combinations:

Herbed Cheese

1/4 teaspoon Lawry's Pinch of Herbs
1/4 teaspoon Lawry's Seasoned Salt
1/4 teaspoon paprika

Garlic-Cheese

1 teaspoon Lawry's Garlic Powder with Parsley
1/2 teaspoon Lawry's Seasoned Salt

Peppery Cheese

1/2 teaspoon Lawry's Seasoned Salt
1/2 teaspoon Lawry's Seasoned Pepper

Blend thoroughly; form into desired shape or pack in container. Refrigerate several hours or overnight. Serve with assorted crackers. Makes 1 1/2 to 2 cups.

Hints:

Be sure tortellini tips are pressed together—moistening with egg white helps.

Made with won ton skins, this version is quick and easy.

1 cup finely chopped, cooked chicken
1/4 cup grated Parmesan cheese
1 egg, separated
1/8 teaspoon grated lemon peel
1/8 teaspoon ground nutmeg
1 teaspoon Lawry's Lemon Pepper Seasoning
Lawry's Seasoned Salt, to taste
1 package (12 oz.) won ton skins, small size (3-inch square)
6 to 8 quarts boiling, salted water
1 package (1 1/2 oz.) Lawry's Spaghetti Sauce Mix with Imported Mushrooms, prepared according to package directions

Mix together chicken, Parmesan cheese, 1 egg yolk, lemon peel, nutmeg and Lemon Pepper Seasoning; blend well. Add Seasoned Salt to taste. Cut a 2-inch diameter circle in each won ton skin. Place 1/4 teaspoon filling in center of circle. Moisten edges with beaten egg white; fold in half and press edges together. Shape into little rings by stretching the tips of each half circle slightly and wrapping the ring around index finger. Gently press tips together. Drop them into boiling water and cook about 8 minutes or until tender. Do a few at a time, so they don't stick together. Drain and serve at once topped with Spaghetti Sauce. Makes approximately 45 tortellini.

Glistening Champagne Punch

This one packs a "punch."

1 1/2 cups sugar
2 cups freshly squeezed lemon juice
2 bottles (750 ml. each) dry white wine, chilled
1 bottle (750 ml.) champagne, chilled
1/2 cup brandy
1/2 cup orange-flavored liqueur (optional)
1 lemon, thinly sliced
1 1/2 cups sliced strawberries, fresh or frozen

Stir sugar into lemon juice until dissolved; chill thoroughly. Just before serving, pour over block of ice in punch bowl. Gently stir in white wine and champagne; add brandy and orange-flavored liqueur, if desired. Garnish with lemon slices and sliced strawberries. Makes 3 1/4 quarts.

Hints:

To make a clear ice mold or ring, use club soda instead of water. If pieces of fruit are to be added to the mold, freeze a layer of soda until almost set, add fruit and freeze again. Add remaining club soda and freeze until firm.

Julie's Sangria

Julie's Sangria

Hints:

Add sugar according to taste preference but don't make it too sweet. Authentic Sangria is full-bodied and fruity but not very sweet.

Sangria is a sensational drink for parties or any time.

2 bottles (750 ml. each) red wine
3 ounces brandy
3 ounces orange-flavored liqueur
Peel (cut in spiral) of 2 lemons and 2 oranges
1 orange, sliced
1 cup fresh or frozen peaches
Sugar to taste
1/2 to 3/4 bottle club soda

Combine all ingredients except club soda; chill several hours to blend flavors. Add club soda before serving. Makes about 2 quarts.

Sober Sangria

Hints:

Garnish with lemon or orange slices.

Another refreshing party beverage.

2 cups cranberry juice, chilled
1 can (6 oz.) frozen orange juice concentrate, prepared according to package directions
2 tablespoons lemon juice
1 quart raspberry OR strawberry soda, chilled

Combine cranberry, orange and lemon juices. At serving time, add chilled raspberry soda. Makes about 2 quarts.

Eric's Orange Sunrise Special

This non-alcoholic drink is as beautiful as a sunrise.

8 ounces orange juice
2 tablespoons grenadine syrup
Crushed ice OR ice cubes, optional
Maraschino cherry OR orange slice

Pour orange juice in tall serving glass; add grenadine and ice, if desired. Garnish with cherry or orange slice and serve with swizzle stick for stirring. Makes 1 serving.

Yeteve's Summer Swizzle

Light and refreshing any time of year.

Ice cubes
2 ounces dry Vermouth
6 to 8 ounces lemon-lime soda
Lemon twist or slice

Fill 8-ounce glass with ice cubes. Pour Vermouth over ice and fill glass with soda. Stir and garnish with twist or slice of lemon. Makes 1 serving.

Special Occasion Dishes

Food has long been considered a symbol of love and hospitality. Mothers traditionally have shown love for their family with food. Visitors were never received nor bid goodbye without first being fed or, at the very least, offered some tempting morsel of refreshment.

Today's lifestyles have changed those traditions somewhat. We have learned other acceptable ways to give and show love. Hospitality is no longer directly linked to the larder. Still, many special occasions in our lives involve some type of food or drink, be it sharing a special wine, a holiday celebration or brunch, lunch or dinner with family and friends.

There are times when we all have an urge to be especially creative and spend extra time in the kitchen. There are also times when we choose to spend a bit more money on a meal or have a special food treat. Everyone has his special occasion dishes—a family favorite, a traditional dish for certain occasions or an often requested dish to share with friends.

The special occasion dishes on the following pages will give you special results. They include entrees, side dishes and desserts. (For vegetables and salad accompaniments, refer to the appropriate chapters.) Some involve a little extra work, some involve a bit more time, while others are more extravagant in terms of cost. The recipes tend to be more dramatic than those normally served for everyday fare. All are designed to bring raves, an added bonus for the cook who makes an extra effort to make an important occasion extra special.

Cioppino

Cioppino

(Italian Fish Stew)

Serving Suggestions:
Warm sourdough or French bread, *Baltic Babushka.*

Hints:
There are several methods for cleaning clams and they all work. First scrub shells. Then let clams stand in cold salted water (1/3 cup salt to 1 gallon water) or in corn meal and water (same proportions as salt) for 15 to 20 minutes. Change water at least twice. Or let stand in plain cold water and change the water several times.

Prepare a day in advance as the flavor "blooms" the second day. For a less expensive version, omit lobster and use more white fish.

1/4 cup olive oil
1 medium onion, finely chopped
2 cloves garlic, crushed
1 can (1 lb. 12 oz.) tomatoes
2 cans (8 oz. each) tomato sauce
2 packages (1 1/2 oz. each) Lawry's Spaghetti Sauce Mix with Imported Mushrooms OR 1 package (3 oz.) Lawry's Economy Size Spaghetti Sauce Mix with Imported Mushrooms
1 teaspoon Lawry's Seasoned Salt
1/4 teaspoon Lawry's Seasoned Pepper
2 cups water
1 cup dry white wine
1 1/2 pounds white fish, such as halibut, cut in large chunks
1 pound raw shrimp, shelled and deveined
4 uncooked lobster tails (about 6 oz. each) fins and soft undershell removed and cut in large chunks, shell and all
1 dozen clams

Heat oil in large Dutch oven or kettle. Add onion and garlic and sauté until tender. Add tomatoes, tomato sauce, Spaghetti Sauce Mix, Seasoned Salt, Seasoned Pepper and water. Bring to a boil, reduce heat and simmer, uncovered, 30 minutes, stirring occasionally. Add wine, fish, shrimp, lobster and clams. Cover and simmer about 15 minutes, stirring occasionally. (Clam shells will open during cooking.) Serve in large soup bowls. Makes 4 quarts—about 8 servings.

Fruit Stuffed Pork Roast

Serving Suggestions:
Eardley's Spoon Bread, cooked green vegetables or tossed green salad.

Hints:
Use a combination of apricots, peaches and prunes for the dried fruit mixture. Use a bed of carrots and celery as a substitute for a roasting rack. The vegetables keep the meat out of the pan drippings and add flavor.

2 cups dried mixed fruit
1 cup dry sherry
4 to 5 pound boned and rolled pork loin OR shoulder roast
1 package Lawry's Pot Roast Seasoning Mix

Marinate dried fruit in sherry 1 to 2 hours. Drain and reserve sherry. Untie roast and stuff with fruit; retie. Rub roast thoroughly with Pot Roast Seasoning Mix. Place roast on a rack in shallow roasting pan. Insert meat thermometer in center of roast if desired. Place roast in 400°F. oven 30 minutes. Reduce heat to 325°F. and continue roasting approximately 30 minutes per pound or 170°F. on meat thermometer. Baste with sherry during the last 30 minutes of roasting time. Let stand 10 minutes before slicing. Makes 8 servings.

Beef Ragout

Another term for stew, this ragout is something special.

3 tablespoons salad oil
2 pounds beef stew meat, cut in 1 1/2-inch cubes
1 cup chopped onion
1 cup chopped celery
1/2 cup chopped green bell pepper
2 cloves garlic, crushed
1 can (10 1/2 oz.) condensed beef broth
1/2 cup water
1 package Lawry's Extra Rich & Thick Spaghetti Sauce Mix
1 can (1 lb.) tomatoes
2 tablespoons chopped parsley
2 teaspoons paprika
2 teaspoons Worcestershire sauce

In 2 tablespoons oil, brown a few cubes of beef at a time in Dutch oven. Remove as browned. Add remaining oil as needed. Sauté onion, celery, green pepper and garlic until tender; drain excess fat. Add beef broth, water, Extra Rich & Thick Spaghetti Sauce Mix, tomatoes, parsley, paprika, Worcestershire and beef. Break up tomatoes with spoon. Bring to a boil, reduce heat and simmer, covered, 1 hour. Uncover and simmer an additional 45 minutes. Makes 6 to 8 servings.

Serving Suggestions:
Cooked rice or broad egg noodles, vegetable relishes.

Hints:
Make ahead and freeze or refrigerate. An easy recipe to double for a crowd.

Zucchini Sausage Lasagna

A wonderful lasagna without the noodles.

1 pound sweet Italian sausage, skinned and crumbled
4 ounces fresh mushrooms, sliced (about 1 1/2 cups)
1 package Lawry's Extra Rich & Thick Spaghetti Sauce Mix
1 can (1 lb.) tomatoes, cut up
1 can (8 oz.) tomato sauce
1/2 cup water
1 teaspoon Lawry's Seasoned Salt
2 pounds zucchini, sliced OR eggplant, cubed
8 ounces Mozzarella cheese, thinly sliced
1/4 cup grated Parmesan cheese

Brown sausage and mushrooms; drain fat. Add Extra Rich & Thick Spaghetti Sauce Mix, tomatoes, tomato sauce, water and Seasoned Salt; blend thoroughly. Bring to a boil, reduce heat and simmer, uncovered, 10 minutes. Meanwhile, cook zucchini or eggplant in boiling water for 5 minutes; drain. Spread 1/3 of meat mixture in the bottom of a 2-quart casserole. Add 1/2 of zucchini and 1/2 of Mozzarella. Repeat procedure ending with meat mixture. Top with Parmesan cheese and bake, uncovered, in 350°F. oven 30 minutes. Makes 6 to 8 servings.

Serving Suggestions:
Marinated Vegetables Italia, Spumoni.

Hints:
Make this dish (or make 2 or 3) ahead and freeze. Thaw before baking.

Arista Fettina Marinato

(Marinated Pork Slices with Avocado)

Serving Suggestions:
Creamy Peanut Soup, White Rice with Artichokes, Flaming Peaches.

Hints:
To prepare avocados, cut into halves lengthwise. Do not remove skin yet. Rotate halves to separate. Strike seed with sharp edge of knife, twist and lift out. Peel and cut.

An unusual and elegant dish.

2 to 3 pound boneless pork roast
Lawry's Seasoned Salt
Lawry's Seasoned Pepper
1 recipe Lemon Garlic Dressing (see page 93)
2 avocados

Rub roast with Seasoned Salt and Seasoned Pepper. Place on a rack in roasting pan and roast in a 325°F. oven 30 minutes per pound or until well done (170°F. on meat thermometer). Let stand 10 minutes; slice fairly thin. Trim off excess fat. Arrange slices, slightly overlapping, in shallow serving platter. Pour 3/4 of Lemon Garlic Dressing over meat; let stand at room temperature 2 hours. Peel and thickly slice avocados lengthwise; arrange around meat. Pour remaining dressing over avocados. Serve at room temperature. Makes 4 to 6 servings.

Sally's Shrimp in Curried Mayonnaise

Serving Suggestions:
Serve as a first course or salad.

Hints:
Substitute chicken or turkey for shrimp.

The combined flavors of curry, papaya and shrimp are divine.

1/2 cup mayonnaise
3/4 teaspoon curry powder
1/2 teaspoon Lawry's Seasoned Salt
1 tablespoon lemon juice
1/2 pound cooked baby shrimp
2 papayas, cut in half, seeded and peeled
Lettuce leaves, radish slices and ripe olives

Combine mayonnaise, curry powder, Seasoned Salt and lemon juice; mix well. Fold in shrimp and chill 1 to 2 hours to blend flavors. Spoon into papaya halves; serve on lettuce leaves. Garnish around papaya halves with radish slices and ripe olives. Makes 4 servings.

Lemon Lettuce Steak

Serving Suggestions:
Cooked rice, *Tomato and Mushroom Salad.*

Hints:
Do the cutting and chopping ahead. Arrange vegetables attractively on a platter and cook (in skillet or wok) just before serving. Invest in some sturdy wooden chopsticks to use for stir-frying.

The lettuce is cooked ever so slightly in this quick, colorful dish.

1 pound round steak, sliced in strips about 1/8-inch thick
1 package Lawry's Tenderizing Beef Marinade, prepared according to package directions
3 bacon slices, chopped
1 head lettuce, cut crosswise in 1/2-inch strips
3 green onions including tops, thinly sliced
6 thin lemon slices (with peel), cut in quarters

Marinate steak strips in Tenderizing Beef Marinade for 5 to 7 minutes **only**. Cook bacon until crisp; remove with slotted spoon. Remove steak strips from marinade and immediately sauté in bacon drippings. Add lettuce, 1/2 of onions, bacon and lemon; sauté quickly. Remove to serving dish and sprinkle with remaining green onions. Makes 4 to 6 servings.

Emilie's Mexican Chicken Kiev

This is an easy way to make a deliciously different Chicken Kiev.

4 whole chicken breasts, halved, boned and skin removed
1 can (7 oz.) whole green chiles, rinsed and seeds removed
1/4 pound Monterey Jack cheese
1/2 cup fine dry bread crumbs
1/4 cup grated Parmesan cheese
1/2 to 1 teaspoon chili powder
1/2 teaspoon Lawry's Garlic Salt
1/4 teaspoon cumin
1/4 teaspoon Lawry's Seasoned Pepper
6 tablespoons butter, melted

Flatten chicken breasts with meat mallet to 1/4-inch thick. Cut chiles and Monterey Jack cheese in 8 pieces. Place a piece of chile and cheese on each chicken breast; roll, tucking in sides. Combine remaining ingredients except butter. Dip each chicken bundle in butter, then crumbs. Place bundles, seam side down, in 13 x 9 x 2-inch baking dish without sides touching. Drizzle with remaining butter. Refrigerate at least 1/2 hour. Bake, uncovered, in 400°F. oven 20 to 25 minutes. Makes 4 servings.

Serving Suggestions:
Fiesta Rice, Mexican Dinner Salad, Mixed Fruit.

Hints:
No need to close the chicken bundles with skewers; the filling will stay inside if you roll tightly and carefully. May be made the day ahead and baked just before serving.

Pasta Verdura

An unusual pasta dish featuring a vegetable sauce.

1/2 cup olive oil
1 medium onion, thinly sliced
4 zucchini, cut in 1/2-inch slices
1 small eggplant, pared and cut in 1-inch squares
1 medium green bell pepper, cut in 1-inch squares
3 medium tomatoes, cut in thin wedges
1 package (1 1/2 oz.) Lawry's Spaghetti Sauce Mix with Imported Mushrooms
1 can (8 oz.) tomato sauce
1 1/2 cups water
Lawry's Seasoned Salt, to taste
1/2 pound noodles or spaghetti, cooked, drained and buttered
1/4 pound Mozzarella cheese, grated

Heat 2 tablespoons oil and sauté onion. Add remaining oil and sauté zucchini, eggplant, green pepper and tomatoes. Add Spaghetti Sauce Mix with Imported Mushrooms, tomato sauce and water. Bring to a boil, reduce heat and simmer, uncovered, about 25 minutes. Add Seasoned Salt. To serve, top noodles with sauce. Sprinkle with cheese and serve immediately. Makes 6 servings.

Serving Suggestions:
Tossed green salad, *Lawry's Garlic Bread.*

Hints:
Buy or make homemade noodles. Italian markets sometimes have homemade pasta available.

Chicken Jerusalem

Serving Suggestions:
Sally's Shrimp in Curried Mayonnaise, Spring Asparagus Salad.

Hints:
May be frozen. When browning chicken or meats, place a square of paper towel over skillet or Dutch oven to absorb spatters. Be careful not to let paper towel extend very far over the sides.

A classic chicken dish. The word Jerusalem indicates the presence of artichokes.

2 whole chicken breasts, halved
3 tablespoons salad oil
1/2 cup dry white wine
1 can (4 oz.) sliced mushrooms, drained
1 can (8 1/2 oz.) artichoke hearts, drained OR 1 package (9 oz.) frozen artichoke hearts
2 tablespoons flour
1/2 teaspoon Lawry's Seasoned Salt
1/4 teaspoon Lawry's Seasoned Pepper
1/2 cup milk
Dash paprika

In large skillet, brown chicken on all sides in oil; drain fat. Add wine, mushrooms and artichokes. Bring to a boil, reduce heat and simmer, covered, 20 minutes. Remove chicken, mushrooms and artichokes to heated platter. Stir flour, Seasoned Salt and Seasoned Pepper into pan juices; heat for 2 to 3 minutes. Blend in milk; stir until thickened. Pour sauce over chicken and sprinkle with paprika. Makes 4 servings.

Chicken Jerusalem

Stuffed Baked Fish

This is a spectacular and delicious entree.

Lawry's Seasoned Salt
1 whole fish (red snapper, sea bass, trout or salmon – 3 to 4 lbs.
  dressed weight) boned and with cavity
1 recipe Savory Bread Stuffing
1/4 cup melted butter OR margarine
1 recipe Gourmet Tomato Sauce

Sprinkle Seasoned Salt in cavity of fish. Pack Savory Bread Stuffing lightly in cavity. Fasten openings with picks or skewers and lace with string. Place fish in greased shallow baking pan. Brush with melted butter and sprinkle with Seasoned Salt. Bake, uncovered, in 350°F. oven about 1 hour or until fish flakes easily. Serve with Gourmet Tomato Sauce. Makes 8 servings.

Savory Bread Stuffing

1/4 cup butter OR margarine
1/2 cup finely chopped onions
1/4 cup finely chopped parsley
1 cup shredded carrots
2 teaspoons Lawry's Seasoned Salt
4 cups small dry bread cubes

In a skillet, melt butter and sauté onions. Place bread cubes in a bowl. Add sautéed onions and remaining ingredients. Toss until blended. Makes 4 cups.

Gourmet Tomato Sauce

1 package (1 1/2 oz.) Lawry's Spaghetti Sauce Mix with Imported
  Mushrooms
1 can (6 oz.) tomato paste
2 cups water
3 tablespoons olive OR salad oil
1/4 cup red wine

Blend Spaghetti Sauce Mix, tomato paste, water and olive oil in saucepan. Bring to a boil, reduce heat and simmer, uncovered, 25 minutes. Add wine and simmer a few minutes more. Makes 2 1/4 cups.

Serving Suggestions:

Lemon Broccoletti, Limelight Salad Marcus.

Hints:

Prepare sauce and stuffing ahead. Fish may be stuffed and refrigerated a few hours before baking. For a stuffing variation use 4 cups total shredded carrot and zucchini plus 1 cup chopped spinach in place of bread cubes. Bake extra stuffing in a small casserole dish.

Paella Valenciana

Serve this classic Spanish dish in a paella pan or a shallow, curved platter.

Serving Suggestions:
Spiked Tomato-Beef Consomme, Cucumber Sour Cream Mousse.

Hints:
If chorizo (Mexican sausage) is not available use a mild Italian version. Make ahead but do not add peas until reheating so they will be bright green and colorful.

2 1/2 pounds chicken breasts, thighs and legs
2 tablespoons salad oil
2 tablespoons olive oil
2 cloves garlic, crushed
1 tablespoon Lawry's Seasoned Salt
1 package Lawry's Mexican Rice Seasoning Mix
5 cups water
2 cups uncooked long-grain rice, toasted
4 ounces chorizo, crumbled
2 cans (7 oz. each) minced clams
2 cups boiling water
24 large fresh shrimp, shelled and deveined
1 can (7 oz.) pitted ripe olives, drained
1 package (10 oz.) frozen peas, thawed

Cut chicken breasts in 4 pieces. Heat oils in a skillet. Brown all chicken pieces until golden; remove from skillet. Combine garlic and Seasoned Salt and blend to make paste. In an 8 to 10-quart Dutch oven, combine Mexican Rice Seasoning Mix, water, rice, chorizo, clams and garlic-Seasoned Salt paste. Blend well and add chicken. Bring to a boil, reduce heat, cover and simmer 1 hour. Stir occasionally. Add boiling water and shrimp. Cover and continue simmering 10 to 15 minutes or until shrimp are tender. Add olives and peas and simmer 5 to 10 minutes longer. Makes about 12 servings.

Pork Chops Olivette

A simple chop dish but different enough for special occasions.

Serving Suggestions:
Potatoes Au Gratin, Orange and Red Onion Salad.

Hints:
Salad dressings make excellent marinades for meat, fish and poultry. Chops may be marinated overnight in the refrigerator.

1 package Lawry's Caesar Salad Dressing Mix
1/2 cup dry white wine
1/2 cup olive oil
1/2 cup sliced green onions
1/2 cup sliced pimiento-stuffed green olives
4 large loin pork chops, about 1-inch thick

Combine Caesar Salad Dressing Mix and wine in a jar; shake well. Add olive oil and shake again. Add onions and olives to dressing. Arrange pork chops in shallow dish. Marinate in refrigerator about 2 hours, turning chops frequently. Remove chops from marinade and brown in skillet on both sides; add marinade. Bring to a boil, reduce heat, cover and simmer 45 minutes or until chops are done. Arrange chops on serving platter; with slotted spoon, remove olives and onions from marinade and place on chops. Makes 4 servings.

Peach 'n Chicken Teriyaki

Colorful, quick and easy, this dish is a good "last-minute company" recipe.

2 1/2 to 3 pounds chicken parts, skin removed
1 bottle (8 oz.) Lawry's Teriyaki Barbecue Marinade
2 tablespoons salad oil
1 can (4 oz.) button mushrooms, drained
1/2 green bell pepper, sliced in thin strips
6 fresh peaches, peeled OR 12 canned peach halves
1 can (20 oz.) pineapple chunks, drained
2 tablespoons toasted sesame seeds

Marinate chicken in Teriyaki Barbecue Marinade for 1 to 2 hours in the refrigerator, turning several times. In large deep skillet, sauté chicken in oil until browned, about 10 minutes. Add marinade, cover and cook on low heat for 20 minutes, turning and basting occasionally. Stir in mushrooms and green pepper. Add peaches and baste with marinade. Top with pineapple and sesame seeds. Cover and heat thoroughly. Makes 6 servings.

Serving Suggestions:
Cooked rice, *Tangy Bean Sprout Toss.*

Hints:
If desired, marinate chicken overnight for more teriyaki flavor. Chicken may be cooked ahead, arranged on a serving platter and refrigerated. Add fruit and vegetables, cover and heat in the oven or microwave before serving.

Peach 'n Chicken Teriyaki

Fettuccine

An Italian favorite.

8 ounces medium width egg noodles
1/4 cup butter
1/4 cup Lawry's Garlic Spread Concentrate
1/2 cup light cream
1/2 cup freshly grated Parmesan OR Romano cheese
2 tablespoons chopped parsley

Cook noodles in unsalted water according to package directions; drain. Melt butter and Garlic Spread Concentrate. Add melted butter-garlic spread mixture, cream and grated cheese to hot noodles. Toss lightly. Serve with a light sprinkle of additional grated cheese and garnish with chopped parsley. Makes 4 servings.

Serving Suggestions:
Serve as a side dish or as an entree with a tossed green salad.

Hints:
Substitute 1/4 teaspoon Lawry's Garlic Powder with Parsley for 1/4 cup Lawry's Garlic Spread Concentrate. Fettuccine noodles are available in Italian markets.

Eardley's Spoon Bread

Serving Suggestions:
Serve in place of potatoes, rice or bread for breakfast, lunch or dinner.

Hints:
Delicious cold or reheated. To reheat, sauté in butter.

A traditional Southern side dish but a favorite everywhere.

6 bacon slices
1 1/2 cups yellow corn meal
1 teaspoon Lawry's Seasoned Salt
4 1/2 cups milk
1/2 cup butter or margarine, melted
4 large eggs, well beaten
1 tablespoon honey

Cook bacon until crisp; drain and crumble. Set aside. Combine corn meal, Seasoned Salt and 1 1/2 cups milk; mix well and set aside. Bring remaining 3 cups milk to a boil; gradually stir in corn meal mixture. Reduce heat and cook until mixture thickens, stirring constantly. Remove from heat and add butter, eggs, honey and bacon. Pour into buttered 4-quart casserole dish. Bake in 325°F. oven 40 to 45 minutes or until a knife inserted in center comes out clean. Serve warm with additional honey if desired. Makes 10 servings.

Eileen's Rice Pilaf

Serving Suggestions:
Serve as a side dish or add cooked meat or poultry strips to make into an entree.

Hints:
Make ahead and reheat just before serving.

A colorful and delicious accompaniment to meat, chicken and poultry entrees.

1 1/2 cups uncooked long-grain white rice
1/4 cup butter, melted
1/4 cup water
2 cans (10 3/4 oz. each) chicken broth
1 1/4 teaspoons Lawry's Seasoned Salt
1/2 teaspoon Lawry's Seasoned Pepper
1/2 teaspoon paprika
1 tablespoon Lawry's Minced Onion with Green Onion Flakes
1 jar (2 oz.) diced pimiento, drained
1/2 pound fresh mushrooms, sliced
2 tablespoons minced fresh parsley
2 green onions, finely chopped

Sauté rice in large skillet with melted butter until golden brown. Gradually add water and chicken broth. Stir in remaining ingredients except parsley and green onions. Bring to a boil, reduce heat, cover and simmer 15 minutes. Stir in parsley and green onions; cover and continue cooking about 5 minutes. Makes 6 to 8 servings.

White Rice with Artichokes

An especially good side dish.

1 medium onion, chopped
2 cups uncooked long-grain rice
1/4 cup olive OR salad oil
1 jar (2 oz.) sliced pimiento, drained
1 package (9 oz.) frozen artichoke hearts
1/2 package (10 oz.) frozen peas
3 1/2 cups chicken broth
Lawry's Seasoned Salt and Seasoned Pepper, to taste

Cook onion and rice in hot oil until rice is golden; stir frequently. Place in 2-quart casserole; add remaining ingredients except Seasoned Salt and Seasoned Pepper. Cover; bake in 350°F. oven until liquid is absorbed, about 40 to 45 minutes. Season to taste. Makes 8 to 10 servings.

Hints:

Make ahead and reheat. Either reheat any leftovers or add chunks of cooked chicken or turkey and top with grated Monterey Jack cheese to create an entree for another meal.

Cassata
Baltic Babushka
Cappuccino Creme

A pastry bag and tip is easy to use with just a little practice. It adds a professional touch to desserts. It's also useful for piping mashed potatoes on casseroles as topping or for making potato rounds on a cookie sheet.

An adaptation of an Italian cake dessert.

1 (1 pound) pound cake
1 1/2 ounces Amaretto OR Grand Marnier
8 ounces ricotta cheese
Grated peel of 1 lemon
1 1/2 cups raspberry jam
2 cups chocolate frosting OR whipped cream

Freeze the pound cake for easier slicing. Trim edges and top so that cake is level and even on all sides. Cut horizontally into 1/2-inch slices. Sprinkle each slice with liqueur; set aside. Combine ricotta and lemon peel; whip with electric mixer until light and fluffy. Spread all but the top slice of cake with ricotta and then with raspberry jam. Stack slices on each other to make the "torte" and top with plain slice of cake. Chill while making frosting. Be sure that frosting is very smooth and creamy. Remove cake from refrigerator and frost top and sides of cake using a pastry bag and star tip to add decorative trim. Makes 8 to 10 servings.

Baltic Babushka

Hints:
If there is some leftover, reshape, mixing the nuts into the cheese, and serve again. Fresh berries are especially nice with this dessert.

A cheesy dessert that's molded in a clay flowerpot.

8 ounces cream cheese
8 ounces ricotta cheese
1/2 cup butter
2 egg yolks
1 cup sifted confectioners' sugar
1 teaspoon vanilla
1/2 cup chopped citron
1 cup toasted whole almonds
Cheesecloth
About 3 cups fruit, frozen or fresh

Combine cheeses, butter and egg yolks; beat well. Beat in sugar; add vanilla, citron and 1/2 cup almonds. Line clean flowerpot with hole for drainage (5-inches in diameter and 4 to 5-inches high) with damp cheesecloth. Pack cheese into pot, covering top with ends of cloth. Set pot in bowl and cover the top with a plate and weight. Let mixture drain overnight in refrigerator. Invert on platter and remove cheesecloth. Stud top and sides with remaining 1/2 cup almonds and surround with fruit. Cut in wedges to serve. Makes 8 to 10 servings.

Dessert Fruit Tacos

Be prepared for raves.

2 cups melon balls or cubes (cantaloupe, watermelon, honeydew)
2 cups strawberries, washed, hulled and halved
2 cups pineapple chunks
1 cup seedless green grapes, halved
1 orange, peeled, sectioned and sliced in 1/2-inch pieces
1 banana, peeled and sliced
1 kiwi, peeled and sliced
1/4 cup confectioners' sugar
1/4 teaspoon cinnamon
1 box (10 shells) Lawry's Super Size Taco Shells
Shredded coconut, to garnish

Combine all fruit in large bowl; chill. Sift together sugar and cinnamon. Heat Taco Shells according to package directions. Lightly sift sugar mixture over inside and outside of heated Taco Shells. Fill each shell with 1 cup mixed fruit; garnish with coconut. Makes 10 servings.

Cappuccino

Specialty coffees such as this one can sometimes double as dessert.

2 tablespoons instant espresso
1 tablespoon cocoa
6 tablespoons sugar
4 1/2 cups hot water
4 1/2 cups light cream
4 ounces brandy
2 ounces rum
1 ounce coffee-flavored liqueur
Whipped cream

Hints:
The coffee mixture may be blended ahead of time.

Combine espresso, cocoa, sugar, water and cream; heat. Pour into 12 (8 oz.) glasses or cups. Combine brandy, rum and coffee-flavored liqueur. Add about 3/4 ounce liquor to each glass. Top with whipped cream. Makes 12 servings.

Cappuccino Creme

A light refreshing dessert.

1 envelope unflavored gelatin
1/2 cup cold water
1 1/2 cups hot Cappuccino, without whipped cream
1/2 pint whipping cream, whipped
Whipped cream
Chocolate curls

Hints:
Chill bowls and beaters before whipping cream. To make chocolate curls, use a vegetable peeler and scrape across bar of semisweet chocolate. Use pressure in order to make curls. If you don't have curls, you will end up with grated chocolate which, while not as fancy, will be fine.

Soften gelatin in water; add to hot Cappuccino; cool. Fold in 1/2 pint whipped cream; pour into sherbet glasses. Chill until set. Garnish with additional whipped cream and chocolate curls. Makes 6 servings.

Avocado Lime Pie

Hints:
Crush gingersnaps in blender or food processor. Or, place whole gingersnaps in paper or plastic bag and roll with rolling pin.

A refreshingly different dessert.

1 1/2 cups finely crushed gingersnaps
1/4 cup sugar
1/4 pound butter, melted
1 or 2 large avocados, peeled and pitted
1 can (14 oz.) sweetened condensed milk
1 teaspoon grated lime peel
1/4 cup lime juice
1/4 cup lemon juice
2 egg yolks, lightly beaten
Dash salt
Lime slices
Fresh mint sprigs

Mix together gingersnaps, sugar and butter; press into 8-inch pie pan. Chill while preparing filling. Mash avocados through a sieve or puree in blender to make 1 cup. Combine milk, lime peel and juices in bowl; stir in egg yolks and salt. Add avocado, stirring until well blended. Do not beat. Pour into chilled crust; refrigerate several hours until set. Garnish with lime slices and mint sprigs. Makes 6 to 8 servings.

Flaming Peaches

Hints:
Substitute canned peach halves for fresh or use a combination of peaches, pears and apricots, fresh or canned.

Fruit desserts of all kinds are becoming increasingly popular.

3/4 cup dried, crumbled macaroons (almond or coconut)
1/4 cup ground almonds
2 tablespoons finely chopped candied orange peel
2 tablespoons melted butter OR margarine
6 ripe yellow peaches, peeled, halved and pitted
Sugar
2 tablespoons Marsala wine
2 tablespoons rum (at least 80-proof)

Combine macaroons, almonds, orange peel and melted butter; mix well. Stuff each peach half with 1 to 2 tablespoons of the mixture. Sprinkle with sugar. Arrange in shallow baking dish; pour 1/2 teaspoon Marsala over each peach half. Bake in 350°F. oven 25 minutes. To serve, heat rum and ignite; pour flaming rum over peach halves. Makes 12 servings.

Lawry's All-Time Favorites

Tastes change, fashions and fads in foods come and go, but the flavor and appeal of the recipes in this chapter have withstood the test of time. Throughout the years, consumers have requested these recipes time and time again, a good measurement of their appeal.

Many of these recipes may look familiar to you. And they probably are, as they have been printed in previous Lawry's cookbooks and other publications. But one more time, we're making sure that you have a copy, just in case you have lost or loaned yours.

Throughout this book, you will see recipes with someone's name in the title—"Richard N. Frank's Famous Leftover Hash" is one example in this chapter. These are recipes created by individuals, either co-workers or consumers, who have generously shared the results of their ingenuity in the kitchen.

As you use the recipes and ideas in this book, you will undoubtedly find your own favorites and, perhaps, create some originals. Cooking is a satisfying and creative outlet so take our ideas and make them even better. Most of all, enjoy!

Sausage and Eggplant Creole

Sausage and Eggplant Creole

Serving Suggestions:
Cream of Romaine Soup, buttered noodles or rice, fresh fruit.

Hints:
Make ahead to the point of adding mushrooms, cheese and parsley. Depending upon taste preferences, use mild or hot Italian sausage. Leave the skin on the eggplant for added color and flavor.

A winning combination.

1 1/2 pounds mild or hot Italian sausage
1 large onion, chopped
1 green bell pepper, chopped
1 cup sliced celery
3 zucchini, halved lengthwise and cut in 1/2-inch slices
1 large eggplant, cut in 1-inch cubes
1 can (1 lb. 12 oz.) tomatoes
1 teaspoon Lawry's Garlic Salt
1 teaspoon Lawry's Seasoned Salt
1 teaspoon sugar
1 teaspoon Lawry's Pinch of Herbs
1/2 pound fresh mushrooms, sliced and sautéed in butter
1/2 pound grated Monterey Jack cheese
1/4 cup chopped parsley

Brown sausage until crumbly; drain fat. Add onion, green pepper, celery, zucchini, eggplant, tomatoes, Garlic Salt, Seasoned Salt, sugar and Pinch of Herbs. Bring to a boil, reduce heat and simmer, covered, 1 hour, stirring occasionally. Top with sautéed mushrooms, cheese and parsley. Cover and cook about 5 minutes or until cheese is melted. Makes 6 to 8 servings.

Richard N. Frank's Famous Leftover Hash

Serving Suggestions:
Wilted Spinach Salad, Dessert Fruit Tacos.

Hints:
Boiled potatoes are best though raw may be used—just cook a bit longer. Frozen hash browns may also be used.

Use leftover beef, steak or roast lamb. Also good when a small portion of corned beef or roast pork is included.

2 onions, sliced in thin rings
Olive oil
1 pound cooked roast beef, cut in 1/4-inch dice
1 pound boiled potatoes, cut in 1/4-inch dice
1 green bell pepper, sliced in thin rings and quartered
Lawry's Seasoned Salt, to taste
Lawry's Pinch of Herbs, to taste
2 hot red Mexican peppers, finely chopped OR cayenne pepper, to
    taste
6 to 8 poached eggs

Cut onion slices in quarters; sauté onions in small amount of olive oil until brown. Remove onions; add meat and cook over high heat until crispy brown. Remove and set aside. Sauté potatoes and green pepper in olive oil until potatoes begin to brown. Add meat and onions and continue cooking about 15 minutes, turning occasionally until mixture is browned. Season generously to taste with Seasoned Salt and Pinch of Herbs. Add chopped hot peppers or cayenne. To serve, top each serving with one poached egg. Makes 6 to 8 servings.

Lasagna

This is one of the best lasagna recipes ever.

1 pound ground beef
2 teaspoons Lawry's Seasoned Salt
1/2 teaspoon Lawry's Seasoned Pepper
2 cloves garlic, crushed
1 can (1 lb. 12 oz.) tomatoes
1 can (8 oz.) tomato sauce
1 package (1 1/2 oz.) Lawry's Spaghetti Sauce Mix with Imported
   Mushrooms
1/2 pound lasagna noodles
1/2 pound Mozzarella cheese, sliced
1/2 pound ricotta cheese
1/2 cup Parmesan cheese

Brown beef in Dutch oven; drain fat. Add Seasoned Salt, Seasoned Pepper, garlic, tomatoes, tomato sauce and Spaghetti Sauce Mix with Imported Mushrooms; stir thoroughly, breaking up tomatoes. Bring to a boil, reduce heat and simmer, covered, 30 minutes. Meanwhile, cook lasagna noodles according to package directions; drain and rinse. Pour 1/4 of meat sauce in 13 x 9 x 2-inch baking dish. Cover meat sauce with 1/3 of cooked lasagna noodles. Arrange 1/3 of Mozzarella cheese and 1/3 of ricotta over lasagna. Repeat the layers 2 more times, ending with meat sauce; top with Parmesan cheese. Bake, uncovered, in 350°F. oven 20 minutes. Let stand 10 minutes before cutting. Makes 6 to 8 servings.

Serving Suggestions:
Tossed green salad, *Lawry's Garlic Bread.*

Hints:
Make ahead and freeze before baking. The meat sauce may be made with 1/2 ground beef and 1/2 crumbled Italian sausage, if desired. When cooking lasagna, add vegetable oil to boiling water to prevent noodles from sticking together. Rinse noodles immediately and arrange, in a single layer, on wax paper. Cottage cheese may be substituted for ricotta; however, drain well.

California Pot Roast

This might also appropriately be called Italian-Style Pot Roast, but then California is a melting pot of nationalities.

3 1/2 to 4 pound 7-bone beef pot roast
3 tablespoons salad oil
2 teaspoons Lawry's Seasoned Salt
1 can (1 lb.) tomatoes
1 cup dry red wine
1 package (1 1/2 oz.) Lawry's Spaghetti Sauce Mix with Imported
   Mushrooms
3/4 cup finely chopped celery
3/4 cup finely chopped onion

Brown meat slowly in salad oil in Dutch oven. Sprinkle with Seasoned Salt. Pour tomatoes and wine over meat. Add Spaghetti Sauce Mix with Imported Mushrooms and stir until mix is dissolved. Add celery and onion. Bring to a boil, reduce heat and simmer, covered, about 2 1/2 hours, stirring occasionally. Serve tomato-wine sauce as gravy and thicken, if desired. Makes 6 servings.

Serving Suggestions:
Buttered egg noodles, *Ensalada Esmeralda, Carrot Cake.*

Hints:
The roast may be baked, rather than simmered, in 350°F. oven for the same length of time. Conserve energy by baking other dishes at the same time. Pot roast freezes well and is handy for a freezer-to-table meal.

Steak au Poivre

Serving Suggestions:
Fettuccine, Limelight Salad Marcus.

Hints:
This dish may be made with less tender beef cuts. Simply marinate in Lawry's Tenderizing Beef Marinade according to package directions and proceed with recipe as directed.

This classic flamed dish is dramatic to prepare at the table.

1 tablespoon Lawry's Seasoned Pepper
2 teaspoons Lawry's Seasoned Salt
1 (2 1/2 pound) sirloin steak, 2-inches thick
2 tablespoons butter
2 tablespoons olive oil
2 tablespoons beef consomme OR bouillon
1/4 cup dry white wine
1/4 cup Cognac OR brandy

Press Seasoned Pepper and Seasoned Salt into both sides of steak. Heat butter and olive oil in a large skillet. Cook steak in butter-oil mixture for 7 to 10 minutes on each side, depending on the degree of rareness desired. Add more oil if necessary. Remove meat. Add consomme and white wine. Heat gently. Pour in Cognac or brandy, heat and carefully ignite. Pour flaming sauce over steak and serve immediately. Makes 4 to 6 servings.

French Onion Soup

Serving Suggestions:
Plenty of French Onion Soup and a tossed green salad.

Hints:
Freshly grated Parmesan should be used for best flavor results. Soup may be made ahead to the point of adding toast slices.

Beef stock is the essence of good French Onion Soup. Au Jus Gravy Mix provides a full-bodied, beefy flavor.

3 medium onions, thinly sliced in rings
1/4 cup butter OR margarine
1 package Lawry's Au Jus Gravy Mix
3 cups water
4 slices sourdough French bread
Butter OR margarine, softened
1/4 cup grated Parmesan cheese

Sauté onions in butter until golden. Combine Au Jus Gravy Mix and water and add to onions. Bring to a boil, reduce heat, cover and simmer 15 minutes. Broil bread on one side until lightly browned. Butter untoasted side and sprinkle each slice with 1 tablespoon cheese. Broil until cheese melts. Pour soup into tureen or individual bowls and float a toast slice on top of each serving. Makes 4 servings.

Pizza Pork Chops

San Fernando Mish Mash

Great for brunch.

1 pound ground beef
1/2 cup chopped onion
1 can (4 oz.) sliced mushrooms, drained
1 package (10 oz.) frozen chopped spinach, thawed
2 teaspoons Lawry's Garlic Salt
1/4 to 1/2 teaspoon Lawry's Pinch of Herbs
4 eggs, lightly beaten

Brown ground beef until crumbly; drain fat. Add onion, mushrooms, spinach, Garlic Salt and Pinch of Herbs. Cook over low heat and stir until onions are tender and spinach is cooked, about 3 to 5 minutes. Add eggs and cook until eggs are set. Serve immediately. Makes 4 to 5 servings.

Serving Suggestions:
Zucchini Vinaigrette, warm sourdough rolls.

Hints:
When using dried leafy herbs (as opposed to ground) rub leaves between palms or crush in mortar and pestle to release flavor.

Salad Bowl a la Lawry's

As served at Lawry's The Prime Rib Restaurants, Beverly Hills and Chicago, from the iced spinning bowl.

1 small head romaine
1 small head lettuce
1/2 cup watercress, torn in sprigs
1 cup shoestring beets, well-drained
1 hard-cooked egg, sieved
Lawry's Seasoned Salt
Lawry's Seasoned Pepper
3/4 cup Lawry's Famous French Dressing
6 cherry tomatoes

Tear romaine and lettuce in pieces. Add watercress, beets and egg. Sprinkle with Seasoned Salt and Seasoned Pepper and toss with Famous French Dressing. Garnish with 1 cherry tomato on each plate. Makes 6 servings.

Serving Suggestions:
Prime ribs of beef, yorkshire pudding, baked potato, *Lawry's Creamed Spinach.*

Hints:
Chill salad plates and salad forks before serving and have all ingredients well chilled. The waitresses at The Prime Rib skillfully spin the salad bowl in a larger bowl of ice, pour the dressing and toss with great flourish. With a little practice, anyone could master this dramatic flair for guests at home.

46

Pizza Pork Chops

Serving Suggestions:
Buttered pasta, *Lila's Creamy Spaghetti Squash, Flaming Peaches.*

Hints:
Make ahead, bake and freeze. Mozzarella is best to use and is traditionally Italian, although Monterey Jack may be substituted.

Pork chops can be prepared in numerous ways. This recipe has been a favorite for years.

8 ounces Mozzarella cheese
8 pork chops, about 1-inch thick, with pocket
1 1/2 teaspoons Lawry's Seasoned Salt
2 tablespoons salad oil
2 packages (1 1/2 oz. each) Lawry's Spaghetti Sauce Mix with Imported Mushrooms OR 1 package (3 oz.) Lawry's Economy Size Spaghetti Sauce Mix with Imported Mushrooms
1 can (1 lb.) tomatoes
1 can (6 oz.) tomato paste
1 medium onion, chopped

Grate 1/4 of cheese; divide remaining cheese into 8 equal slices. Place slice of cheese in each pork chop pocket. Close each pocket with a toothpick. Sprinkle Seasoned Salt on both sides of pork chops and rub in. Heat oil in large skillet. Brown chops thoroughly on both sides; remove and drain fat. In same skillet combine Spaghetti Sauce Mix with Imported Mushrooms, tomatoes, tomato paste and onion; break up tomatoes. Bring to a boil. Place browned pork chops in large baking dish. Pour tomato mixture over chops. Cover and bake in 350°F. oven 1 hour. Sprinkle grated Mozzarella cheese over cooked chops. Makes 8 servings.

Sherried Chicken

Serving Suggestions:
Fluffy rice or mashed potatoes, *Gingered Carrots,* tossed green salad.

Hints:
Make ahead and reheat before serving. Or, prepare chicken breasts and freeze. Make sauce separately and freeze without the sour cream, then add sour cream just before serving.

One of the most frequently requested recipes in the Lawry's collection.

3 whole chicken breasts, halved
Lawry's Seasoned Salt, as needed
3 to 4 tablespoons butter
1/2 cup sherry
1 can (4 oz.) button mushrooms
1 package Lawry's Chicken Gravy Mix
1 cup dairy sour cream

Lighty sprinkle chicken with Seasoned Salt. Brown in butter in Dutch oven. Add sherry and liquid from can of mushrooms. Cover and bake in 350°F. oven 45 minutes to 1 hour until chicken is tender. Remove chicken to serving dish. Measure pan juices and add water, if necessary, to make 1 1/4 cups liquid. Carefully blend liquid and Chicken Gravy Mix in Dutch oven. Bring to a boil, reduce heat and simmer, uncovered, 5 minutes, stirring continually. Blend in sour cream and add mushrooms. When sauce is smooth and hot, pour over chicken breasts. Makes 6 servings.

Holiday Roast Turkey with Herbed Corn Bread Dressing

Roast turkey is a holiday tradition that is becoming more popular for year 'round good eating.

Use 1/2 teaspoon Lawry's Seasoned Salt per pound of turkey. Rub Seasoned Salt inside cavities and on outside of the bird. Loosely fill cavities with Corn Bread Dressing. Skewer openings closed and roast as desired. Baste with melted butter during roasting.

1 pound bulk pork sausage
1 1/2 cups chopped onion
1 cup chopped celery
4 teaspoons Lawry's Pinch of Herbs
6 cups coarsely crumbled corn bread
1/4 cup dry sherry
1/4 cup light cream

Cook sausage meat until crumbly; add onion and celery. Cook until tender. Drain fat; add Pinch of Herbs, corn bread, sherry and cream. Mix lightly; pack dressing loosely in turkey cavities. Leftover dressing may be baked in a covered casserole. Makes 9 cups dressing, enough for a 14 pound turkey.

Serving Suggestions:
Your traditional holiday dinner and trimmings.

Hints:
Use a sausage that is lightly seasoned and a corn bread mix or recipe with a minimum amount of sugar. Remember to stuff the turkey just before roasting, though the dressing may be made in advance and refrigerated.

Chicken Marengo

In this recipe, Spaghetti Sauce Mix is used as a seasoned coating rather than as a sauce.

2 to 2 1/2 pounds chicken parts
1 teaspoon Lawry's Seasoned Salt
1 package (1 1/2 oz.) Lawry's Spaghetti Sauce Mix with Imported Mushrooms
1/2 cup bread crumbs
1/4 cup salad oil
1/2 cup dry white wine
3 tomatoes, peeled and quartered
2 cups sliced fresh mushrooms

Sprinkle chicken pieces with Seasoned Salt. Blend Spaghetti Sauce Mix and crumbs. Roll chicken in seasoned crumb mixture. Fry in hot oil in skillet. Add wine, tomatoes, mushrooms and remaining crumb mixture. Bring to a boil, reduce heat and simmer, covered, about 45 minutes or until chicken is tender. Makes 4 servings.

Serving Suggestions:
Artichokes Vinaigrette, Eggplant Cheese Casserole.

Hints:
For a spicier version, use Chili Seasoning Mix in place of Spaghetti Sauce Mix.

The Cartwheel Salad

As served at Lawry's California Center for the Fiesta Dinner, with a choice of the following four dressings.

1 small head iceberg lettuce, torn in bite-size pieces
1 small head romaine, torn in bite-size pieces
1/2 cup garbanzo beans
1 cup cherry tomato halves
1/4 cup sliced ripe olives
1/4 cup shoestring beets
1/4 cup sliced radishes
Tortilla strips

Have all ingredients except tortilla strips prepared and chilled. To prepare tortilla strips, slice 6 corn tortillas into 1/4-inch strips; fry in hot oil until crisp. In large, shallow salad bowl, make a bed with lettuce and arrange toppings in cartwheel design. To serve, toss with your choice of salad dressing. *Makes 6 to 8 servings.*

Confetti Dressing

1 package Lawry's Italian Salad Dressing Mix, prepared according to package directions
2 tablespoons chopped green bell pepper
2 tablespoons chopped pimiento
2 tablespoons chopped hard-cooked egg
2 tablespoons chopped pickled beet

Combine all ingredients and shake well, about 30 seconds. Makes 1 1/2 cups.

Mexican Caesar Dressing

2 tablespoons chopped toasted almonds
2 tablespoons diced green chiles
1 tablespoon chopped pimiento
1 package Lawry's Caesar Salad Dressing Mix, prepared according to package directions

Add chopped ingredients to prepared salad dressing; blend. Chill before serving. Makes 1 1/2 cups.

The Cartwheel Salad

Creamy Mexican Dressing con Cilantro

3/4 cup dairy sour cream
1/3 cup mayonnaise
1/3 cup buttermilk
1 tablespoon lemon juice
1 tablespoon water
1/2 teaspoon Lawry's Seasoned Salt
1/8 teaspoon Lawry's Garlic Powder with Parsley
1/8 teaspoon oregano
1/4 teaspoon basil
1/4 teaspoon dry mustard
1/4 teaspoon Lawry's Seasoned Pepper
3 to 4 tablespoons minced cilantro

Combine all ingredients with whisk or fork; blend thoroughly. Refrigerate several hours or overnight for best flavor. Makes about 1 1/2 cups.

Creamy Green Goddess Dressing

3 tablespoons tarragon vinegar
1 tablespoon water
1 tablespoon finely minced parsley
1 teaspoon Lawry's Minced Onion with Green Onion Flakes
3/4 teaspoon tarragon leaves, crushed
1/4 teaspoon sugar
1/4 teaspoon Lawry's Seasoned Salt
1/4 teaspoon Lawry's Garlic Powder with Parsley
1 drop green food coloring
4 anchovy fillets, finely minced
3/4 cup mayonnaise

Hints:
For fewer calories, use plain yogurt instead of mayonnaise.

Combine all ingredients except mayonnaise in a jar; shake well. Add mayonnaise and blend thoroughly. Chill several hours before serving. Makes about 1 cup.

Parmesan Fried Chicken

One of the first recipes ever created for Lemon Pepper Seasoning.

1 egg
2 tablespoons water
2/3 cup fine dry bread crumbs
1/3 cup grated Parmesan cheese
2 teaspoons Lawry's Lemon Pepper Seasoning
1 teaspoon Lawry's Seasoned Salt
2 1/2 to 3 pounds chicken parts
1/4 cup butter and 2 tablespoons salad oil

Serving Suggestions:
Sliced tomatoes, *Sally's Baked Potato Casserole.*

Hints:
This fried chicken is best served warm.

Beat egg and water together. Combine bread crumbs, Parmesan cheese, Lemon Pepper Seasoning and Seasoned Salt. Dip chicken pieces in egg, then bread crumbs. Brown in butter-oil mixture. Cover; cook 25 to 30 minutes or until tender. Remove cover during last 5 minutes of cooking time to crisp chicken. Makes 4 to 6 servings.

Green Chile Enchiladas

Serving Suggestions:
Open Face Pattypan Squash, Jicama Salad.

Hints:
Make ahead and bake just before serving. The sour cream sauce is wonderful over chicken breasts or vegetables.

Good as an entree or side dish.

1 dozen corn tortillas
1/2 cup salad oil
2 cups grated Monterey Jack cheese
3/4 cup chopped onion
2 packages Lawry's Chicken Gravy Mix
1 cup dairy sour cream
1 can (4 oz.) diced green chiles
Lawry's Chunky Taco Sauce

In a skillet, cook tortillas, one at a time, in hot oil for 15 seconds on each side. (Do not overcook or they won't roll.) Combine 1 cup grated cheese and onion. Place about 3 tablespoons on each tortilla; roll up. Place tortillas, seam side down, in 13 x 9 x 2-inch baking dish. In saucepan, prepare Chicken Gravy Mix according to package directions. Stir in sour cream and chiles; cook until heated through but do not boil. Pour over tortillas in baking dish. Bake, uncovered, in 425°F. oven 20 minutes. Sprinkle remaining cheese on top; return to oven 5 minutes more or until cheese melts. Serve with Chunky Taco Sauce if desired. Makes 6 servings.

Lawry's Creamed Spinach

Serving Suggestions:
Traditionally served with prime ribs of beef, yorkshire pudding and baked potatoes. Good any time a creamed vegetable complements a meal.

Hints:
One bunch chopped, cooked fresh spinach may be used. Use 1/4 teaspoon Lawry's Garlic Powder with Parsley instead of the garlic clove, if desired. When using fresh garlic, either mince or crush with garlic press.

Even non-spinach fanciers have been known to enjoy this tempting dish served at Lawry's The Prime Rib Restaurants.

1 package (10 oz.) frozen chopped spinach
2 bacon slices, finely chopped
1/2 cup finely chopped onion
2 tablespoons flour
1 teaspoon Lawry's Seasoned Salt
1/4 teaspoon Lawry's Seasoned Pepper
1 clove garlic, minced
1 cup milk

Cook spinach according to package directions but do not add salt; drain well. Fry bacon and onions together until onions are tender, about 10 minutes. Remove from heat. Add flour, Seasoned Salt, Seasoned Pepper and garlic. Blend thoroughly. Slowly add milk, return to heat and stir until thickened. Add spinach and mix thoroughly. Makes 4 servings.

Lemon Lamb Lawry's

Lamb, lemon and green beans are a sensational combination.

2 teaspoons Lawry's Lemon Pepper Seasoning
1 cup water
2 pounds boneless lamb, cut in 1-inch cubes
2 tablespoons salad oil
1 large onion, sliced
1 tablespoon olive oil
1/2 cup lemon juice
1 teaspoon Lawry's Seasoned Salt
1 1/2 pounds fresh green beans, cut in 1-inch pieces
1 teaspoon leaf oregano, crushed

Combine Lemon Pepper Seasoning and water; let stand while browning lamb. In a large skillet or Dutch oven, brown lamb well in salad oil; add onion and sauté. Add olive oil and toss with lamb and onion to coat. Add water, lemon juice, Seasoned Salt, green beans and oregano. Bring to a boil, reduce heat and simmer, covered, 1 hour, stirring occasionally. Add an additional 1/4 cup water during cooking if necessary. Makes 6 servings.

Serving Suggestions:

Ginger Avocado Soup, tossed green salad.

Hints:

May use 2 pounds ground lamb in place of lamb cubes. Shape into 16 to 20 meatballs. This dish may be baked in 350°F. oven 1 1/2 hours rather than simmered, if desired. Fresh beans are preferable to frozen, when available.

Sour Cream Tortilla Casserole

Serving Suggestions:
Barbecued or broiled steak or fish, *The Cartwheel Salad.*

Hints:
For a slightly different flavor, a package of Lawry's Chili Seasoning Mix may be used in place of Mexican Rice Seasoning Mix. Frying the tortillas in oil adds flavor but this step may be eliminated to reduce calories.

Enjoy this meatless casserole as an entree or a side dish. Served at Lawry's California Center.

1/2 cup chopped onion
2 tablespoons salad oil
1 can (1 lb. 12 oz.) tomatoes
1 package Lawry's Mexican Rice Seasoning Mix
2 tablespoons salsa jalapeña
12 corn tortillas
1/2 cup salad oil
3/4 cup chopped onion
1 pound Monterey Jack cheese, grated
2 cups dairy sour cream
1 teaspoon Lawry's Seasoned Salt
Lawry's Seasoned Pepper

Sauté 1/2 cup onion in 2 tablespoons salad oil until tender. Add tomatoes, Mexican Rice Seasoning Mix and salsa jalapeña, breaking up tomatoes. Bring to a boil, reduce heat and simmer, uncovered, 15 to 20 minutes. Set aside to cool. Fry tortillas lightly in a small amount of oil, 10 to 15 seconds on each side (do not let them get crisp). Pour 1/2 cup of sauce in the bottom of 13 x 9 x 2-inch baking dish. Arrange a layer of tortillas over the sauce (tortillas can overlap). Top with 1/3 of sauce, onions and cheese. Repeat the procedure twice, making 3 layers of tortillas. Combine sour cream and Seasoned Salt; spread over cheese to edges of dish. Sprinkle lightly with Seasoned Pepper. Bake, uncovered, in 325°F. oven 25 to 30 minutes. To serve, cut in squares. Makes 10 to 12 servings.

Coleslaw with Peanuts

Serving Suggestions:
A corned beef dinner or any hearty meat sandwich.

Hints:
Keeps for several days in the refrigerator. Easy to double or triple the recipe for larger groups.

A long time favorite and a very different way to prepare coleslaw. Served at **The Great Scot Restaurant.**

4 cups shredded cabbage
1/2 cup chopped green onion, including tops
1 cup chopped celery, including leaves
1/4 cup chopped cocktail peanuts
1/2 teaspoon Lawry's Seasoned Salt
1/4 teaspoon Lawry's Seasoned Pepper
1/3 cup Lawry's Italian Salad Dressing, made from mix, prepared according to package directions

Toss cabbage, onions, celery and peanuts together lightly. Sprinkle with Seasoned Salt and Seasoned Pepper. Pour salad dressing over salad and toss. Chill thoroughly. Makes 4 to 6 servings.

Sherry Trifle

A sinfully rich and wonderful dessert classic served at Lawry's The Prime Rib Restaurants.

1 package (4 1/2 oz.) vanilla pudding and pie filling mix
2 cups light cream
2 tablespoons dark rum
2 1/4 cups whipping cream
3 tablespoons sugar
2 tablespoons red raspberry preserves
1 (10-inch) round sponge, angel food OR pound cake
1/4 cup brandy
1/4 cup dry sherry
30 whole strawberries

Combine pudding mix and light cream. Cook, stirring constantly, until mixture comes to a boil and thickens. Add rum; chill. Whip 1 1/4 cups whipping cream and 1 tablespoon sugar until stiff. Fold into chilled pudding. Coat the inside of a deep 10-inch bowl with raspberry preserves to within 1 inch of the top. Slice cake horizontally into fourths. Place top slice, crust side up, in bottom of bowl, curving edges of cake upward. Combine brandy and sherry; sprinkle about a fourth of the mixture (about 2 tablespoons) over the cake slice. Spread one third of chilled pudding mixture over cake slice. Repeat procedure two additional times. Arrange 15 strawberries on top of layer of pudding. Cover with remaining cake layer, crust side down. Sprinkle with remaining brandy-sherry mixture. Whip remaining 1 cup cream and 2 tablespoons sugar until stiff. Place whipped cream in pastry bag with fluted tip. Make 12 mounds around edge of bowl and 3 mounds across diameter. Top each mound with a strawberry. Chill at least 6 hours. Makes 12 servings.

Hints:

This is a good dessert for a large party and, since most people want a very small serving, the recipe will easily serve 20. Additional sherry may be sprinkled over individual servings if desired.

Sherry Trifle
Carrot Cake
Peach Pudding Cake

Hints:

This cake freezes beautifully. Bake in 13 x 9 x 2-inch pan, frost, cut in squares and freeze individual portions. Easy to defrost for a quick dessert or unexpected guests.

An adaptation of the popular carrot cake served at Lawry's California Center.

1 1/2 cups sugar
1 1/2 cups salad oil
4 eggs
2 cups flour
2 teaspoons baking powder
1 1/2 teaspoons baking soda
1 teaspoon salt
2 teaspoons cinnamon
2 cups grated, raw carrots
1 can (8 3/4 oz.) crushed pineapple, drained
1 cup golden raisins
1/2 cup chopped nuts
Cream Cheese Frosting

Mix together sugar, oil and eggs. Sift together flour, baking powder, baking soda, salt and cinnamon. Combine with egg mixture. Add carrots, pineapple, raisins, nuts and blend. Turn into 2 greased and floured 9-inch layer pans or one 13 x 9 x 2-inch baking pan. Bake at 350°F. 25 to 30 minutes for 9-inch, 35 to 50 minutes for larger pan. Cool a few minutes in pans. Turn out and cool on wire racks; frost.

Cream Cheese Frosting

1/2 cup butter
1 package (8 oz.) cream cheese, softened
1 teaspoon vanilla
1 pound confectioners' sugar, sifted

Combine butter, cheese, vanilla and cream well. Add sugar gradually, beating well. If too thick, add small amount of milk.

Peach Pudding Cake

Hints:

This is best baked and served immediately, though it can be made ahead and reheated. Do serve warm. Top with vanilla ice cream if desired.

Everybody loves this cake! Best served warm.

1 package (3 oz.) instant French vanilla pudding and pie filling mix
2 cups yellow OR white cake mix
1 egg
2 cups milk
1 1/2 teaspoons almond extract
1 can (1 lb. 13 oz.) sliced peaches, undrained
1/4 pound butter, melted
1/2 pint whipping cream, whipped
Ground nutmeg

Combine pudding mix, cake mix, egg and milk. Stir in almond extract and peaches with their juice; mix well. Coat a 13 x 9 x 2-inch baking dish with some of the melted butter. Pour batter into baking dish; pour butter over top. Bake in a 350°F. oven 1 hour until golden. Serve warm topped with whipped cream and a dash of nutmeg. Makes 12 servings.

Mexican Specialties

Mexican cuisine is one of the oldest in the world. Historical records mention Mexican cooking dating back from 300 to 900 A.D., which was during the peak of Mayan civilization. French cuisine, often thought of as ancient, is only about 400 years old.

Mexican cuisine is simple yet subtle. Foods are exotic in their seasonings and call upon a wide range of spices, herbs and chile peppers, which are used in abundance. Mexican cooking is also distinguished by the types of sauces used. The most well known is a complementary sauce known as salsa. Salsas, of which there are many different types, are basically tomatoes, onions, peppers and seasonings and are used to enhance the delicate flavors of corn, avocado, beans and vegetables, as well as meats. The ever-intriguing Mexican cuisine basically centers around tortillas, beans and chiles which, in combination with other ingredients, are prepared in virtually hundreds of ways.

When the Spanish began exploration of the West Coast from their base in Mexico, they brought this marvelous cuisine to California where it has thrived and grown in popularity. In recent years, tacos, enchiladas, burritos and tostadas have become as American as pizza and chow mein.

Lawry's enthusiasm for the culture and cuisine of Mexico is apparent upon visiting Lawry's California Center, a beautiful complex inspired by the art and architecture of Mexico. Some time ago, Lawry's realized that, while many people enjoyed eating Mexican food in restaurants, they were reluctant to prepare these same foods at home. Unfamiliar and sometimes unavailable ingredients were part of the problem. Lawry's packaged the essence of the delightful Mexican flavor, the seasonings, and made Mexican easy!

This chapter emphasizes the unusual, less well-known Mexican dishes. You'll find the more familiar tacos, burritos and tostadas in other chapters. Enjoying ethnic foods prepared in your own "Cocina" (ko-see'-na) or kitchen is a grand way to absorb a part of the culture of other countries without ever leaving home.

Elvira's Aji de Salmon

56

Elvira's Aji de Salmon

(Salmon with Spicy Sauce)

Serving Suggestions:
Ensalada Tropical, Tortilla Flats, Mexican Coffee.

Hints:
Sauce may be made ahead and vegetables cooked and reheated just before serving. Assemble just before serving.

This is a beautiful and elegant dish. The salmon sauce contrasted with crisp lettuce and vegetables is most unusual and delicious.

1 package Lawry's Enchilada Sauce Mix
1 can (8 oz.) tomato sauce
1 medium onion, chopped
5 green onions, including tops, chopped
1 stalk celery, chopped
3 tablespoons olive oil
3 cans (7 3/4 oz. each) salmon, drained, bones and skin removed
Lawry's Seasoned Salt, to taste
Lawry's Seasoned Pepper, to taste
3 boiling potatoes, peeled, cooked and quartered
2 ears corn, cut in 2-inch pieces, cooked
3 hard-cooked eggs, quartered
6 ounces Monterey Jack cheese, cut in wedges
1/3 cup chopped parsley
Crisp lettuce leaves
Pitted ripe olives

Prepare Enchilada Sauce Mix according to package directions using tomato sauce. Reserve some green onions for topping; sauté remaining onions and celery in olive oil. Add salmon and prepared enchilada sauce; bring to a boil, reduce heat and simmer, uncovered, 30 minutes. Season to taste. To serve, arrange potatoes and corn on a platter, pour salmon mixture over and garnish with hard-cooked eggs and cheese wedges. Sprinkle with parsley and green onions. Place platter in hot oven 5 to 10 minutes or until cheese is melted. Serve with fresh cold lettuce leaves and ripe olives. Makes 8 to 10 servings.

Chile Verde

Serving Suggestions:
Serve over cooked rice with warmed corn or flour tortillas on the side. Also good as a filling for burritos.

"Verde" means green in Spanish.

1 1/2 pounds lean pork, cut in 3 x 1/2-inch strips
1 tablespoon shortening
1 can (1 lb.) tomatoes, cut up
3 cans (4 oz. each) whole green chiles, rinsed and seeds removed, cut in narrow lengthwise strips
1/4 teaspoon leaf oregano, crushed
1/2 teaspoon Lawry's Garlic Powder with Parsley
1 tablespoon Lawry's Minced Onion with Green Onion Flakes
1 package Lawry's Brown Gravy Mix
1/4 cup water
Lawry's Seasoned Salt, to taste

Brown pork strips in shortening. Add remaining ingredients. Bring to a boil, reduce heat, cover and simmer 35 to 40 minutes or until meat is tender; stir occasionally. Makes 6 servings.

Chicken Tortilla Stack

A layered tortilla dish that is easy to prepare and makes wonderful eating.

1/2 to 3/4 pound cooked, boned and shredded chicken
1 package Lawry's Chicken Taco Seasoning Mix
1 cup water
1 can (8 oz.) tomato sauce
4 corn tortillas
1 can (4 1/4 oz.) chopped ripe olives
1 can (4 oz.) whole green chiles, rinsed and seeds removed
1/2 pound grated Monterey Jack OR Cheddar cheese

In a large skillet combine chicken, Chicken Taco Seasoning Mix, water and tomato sauce. Bring mixture to a boil, reduce heat and simmer, uncovered, 10 minutes. Coat a 2-quart casserole dish with vegetable spray. Dip one tortilla in chicken mixture. Place tortilla in bottom of casserole, top with 1/2 of chicken mixture. Sprinkle with 1/4 of cheese and top with a tortilla. Layer whole chiles on top of tortilla. Sprinkle with olives, reserving 2 tablespoons for garnish. Sprinkle 1/4 of grated cheese over olives. Top with tortilla, remaining chicken mixture, 1/4 of grated cheese and the last tortilla. Garnish with remaining cheese and chopped olives. Bake, uncovered, in 350°F. oven 15 to 20 minutes. Cut each stack in half to serve. Makes 4 servings.

Serving Suggestions:
Creamy Chayote Soup, Mixed Fruit.

Hints:
If made in advance, cover tightly so tortillas do not dry out.

Chicken Flautas

The word "flauta" describes the flute shape of these filled and rolled tortillas.

3 cups (about 3/4 pound) shredded or diced cooked chicken
1 package Lawry's Chicken Taco Seasoning Mix
1 cup water
1 dozen (8-inch) flour tortillas
Salad oil for frying
Dairy sour cream
Guacamole (see page 9)

In large skillet, combine chicken, Chicken Taco Seasoning Mix and water. Bring to a boil, reduce heat and simmer, uncovered, 10 minutes; set aside. In large skillet, heat 1/2-inch oil to about 375°F. On each flour tortilla, place 1 to 2 tablespoons of prepared chicken filling in long strip. Roll up tightly to form a tube (like a crepe). Hold flap firmly with tongs and place in hot oil. Hold until flap fries firmly closed. Lightly brown all sides. Remove and drain on paper towels. Serve immediately topped with sour cream and guacamole. Makes 12 flautas.

Serving Suggestions:
Serve as an entree with *Fiesta Rice* and *Refried Beans* or cut in half, once fried, and serve as an appetizer with sour cream and guacamole for dipping.

Hints:
May use shredded or diced cooked turkey or 1 pound ground turkey, browned and crumbled. May make ahead and reheat on baking sheet in 300°F. oven to crisp.

Creamy Chayote Soup

Serving Suggestions:
Red Snapper Veracruz, fluffy rice or fresh corn tortillas.

Hints:
Make ahead up to the point of adding sour cream. Zucchini or potato may be substituted for chayote.

Chayotes, a member of the squash family, are botanically a fruit but are prepared and eaten as a vegetable. Chayotes are light green or white on the outside and pear-shaped.

3 tablespoons butter
1 small onion, chopped
3 tablespoons flour
1 quart chicken broth
1 large tomato, peeled, seeded and chopped
1/4 cup uncooked long-grain rice
3/4 teaspoon thyme leaves
1/2 teaspoon chili powder
1/4 teaspoon hot pepper sauce
2 small chayotes (about 1 pound), peeled, seed removed and cut in
    1/4-inch cubes
3/4 cup dairy sour cream
Lawry's Seasoned Salt
Lawry's Seasoned Pepper

In a 3-quart saucepan, melt butter and sauté onion until soft. Add flour and stir until mixed. Gradually add chicken broth, stirring constantly until thickened. Add tomato, rice, seasonings and chayote. Bring to a boil, reduce heat, cover and simmer 20 to 25 minutes, stirring occasionally. Blend in sour cream and heat. Season with Seasoned Salt and Seasoned Pepper. Makes 6 to 8 servings.

Chili Albondigas

Serving Suggestions:
Large bowls of Albondigas, corn tortillas and butter, *Yolanda's Capirotada*.

Hints:
Make ahead, as the flavor improves. Also freezes well.

A traditional Mexican meatball soup, hearty and filling as an entree soup or, served in small cups or bowls, a nice beginning for a meal.

1 pound ground beef
1/4 cup instant rice
1/4 cup ice water
1 1/2 teaspoons Lawry's Seasoned Salt
1 package Lawry's Chili Seasoning Mix
1 1/2 cups water
1 can (1 lb.) tomatoes
1 can (15 oz.) kidney beans
1/2 cup slivered onion
1 bay leaf

Combine ground beef, rice, ice water and 1 teaspoon Seasoned Salt; mix lightly. Form into 20 meatballs. Mix together Chili Seasoning Mix, water and tomatoes. Add beans, onion, bay leaf and remaining 1/2 teaspoon Seasoned Salt. Bring to a boil, add meatballs. Reduce heat, cover and simmer 20 minutes, stirring occasionally. Makes 5 servings of 4 meatballs each or about 1 1/3 cups soup per serving.

Tortilla Soup

This soup base is wonderfully versatile and easily varied by adding the listed ingredients. Also good served as a broth.

2 cans (10 1/2 oz. each) beef broth
2 cans (10 1/2 oz. each) water
1 can (8 oz.) tomato sauce
1 package (1 1/2 oz.) Lawry's Spaghetti Sauce Mix with Imported
  Mushrooms
6 corn tortillas, torn in bite-size pieces
Garnishes

Combine broth, water, tomato sauce and Spaghetti Sauce Mix. Bring to a boil, reduce heat and simmer, uncovered, 10 minutes, stirring occasionally. Add tortillas and simmer 2 minutes longer. Top soup with any of the following garnishes: sour cream, chopped cilantro, dried pork cracklings, sliced avocado, chopped onion or grated cheese. Makes 5 servings.

Serving Suggestions:
Good with meat or fish dishes.

Hints:
Soup base may be frozen. Whole tortillas may also be frozen so the makings can always be on hand. Use homemade beef stock in place of canned broth if available.

Gazpacho

Gazpacho doubles as a cold soup or a salad.

1 clove garlic, halved
1 package Lawry's Mexican Rice Seasoning Mix
1 cup tomato juice
1 1/2 pounds fresh tomatoes
1 medium cucumber, peeled and chopped
1/4 cup minced green bell pepper
3/4 cup minced green onion
2 tablespoons olive oil
1 tablespoon vinegar
1 tablespoon chopped cilantro, optional
Lawry's Seasoned Pepper

Rub large bowl with garlic. Empty Mexican Rice Seasoning Mix into bowl. Add tomato juice and stir thoroughly. Peel tomatoes, remove cores and chop in small pieces. Add tomatoes, cucumbers, green pepper and green onion to seasoned tomato juice. Add olive oil, vinegar and cilantro; mix thoroughly. Chill well before serving. Add a sprinkle of Seasoned Pepper. Makes 5 to 6 servings.

Serving Suggestions:
Machaca de Huevos, Arroz con Pollo or *Torta Mexican-Style.*

Hints:
May use 1 package (1 1/4 oz.) Taco Seasoning Mix and 1 1/2 cups tomato juice, if desired. Keeps nicely in refrigerator for several days.

Ensalada Tropical

Serving Suggestions:
Serve with distinctively flavored and/or hearty dishes either as a salad course or dessert.

Hints:
Make ahead as marinating improves the flavor. The salad may be served plain or on lettuce leaves with a light garnish of coarsely chopped fresh cilantro. A little more of the chili powder may be added to each serving as a final touch.

In Mexico, fresh tiny lime wedges accompany all fruit dishes and are served as a seasoning for fish and soups. Very refreshing and flavorful.

Equal parts of jicama, orange sections and cubed fresh pineapple
Fresh lime juice
Fresh lemon juice
Chili powder

Peel and cut jicama into fine julienne and place in slightly salted ice water to stay crisp while you peel and section the oranges and cube the pineapple. Mix ingredients and dress rather liberally with 1/2 lime and 1/2 lemon juice. Sprinkle lightly with chili powder to produce some red flecks throughout the salad; toss lightly.

Mexican Dinner Salad

Serving Suggestions:
A basic green salad to accompany any Mexican meal.

Hints:
Wash and carefully drain greens, chop and measure other ingredients. Store in plastic bags; combine and toss just before serving.

The cilantro gives this salad a refreshingly different flavor.

2 medium heads butter lettuce
1 medium red or green bell pepper, slivered
1/4 to 1/2 cup cilantro sprigs (or watercress)
1/2 cup sliced ripe olives
1/2 cup garbanzo beans
1 bottle (8 oz.) Lawry's San Francisco Dressing

Tear lettuce in bite-size pieces. Add bell pepper, cilantro sprigs, olives and beans. Toss with San Francisco Dressing to coat. Makes 4 to 6 servings.

Ensalada de Noche Buena
(Christmas Eve Salad)

Serving Suggestions:
Turkey or Chicken Molé, Mexican Coffee.

Hints:
Prepare fruits and dressing in advance and assemble just before serving.

Traditionally served with Chicken or Turkey Molé for the Christmas Eve celebration.

1 head lettuce, shredded
3 oranges, peeled and sectioned
2 firm bananas, sliced crosswise 1/4-inch thick
1 large apple, cored and diced, unpeeled
1 cup pineapple chunks, fresh or canned
1 cup sliced canned beets
1/2 cup coarsely chopped toasted peanuts
Seeds of 1 pomegranate OR 1/4 cup whole cranberry sauce (canned)
1 recipe French Vinaigrette Dressing (see page 94) OR 1 bottle Lawry's Red Wine Vinegar & Oil Dressing

Arrange shredded lettuce on platter; arrange fruit and beets; sprinkle with pomegranate seeds and nuts. Serve with French Vinaigrette Dressing. Makes 10 servings.

Luncheon Tostada Salad

Serving Suggestions:
Julie's Sangria and/or fresh fruit.

Hints:
To make ahead, prepare the taco meat and cut all vegetables. At serving time, reheat meat and toss salad.

As served at Lawry's California Center and several other fine restaurants in Los Angeles.

1 pound ground beef
1 package (1 1/4 oz.) Lawry's Taco Seasoning Mix
3/4 cup water
3/4 teaspoon Lawry's Seasoned Salt
1 can (14 oz.) red kidney beans, drained
4 tomatoes, cut in wedges
1 avocado, peeled and cut in thin slices
1 package (6 1/4 oz.) tortilla chips
1 head lettuce, torn in small pieces
4 ounces Cheddar cheese, grated
1 cup chopped onion
3/4 cup Lawry's Chunky Taco Sauce OR Mexican Dressing

Brown ground beef; drain fat. Add Taco Seasoning Mix, water, Seasoned Salt and beans. Bring to a boil, reduce heat, cover and simmer 10 minutes. Reserve some tomato wedges, avocado slices and tortilla chips for use as a garnish. Combine all remaining ingredients in a large salad bowl; add hot ground beef mixture and lightly toss all ingredients. Garnish with reserved tomato, avocado and chips. This salad is best served immediately. Makes 6 to 8 servings.

Mexican Dressing

A Mexican-style Thousand Island dressing.

1/2 cup Lawry's Chunky Taco Sauce
1/3 cup mayonnaise

Blend ingredients together thoroughly. Chill and serve over salad greens or as a relish or dip. Makes about 3/4 cup.

Nopalitos Salad

Serving Suggestions:
A good marinated salad to serve with most Mexican dishes. Also good topped with your favorite tuna salad and garnished with hard-cooked eggs.

Diced cactus (nopalitos) is available in jars, either plain or marinated. Buy the "plain" for this recipe.

1 jar (16 oz.) nopalitos, rinsed and drained
2 green onions, chopped
1 1/2 to 2 teaspoons chopped cilantro
1 tomato, diced
2 tablespoons diced green chiles
2 tablespoons grated Romano OR Parmesan cheese
1/2 cup French Vinaigrette Dressing (see page 94)

Combine all ingredients and toss. Chill for several hours to blend flavors. Makes 6 servings.

Pork 'n Raisin Enchiladas

Raisins are used in a variety of Mexican dishes. Here's one you'll enjoy.

1 package Lawry's Enchilada Sauce Mix, prepared according to package directions
1 medium onion, chopped
1 tablespoon bacon drippings OR butter
2 cups diced, cooked pork
2 tablespoons diced green chiles
1/4 cup raisins
2 tablespoons chopped ripe olives
8 corn tortillas
Salad oil for frying
1 cup grated Cheddar cheese

Combine 1 cup Enchilada Sauce with onion, bacon drippings or butter, pork, green chiles, raisins and olives; set aside. Soften each tortilla in hot oil but do not cook or crisp. Place about 1/4 cup pork mixture on each tortilla and roll up. Place enchiladas, seam side down, in 12 x 8 x 2-inch baking dish; pour remaining Enchilada Sauce over. Top with grated cheese. Bake, uncovered, in 350°F. oven 25 minutes. Makes 4 servings.

Serving Suggestions:
Mexican Dinner Salad, Jicama Custard Dessert.

Hints:
Enchiladas are a wonderful way to use leftover meat and poultry. This dish may be frozen. Add grated cheese just before baking for fresher appearance and flavor.

Tortilla Flats

A delightful dessert served at Lawry's California Center...not authentically Mexican though the base is a tortilla.

1 (6-inch) flour tortilla
Salad oil for frying
Melted butter, about 1 tablespoon
Sugar/cinnamon mixture, about 2 teaspoons
Scoop of vanilla ice cream
Fresh fruit such as strawberries, peaches, raspberries, boysenberries OR Mexican Fudge Sauce
Slivered toasted almonds, optional

Fry tortilla in hot oil until golden and puffy; drain on paper towels. Brush with melted butter, generously sprinkle with sugar/cinnamon mixture and top with vanilla ice cream. Garnish with fruit and nuts as desired or serve with Mexican Fudge Sauce. Makes 1 serving.

Note: For sugar/cinnamon mixture, mix together 1/4 cup sugar and 1 teaspoon cinnamon.

Serving Suggestions:
Any Mexican meal where a hearty dessert is desired.

Hints:
Flour tortillas, when fried, taste just like pastry. Prepare the tortillas early in the day and store loosely covered until serving time.

Mexican Fudge Sauce

1 cup hot fudge sauce
1 tablespoon vanilla extract
1 teaspoon cinnamon

Heat fudge sauce in top of double boiler; add vanilla and cinnamon, blending thoroughly. Serve over ice cream, brownies, angel food cake or other dessert items. Makes about 1 cup.

Mexican Coffee

Mexican Coffee

Serving Suggestions:
A perfect ending for any Mexican meal.

A lovely way to complete a meal. The combination of cocoa and coffee with cinnamon is delicious. Serve each cup with a cinnamon stick garnish, if desired.

Hints:
The drip or filter method also works successfully.

1/4 cup unsweetened cocoa
1 cup brown sugar
2 teaspoons cinnamon
4 cups water
4 1/2 teaspoons ground coffee
Brandy
Whipped cream

Mix cocoa, brown sugar, cinnamon and water in bottom of a perculator. Place coffee in basket; perk. To serve, add brandy to taste and top each serving with whipped cream. Makes 4 1/2 cups.

Margaritas

Serving Suggestions:
Serve in an iced pitcher with Mexican meals or for parties.

Everyone's Mexican favorite.

Hints:
May use about 8 ounces sweet-and-sour bar mix in place of fresh lime juice and sugar. To make Strawberry Margaritas, blend in about 1 to 1 1/2 cups fresh strawberries.

8 ounces tequila
4 ounces Triple Sec
8 ounces fresh lime juice
1/4 cup sugar
Crushed ice
Lime juice
Coarse or kosher salt

Mix tequila, Triple Sec, lime juice, sugar and crushed ice in a blender until frothy. Dip rim of glass in lime juice, then in salt; fill with Margarita mixture. Makes 4 servings.

Yolanda's Capirotada

A deliciously different dessert—a Mexican version of bread pudding with fruit and cheese added.

Butter
1 loaf (1 lb.) sliced French bread
8 ounces Monterey Jack cheese, cut in strips
4 bananas, sliced crosswise 1/4-inch thick
1 cup raisins
2 cups crushed walnuts
Milk
Syrup: 2 cups water
         2 sticks cinnamon
         2 cloves
         1/2 pound brown sugar
         Combine water, cinnamon and cloves;
         boil for 5 minutes. Add brown sugar and
         continue cooking 5 to 10 minutes until
         slightly thickened.

Butter bread on both sides; toast lightly. Cover bottom of 13 x 9 x 2-inch baking dish with 1/2 of bread slices. Top with 1/2 of cheese, bananas, raisins and walnuts. Moisten with milk and pour over 1/2 of the syrup. Repeat to make two layers. Bake, uncovered, in 350°F. oven 30 minutes. Serve hot. Makes 8 to 10 servings.

Serving Suggestions:
Serve with light meals—soup, a fish dish and salad.

Hints:
Assemble in advance and bake at serving time. Or bake ahead and reheat.

Arroz con Pollo

No collection of Mexican recipes would be complete without this popular chicken and rice dish. It's a one dish meal so perfect for today's busy pace and budget.

2 1/2 to 3 pounds chicken parts
1/2 cup seasoned flour
1/3 cup salad oil
1 package Lawry's Mexican Rice Seasoning Mix
2 cups water
1 teaspoon Lawry's Seasoned Salt
1/4 cup medium-dry sherry
1 cup uncooked long-grain rice

Roll chicken in seasoned flour. In a large skillet or Dutch oven, brown chicken pieces in hot oil. Remove pieces as they brown and drain on paper towels. In 13 x 9 x 2-inch casserole, combine Mexican Rice Seasoning Mix, water, Seasoned Salt, sherry and rice; mix well. Place chicken pieces on top of mixture. Cover and bake in 350°F. oven about 45 minutes or until chicken and rice are cooked. Makes 4 servings.

Note: May use 1 1/2 pounds boneless chicken breasts.
Seasoned Flour: Mix 1/2 cup flour with 1 teaspoon Lawry's Seasoned Salt and 1/2 teaspoon Lawry's Seasoned Pepper.

Serving Suggestions:
Ensalada Esmeralda, Yolanda's Capirotada.

Hints:
Add a package of frozen peas, thawed, to the rice mixture the last 20 minutes of baking time, if desired. Bake ahead and freeze or refrigerate; keeps well.

Serving Suggestions:
A salad is all that's needed to complete the meal.

Hints:
Prepare taco meat mixture in advance and refrigerate. Prepare remaining ingredients, assemble and bake before serving. Make in 4 separate au gratin dishes and serve as an entree.

Nachos can be as simple as grated cheese and an olive slice on tortilla chips or expanded into an entree dish such as this.

1 pound lean ground beef
1 large onion, chopped
1 teaspoon Lawry's Seasoned Salt
1/2 teaspoon ground cumin
2 cans (1 lb. each) refried beans
1 package (1 1/4 oz.) Lawry's Taco Seasoning Mix
2 cups grated Monterey Jack cheese
1 can (4 oz.) chopped green chiles
1 cup grated Cheddar cheese
3/4 cup Lawry's Chunky Taco Sauce
Tortilla chips
Garnish with any or all of the following:
1 cup guacamole (see page 9)
1/2 cup dairy sour cream
1/2 cup chopped green onions
1 cup sliced ripe olives

Brown meat and onion; drain well and add Seasoned Salt and cumin. Combine beans, Taco Seasoning Mix and Monterey Jack cheese; mix well. Spread beans in a shallow, oval (15 x 10-inch) baking dish. Cover with meat mixture. Sprinkle chiles over meat; top with Cheddar cheese. Pour Chunky Taco Sauce over cheese. Bake, uncovered, in a 400°F. oven 20 to 25 minutes or until thoroughly heated. Tuck tortilla chips around edge of platter and garnish as desired. Makes 4 to 6 main dish servings or 10 to 12 appetizer servings.

Supper Nachos

Mixed Fruit

Fruit desserts are a refreshing accompaniment to a Mexican meal.

1 bottle (12 oz.) grenadine syrup
1 tablespoon cornstarch combined with 1 tablespoon water
1/2 cup rum
1 cup each:
        Fresh pineapple chunks
        Papaya chunks
        Orange chunks
        Dark pitted cherries
Lime sherbet

Combine grenadine and cornstarch-water mixture in a saucepan and bring to a boil; reduce heat and simmer, stirring frequently, until thick and smooth (about 8 minutes); cool. Add rum. Combine fruits and sauce and refrigerate for at least 2 hours. Spoon over lime sherbet. Makes 8 servings.

Serving Suggestions:
Especially good with enchiladas of all kinds, *Tamale Casserole or Tijuana Torte.*

Hints:
Use any combination of favorite fruits in season. Keeps well, covered, in the refrigerator for about 2 days though for optimum appearance, serve the same day.

Chicken or Turkey Molé

A traditional dish served on Christmas Eve as well as throughout the year. The richly flavored molé sauce contains chocolate and peanut butter, which are interesting flavors to combine with the chili seasoning.

2 quarts water
2 tablespoons Lawry's Seasoned Salt
2 broiler-fryers (2 1/2 to 3 lbs. each), cut up
1 medium onion, finely chopped
3 tablespoons salad oil
1 can (1 lb.) tomatoes
2 packages Lawry's Chili Seasoning Mix
3 cups chicken broth (from simmered chicken)
1/3 cup chunky style peanut butter
1 tablet (3 to 4 oz.) Mexican chocolate, grated
1 tablespoon sesame seeds, toasted

In a Dutch oven, combine water, Seasoned Salt and chicken. Bring to a boil, reduce heat, cover and simmer about 45 minutes, or until tender. Save broth to use in molé sauce. Meanwhile, in a large skillet, sauté onion in hot oil. Add tomatoes and Chili Seasoning Mix. Combine thoroughly, breaking up tomatoes with a spoon. Add chicken broth. Bring to a boil, add peanut butter and Mexican chocolate. Stir thoroughly. Reduce heat and simmer, uncovered, 15 minutes, stirring occasionally. Place chicken in large shallow casserole. Pour molé sauce over chicken. Bake in 350°F. oven 20 to 30 minutes. Sprinkle with toasted sesame seeds. Makes 8 to 10 servings.

Note: 5 to 6 pounds turkey parts may be substituted for chicken. If this is done, remove turkey meat from bone after simmering and cut into 1 1/2-inch pieces. Use turkey broth.

2 squares (1 oz. each) semi-sweet chocolate, 2 tablespoons sugar and 1/4 teaspoon cinnamon may be substituted for the Mexican chocolate.

Serving Suggestions:
Warmed corn or flour tortillas or fluffy rice, *Ensalada de Noche Buena.*

Hints:
May be made ahead and baked just before serving or baked ahead and reheated. Mexican chocolate may be purchased in an ethnic market, or use the substitution given in recipe.

Steak Picado

Serving Suggestions:
Fiesta Rice, green salad, *Tortilla Flats*.

Hints:
Flavor improves if made a day ahead. If desired, eliminate the steps involving Tenderizing Beef Marinade and brown the meat in hot oil, add to enchilada sauce and simmer, covered, 1 to 1 1/2 hours, stirring frequently. Proceed with the remainder of the recipe.

A well known Mexican specialty served over rice or as a filling for burritos.

1 can (1 lb.) tomatoes, cut up
Water
1 package Lawry's Enchilada Sauce Mix
2 pounds chuck steak
1 package Lawry's Tenderizing Beef Marinade, prepared according to package directions
Grated Cheddar cheese
Chopped green onion, including tops

Combine tomatoes and enough water to make 3 cups. In a saucepan, blend Enchilada Sauce Mix and tomato/water mixture. Bring to a boil, reduce heat and simmer, uncovered, 15 minutes. Meanwhile, thoroughly pierce both sides of steak with tines of fork. Cut into chunks and place in prepared Tenderizing Beef Marinade. Marinate **10 minutes only**, turning pieces several times. Add marinated steak pieces to sauce and simmer, covered, 30 minutes. Top with cheese and onions before serving. Makes 4 to 6 servings.

Mexican Lasagna

Serving Suggestions:
Mexican Dinner Salad, Mixed Fruit.

Hints:
May be made early in the day and refrigerated. Add 10 to 15 minutes to the baking time. Or, freeze and defrost before baking.

This hearty dish uses tortillas in place of lasagna noodles; also the sauce is a little zingier than regular lasagna.

1 1/2 pounds ground beef
1 teaspoon Lawry's Seasoned Salt
1 package (1 1/4 oz.) Lawry's Taco Seasoning Mix
1 cup diced tomatoes, fresh or canned
2 cans (8 oz. each) tomato sauce
1 can (4 oz.) diced green chiles
8 ounces ricotta cheese
2 eggs
9 corn tortillas
10 ounces Monterey Jack cheese, grated

Brown ground beef until crumbly; drain fat. Add Seasoned Salt, Taco Seasoning Mix, tomatoes, tomato sauce and chiles. Bring to a boil, reduce heat and simmer, uncovered, 10 minutes. Combine ricotta cheese and eggs. In bottom of 13 x 9 x 2-inch baking dish, spread 1/2 of meat mixture. Top with 1/2 of tortillas; spread 1/2 ricotta cheese and egg mixture over tortillas and top with 1/2 grated Jack cheese. Repeat once more, ending with grated cheese. Bake in 350°F. oven 20 to 30 minutes. Let stand 10 minutes before cutting into squares. Makes 8 servings.

Tamale Casserole

There are many versions of this recipe—this one is outstanding and easy too. The corn meal mixture is used as a topping only; many recipes also have a corn meal crust.

1 1/2 pounds ground beef
1/2 cup chopped onion
1/2 cup chopped green bell pepper
1 teaspoon Lawry's Seasoned Salt
1 package Lawry's Chili Seasoning Mix
1 can (1 lb.) tomatoes
1 can (12 oz.) whole kernel corn, drained
1 can (3 1/4 oz.) small pitted ripe olives, drained (about 1 cup)
1 cup yellow corn meal
1 teaspoon salt
2 1/2 cups cold water
1 cup grated Cheddar cheese

Brown ground beef in skillet until crumbly; drain fat. Add onion, green pepper, Seasoned Salt, Chili Seasoning Mix and tomatoes. Combine thoroughly. Bring to a boil, reduce heat and simmer, uncovered, 10 minutes. Add corn and olives. Spread mixture in 2-quart oblong baking dish. Combine corn meal, salt and cold water. Cook until thick, about 15 minutes. Spread cooked corn meal evenly over beef mixture or pipe with pastry bag. Bake in 350°F. oven 40 minutes. Sprinkle grated cheese over top and bake 5 minutes longer. Makes 6 to 8 servings.

Serving Suggestions:
Creamy Chayote Soup, Mexican Dinner Salad.

Hints:
Make ahead and refrigerate; just add 10 to 15 minutes to the baking time if the dish comes directly from the refrigerator. When using whole canned tomatoes, cut up tomatoes with a knife or kitchen scissors before adding to a recipe. The whole pieces are too large to mix with the other ingredients.

Tamale Casserole

Jicama Custard Dessert

Serving Suggestions:
Serve with hearty entrees such as *Chile Verde* or enchiladas.

Hints:
Make ahead and serve chilled or reheat just before serving.

Jicama, a root vegetable resembling a turnip in shape but with a brown skin, is crisp and delicious in salads or served plain with lime juice and Seasoned Salt. This dessert recipe is an unusual way to use jicama.

1 1/2 pounds jicama, peeled and coarsely grated
1 can (8 oz.) beer
4 eggs, beaten
1/3 cup light cream
3/4 cup sugar
1/2 teaspoon vanilla
2 tablespoons butter

Combine jicama and beer in a saucepan. Bring to a boil, reduce heat and simmer, uncovered, until liquid is absorbed. Cool slightly. Combine eggs, light cream, sugar and vanilla; stir into jicama. Pour mixture into a buttered, 8 x 8 x 2-inch dish. Dot top with butter. Set in a pan containing 1-inch of water and bake, uncovered, in 350°F. oven 45 to 50 minutes. Cover with foil if top browns too quickly. Serve warm or chilled. Makes 6 to 8 servings.

Poached Chicken in Chunky Taco Sauce

Hints:
May be frozen.

A basic filling to use for tacos, enchiladas and burritos.

1 quart water
3/4 teaspoon Lawry's Seasoned Salt
1/4 teaspoon Lawry's Garlic Powder with Parsley
1/4 teaspoon Lawry's Seasoned Pepper
3 pounds boneless, skinned chicken breasts
1 bottle Lawry's Chunky Taco Sauce

Combine water and seasonings in Dutch oven. Bring to a boil, add chicken, cover and poach until done, about 20 minutes. Drain and cool. Shred chicken and add Chunky Taco Sauce. Makes 4 cups.

Chimichangas

(Fried Burritos)

Serving Suggestions:
Nopalitos Salad, Julie's Sangria.

Hints:
Tortillas must be very fresh to be pliable enough to roll or fold without cracking.

Burritos, when fried until crisp, are called chimichangas.

8 (12-inch) flour tortillas
1 can (1 lb. 4 oz.) refried beans, heated
4 cups grated Monterey Jack cheese
1 recipe Poached Chicken in Chunky Taco Sauce
Salad oil for frying

On each tortilla place (in a long strip down center of tortilla) 1/4 cup beans, 1/2 cup cheese and 1/2 cup Poached Chicken. Fold in sides of tortilla and roll up like a burrito. Heat oil (about 1-inch deep) in skillet. Fry burritos, turning once, until golden. Drain on paper towels and serve hot. Makes 8 chimichangas.

Torta Mexican-Style

A beautiful blend of flavors, colors and textures. Good for brunch, lunch or supper and convenient to have on hand for emergencies.

1 package (13 3/4 oz.) hot roll mix
1 pound ground beef
1 package (1 1/4 oz.) Lawry's Taco Seasoning Mix
1 package (10 oz.) frozen chopped spinach, thawed
1/2 pint cottage OR ricotta cheese, drained
1 egg, beaten

Prepare hot roll mix according to package directions. While bread is rising, prepare beef with Taco Seasoning Mix according to package directions. Squeeze excess moisture from spinach and combine with cheese. When fillings are prepared, divide dough into three portions and roll each into a 10-inch round. Fit one portion into a buttered 10-inch springform pan. Spread meat almost to edges of dough. Add next layer of dough and allow to rise 10 minutes. Spread with spinach mixture. Place last portion of dough on top and cover with damp cloth. Set Torta in warm place to rise about 40 minutes. When about double in size, score top with a sharp knife into 8 pie-shaped wedges. Brush top with egg. Bake on lower rack of 350°F. oven 50 to 60 minutes or until bread is deep golden brown. Makes 8 servings.

Serving Suggestions:
Gazpacho, Mexican Coffee.

Hints:
Make ahead, bake and freeze. Reheat, frozen and covered, in a 350°F. oven 45 minutes. May use frozen chopped broccoli in place of spinach or frozen bread dough (1 lb. loaf) instead of hot roll mix.

Enchiladas Suisse

An elegant and colorful enchilada dish made with both white and red sauce.

1 onion, finely chopped
1/8 teaspoon Lawry's Garlic Powder with Parsley
2 tablespoons salad oil
1 package Lawry's Enchilada Sauce Mix, prepared according to package directions
2 tablespoons chopped green chiles, optional
3 cups cooked, shredded chicken
Lawry's Seasoned Salt, to taste
Lawry's Seasoned Pepper, to taste
3 chicken bouillon cubes
2 cups whipping cream
12 corn tortillas
Salad oil for frying
1/2 pound grated Monterey Jack cheese

In large skillet sauté onion and Garlic Powder with Parsley until onion is tender. Add 2 cups prepared Enchilada Sauce, green chiles (if desired), shredded chicken, and season to taste; simmer, uncovered, 5 minutes. Pour remaining Enchilada Sauce in bottom of 13 x 9 x 2-inch baking dish; set aside. Meanwhile combine bouillon and cream; heat until bouillon cubes dissolve; keep warm. To assemble enchiladas, soften each tortilla in hot oil and dip in hot cream mixture. Place 1/4 cup chicken on each tortilla and roll up. Place, seam side down, on sauce in baking dish. Pour remaining cream mixture over enchiladas and top with grated cheese. Bake, uncovered, in 350°F. oven 20 to 25 minutes or until cheese is melted. Makes 6 to 8 servings.

Serving Suggestions:
Gazpacho, buttered zucchini.

Hints:
Make ahead and refrigerate until ready to bake. Cooked shredded turkey may be substituted for chicken.

Torta Mexican-Style

Red Snapper Veracruz

Serving Suggestions:
Fluffy rice, *Ensalada Esmeralda*, *Jicama Dessert*.

Hints:
Sauce may be made ahead. Use any fresh fish fillets in season; shrimp is also good made Veracruz-style.

Fresh fish, popular in coastal regions of Mexico, is often served with tomato-onion sauce. This one has the added flavors of olives and capers.

1 pound red snapper fillets
Lemon juice
Lawry's Seasoned Salt
Lawry's Seasoned Pepper
3 tablespoons salad oil
1/2 cup chopped onion
2 cloves garlic, minced
1 can (1 lb.) tomatoes, drained
3 tablespoons chopped parsley
1 tablespoon vinegar
1 teaspoon Lawry's Seasoned Salt
1 bay leaf
1/4 teaspoon Lawry's Pinch of Herbs
1 teaspoon sugar
1/4 cup water
1/4 cup sliced pimiento-stuffed green olives
2 teaspoons capers
2 tablespoons chopped green chiles
2 tablespoons olive oil

Rub fish with lemon juice; sprinkle with Seasoned Salt and Seasoned Pepper. Fry in hot oil 1 minute per side; remove to baking dish. Sauté onion, garlic and tomatoes in remaining oil 5 minutes; add more oil if necessary. Add parsley, vinegar, Seasoned Salt, bay leaf, Pinch of Herbs, sugar and water; cook an additional 2 minutes. Top fish with olives, capers and chiles; pour sauce over all. Drizzle with olive oil and bake, uncovered, in 300°F. oven until fish flakes, about 30 minutes. Makes 4 servings.

Chicken Avocado Enchiladas

Avocados are an unusual flavor and textural addition to this chicken filling.

8 corn tortillas
1/2 cup salad oil
2 cups Poached Chicken in Chunky Taco Sauce (see page 71)
1 large avocado, peeled and sliced in 8 slices
1 cup dairy sour cream, at room temperature
1 can (4 oz.) diced green chiles
2 packages Lawry's Chicken Gravy Mix, prepared according to package directions
1/2 cup grated Monterey Jack cheese
Lawry's Chunky Taco Sauce

In skillet, cook tortillas, one at a time, in hot oil for 15 seconds on each side. (Do not overcook or they will not roll.) Place about 1/4 cup Poached Chicken and 1 avocado slice on each tortilla; roll up. Place seam side down in 12 x 8 x 2-inch baking dish; repeat for remaining tortillas. In saucepan, add sour cream and chiles to prepared Chicken Gravy; cook until thoroughly heated but do not boil. Pour over tortillas in baking dish. Bake, uncovered, in 425°F. oven 20 minutes. Sprinkle cheese over top; return to oven 5 minutes longer or until cheese melts. Serve with Chunky Taco Sauce as a topping. Makes 4 servings.

Serving Suggestions:
Fiesta Rice, Ensalada Tropical.

Hints:
To ripen avocados, leave at room temperature. When ripe, store in refrigerator until ready to use.

Machaca de Huevos

(Spiced Beef with Scrambled Eggs)

Machaca, a seasoned beef often served alone, is here combined with eggs, cheese and vegetables.

Salad oil
1 1/2 pounds flank steak
Lawry's Seasoned Salt
Lawry's Seasoned Pepper
2 cups water
4 onions, halved and sliced
1 green bell pepper, diced
2 tomatoes, diced
1 dozen eggs, beaten
2 cups grated Cheddar cheese
8 flour tortillas, optional
Lawry's Chunky Taco Sauce, optional

To prepare beef, heat oil in large skillet. Season flank steak liberally with Seasoned Salt and Seasoned Pepper. Brown meat on both sides; add water, bring to a boil, reduce heat and simmer, covered, 2 hours or until tender. Add more water during cooking if necessary. When meat is tender, shred into medium-size pieces. Machaca: Heat 2 to 3 tablespoons oil in large skillet; quickly sauté onions, green pepper and tomatoes. Add meat, eggs and cheese. Continue cooking as for scrambled eggs. Serve as entree or use as burrito filling. To make burritos, place about 1 cup filling in center of flour tortilla, fold sides in and roll up. Serve with Chunky Taco Sauce, if desired. Makes 6 servings or 8 burritos.

Serving Suggestions:
As an entree with warmed tortillas and fresh fruit with lime wedges.

Hints:
Prepare beef ahead, shred and freeze or refrigerate. To make burritos, warm tortillas before filling and rolling to prevent cracking.

Glossary of Mexican Foods and Ingredients

ALBONDIGAS (al-bohn'-dee-gahs) Meatballs usually served with vegetables in a broth.

BURRITO (boo-rree'-toe) Flour tortillas wrapped around fillings such as meats, beans or vegetables. May be fried, baked, warmed or served cold.

CHAYOTE (chy-oh'-tay) A pear-shaped, light green squash which must be peeled before cooking. Zucchini or potato may be substituted.

CHILES (chee'-lehs) Though there are many different kinds of fresh chiles, the green chiles called for in these recipes are available canned, either diced or whole, and vary in "hotness." If using the whole canned chiles, rinse and remove the seeds and veins.

CHORIZO (chor-ee'-so) A typical Mexican spicy sausage, available in ethnic markets. Regular pork sausage, though not the same flavor, may be substituted.

CILANTRO (see-lahn'-tro) Also called Chinese parsley, cilantro is fresh coriander. Sold in bunches, the cilantro leaves are broad and flat. It has a distinctive flavor.

ENCHILADAS (en-chee-lah'-das) Corn tortillas rolled around a filling of meat, poultry, seafood, cheese or chiles, covered with a sauce and baked.

FRIJOLES (free-ho'-lays) **REFRITOS** (rreh-free'-tohs) Cooked beans which have been flavored with lard. Available canned and called Refried Beans.

GAZPACHO (gahs-pah'-cho) A cold soup made with tomatoes and chopped vegetables.

GUACAMOLE (wah-kah-moh'-leh) Dip or sauce made of mashed avocados and seasonings.

JICAMA (hee'-kah-mah) A brown skinned root vegetable, shaped like a turnip. The edible interior is white, sweet and crisp, similar in texture to a water chestnut. Usually served raw, it also may be cooked.

MASA (mah'-sah) Dough made of corn flour to make tortillas and tamales. Flour, available in most supermarkets, is called masa harina.

MOLÉ (moh'-lay) A thick, flavorful sauce made with tomatoes, chiles, chocolate and nuts. Cooked with chicken or turkey, this is a traditional Christmas Eve dish.

NOPALES (no-pah'-les) The leaves of the prickly pear cactus. Available fresh in ethnic markets and canned (called nopalitos) either marinated or plain.

TACOS (tah'-kohs) Corn or flour tortillas, filled with seasoned meat, chicken or other fillings, folded in half and generally fried. Served garnished with shredded lettuce and chopped tomatoes, onions, olives and grated cheese.

TAMALES (tah-mah'-les) Made of masa dough which is spread on corn husks, topped with a filling, tied and steamed.

TORTILLA (tor-tee'-ya) Flat, round unleavened bread made with masa or flour. Available fresh, frozen or canned.

TOSTADA (tos-tah'-da) Tortillas, fried crisp and flat, and topped with refried beans, meat, fish or poultry, cheese, shredded lettuce and chopped tomatoes. Sometimes called an open-face taco.

QUESO (keh'-so) Means cheese in Spanish.

VERDE (verr'-deh) Means green in Spanish.

SALADS AND MORE SALADS

No story about salads or about Lawry's can be told without going back to the beginning. In 1938, Lawry's The Prime Rib opened in Beverly Hills and was one of the first restaurants anywhere to feature a tossed green salad as a first course—before the entree. Tossed at the table in a salad bowl spinning on a bed of ice, the novel salad was dramatically topped with the "house" salad dressing. Because of the dressing's popularity it was later bottled and sold by Lawry's Foods. The company has since added a number of salad dressing flavors, both in bottled and dry mix form. Through the years Lawry's has earned a reputation for fine salad making.

The basics of salad making are quality ingredients thoroughly washed, drained and chilled, then lightly tossed with a complementary dressing to marry the flavors. The dressing is like the perfect accessory for an outfit—it shouldn't be the central focus yet it should pull together the various components. For the finishing touch provide chilled salad forks and serve the salad on thoroughly chilled plates.

The salads in this chapter include tossed, molded and marinated; pasta and potato; classics; and meat, chicken and seafood. In addition to the Lawry's dressings, "from scratch" salad dressings for all types of salads are included.

In salad making, creativity and imagination count far more than cooking knowledge. It's a real opportunity for artistry in the kitchen!

Marinated Summer Salad
Apple Valley Salad
Capri Salad

———————————— # Apple Valley Salad

Hints:
Chill salad plates or bowls and salad forks before serving.

4 cups shredded cabbage
2 medium apples, quartered, cored and diced
1/4 cup chopped green onion
1/2 medium green bell pepper, slivered
1 teaspoon sugar
1 teaspoon Lawry's Seasoned Salt
1/4 teaspoon Lawry's Seasoned Pepper
1/2 cup Lawry's Canadian Dressing

Toss cabbage, apples, green onion and green pepper. Sprinkle with sugar, Seasoned Salt and Seasoned Pepper. Add Canadian Dressing and toss. Makes 6 servings.

Capri Salad

Hints:
Add interest to salads by varying the ways of cutting, chopping or slicing vegetables, meats and cheeses.

1 head cauliflower, broken into flowerets
1 onion, sliced in rings
3 zucchini, sliced 1/8-inch thick
1 green bell pepper, diced
1/2 cup diced celery
1 can (6 oz.) pitted ripe olives, drained
1 bottle Lawry's Red Wine Vinegar & Oil Dressing

Combine vegetables in large bowl. Heat Red Wine Vinegar & Oil Dressing but do not boil. Add hot dressing to vegetables; toss. Cover and refrigerate at least 4 hours, tossing several times. Makes 10 to 12 servings.

Marinated Summer Salad

Hints:
Raw broccoli, cauliflower, jicama and water chestnuts add interest and variety.

Use remainder of broccoli in soup or stew or slice thinly and use in a stir-fry dish.

As served at Lawry's California Center.

1 bunch broccoli
1 red onion, diced
1 large tomato, diced
1 cup grated Cheddar cheese
1 package Lawry's Italian Salad Dressing Mix, prepared according to package directions

Use only the buds and uppermost part of broccoli stalk and chop. Add remaining ingredients and marinate overnight. Makes 10 servings.

Tangy Bean Sprout Toss

Hints:
Alfalfa and bean sprouts are popular and flavorful salad additions.

1 pound fresh bean sprouts, rinsed
1 zucchini, thinly sliced
1 tablespoon chopped pimiento
1/2 cup Lawry's Red Wine Vinegar & Oil Dressing

Blanch bean sprouts and zucchini in boiling water; drain. Combine all ingredients and toss lightly. Chill several hours before serving. Makes 6 servings.

Marinated Vegetables Italia

1 can (1 lb.) shoestring beets, well drained
1 carrot, coarsely grated
3 radishes, thinly sliced
1 box cherry tomatoes, (about 24) halved
1 package (10 oz.) frozen asparagus, cooked and drained
1 package (10 oz.) frozen broccoli, cooked and drained
1/4 pound sliced fresh mushrooms
1/2 cup Lawry's Red Wine Vinegar & Oil Dressing
1 quart torn lettuce
1 tablespoon Lawry's Bacon Onion Seasoning

Hints:
Marinated salad ingredients may be served as is on a bed of lettuce or tossed with greens as part of a larger salad. Often the marinade (usually oil and vinegar base) may be used as the dressing for the tossed salad.

Combine all ingredients, except lettuce and Bacon Onion Seasoning. Marinate several hours or overnight, stirring occasionally. Just before serving, add lettuce and Bacon Onion Seasoning and toss. Makes 10 servings.

Wilted Spinach Salad

3 quarts torn spinach, stems removed (approximately 2 bunches)
6 bacon slices
1/2 cup chopped green onions
1/3 cup vinegar
1/3 cup water
1 package Lawry's Italian Salad Dressing Mix
2 teaspoons sugar

Hints:
Use 3 quarts lettuce for wilted lettuce version.

To wash spinach, cut off roots and swish leaves in a sink full of lukewarm water. Change water several times. Dry thoroughly.

Place spinach in large salad bowl. Fry bacon until crisp; drain, reserve drippings and crumble. Add bacon and onions to spinach; toss. Add vinegar, water, Italian Salad Dressing Mix and sugar to bacon drippings. Heat to boiling point; pour over spinach. Toss and serve immediately. Makes 6 to 8 servings.

Eggplant Relish Salad

2 eggplants, diced
2 teaspoons Lawry's Seasoned Salt
1/2 cup olive oil
1 package Lawry's Italian with Cheese Salad Dressing Mix
1/4 cup olive oil
2 tomatoes, diced
2 stalks celery, diced
1 tablespoon vinegar
1 teaspoon sugar
1/2 teaspoon Lawry's Seasoned Pepper
1 can (2 1/4 oz.) sliced ripe olives
2 tablespoons capers

Sprinkle eggplant with Seasoned Salt; let stand 10 minutes. Pat dry with paper towels; sauté in 1/2 cup olive oil until brown. In a large saucepan, combine Italian with Cheese Salad Dressing Mix, olive oil, tomatoes, celery, vinegar, sugar and Seasoned Pepper; heat thoroughly. Add eggplant; cook an additional 10 minutes. Transfer to serving dish; chill. Garnish with olives and capers. Makes 8 to 10 servings.

Zucchini Vinaigrette

Hints:
Parsley and watercress should be immersed in water to clean thoroughly.

As served at Lawry's California Center.

1 package Lawry's Italian Salad Dressing Mix
2 tablespoons water
1/4 cup white wine vinegar
1/4 cup white wine
1/2 cup salad oil
2 tablespoons finely chopped green bell pepper
2 tablespoons chopped parsley
2 tablespoons finely chopped green onion
3 tablespoons sweet pickle relish
5 or 6 medium-size zucchini, diagonally sliced about 1/4-inch thick

Combine Italian Salad Dressing Mix and water in a jar; shake well. Add vinegar, wine and salad oil; shake about 30 seconds. Add remaining ingredients except zucchini and shake again. Pour vinaigrette sauce over zucchini. Marinate several hours or overnight. Serve as a relish or mix with salad greens. Makes 8 servings.

Artichokes Vinaigrette

Hints:
Salads are versatile and may be served as an appetizer or first course, an accessory to the entree, as a main course or dessert (fruit salad).

2 packages (9 oz. each) frozen artichoke hearts
1/4 cup lemon juice
1/2 cup salad oil
1 teaspoon Lawry's Seasoned Salt
1/4 teaspoon Lawry's Seasoned Pepper
2 tablespoons minced pimiento-stuffed green olives
2 tablespoons minced green onion
2 tablespoons sweet pickle relish, drained

Cook artichokes according to package directions except cook only about 3 minutes or until just tender; drain. Combine remaining ingredients in a jar; shake well. Pour over warm artichokes and marinate overnight. Makes 6 servings.

Vegetable Medley

1 pound green beans
1 bunch carrots, peeled
1 can (1 lb.) small whole potatoes
1/2 cup Lawry's San Francisco Dressing

Cut ends from green beans and leave whole. Cut carrots in lengthwise strips about size of beans. Cook beans and carrots separately in boiling salted water until almost tender; drain. Rinse potatoes in cold water; drain. Arrange vegetables in shallow dish. Add dressing and refrigerate several hours or overnight. Makes 6 to 8 servings.

Limelight Salad Marcus

Limelight Salad Marcus

Serve with a simple entree, for this salad will be center stage.

1 quart torn lettuce
2 tomatoes, cut in wedges
1/2 papaya, peeled, seeded and cubed
1/2 large pink OR white grapefruit, peeled and sectioned
1/4 pound sharp Cheddar cheese, cubed
1/2 cup dry roasted cashews
1 avocado, peeled, seeded and cubed
Juice of 1 small lime
1/4 cup safflower oil
Lawry's Lemon Pepper Seasoning

Combine all ingredients except lime juice, oil and Lemon Pepper Seasoning. Mix lime juice and oil in a jar; shake well. Add to salad; sprinkle generously with Lemon Pepper Seasoning; toss. Makes 4 servings.

Hints:

When in season, mangoes, kiwis, pomegranates or jicama are colorful additions.

Use crunchy ingredients for texture—nuts, croutons, Chinese noodles, toasted sesame seeds, wheat germ or bulgar, sunflower seeds, pine nuts, crisp fried tortilla strips or small size corn chips.

Orange and Red Onion Salad

2 bunches fresh spinach, washed and drained
4 medium oranges, peeled and sectioned
2 medium red onions, peeled and thinly sliced in rings
1 recipe French Vinaigrette Dressing (see page 94)

Combine all ingredients and toss. Makes 6 servings.

Hints:

Select the freshest, top quality salad greens, using two or more varieties for interesting contrast in flavor and texture.

Lima-Mushroom Vinaigrette

Hints:
The fresh and frozen vegetables specified in these recipes are interchangeable. Use fresh when in season if desired.

1 package (10 oz.) frozen baby lima beans, cooked and drained
1 1/2 cups sliced fresh mushrooms
3/4 cup finely chopped onion
1 teaspoon dried parsley flakes
2 teaspoons Lawry's Pinch of Herbs
1/2 teaspoon Lawry's Seasoned Salt
1/2 teaspoon Lawry's Seasoned Pepper
1/3 cup red OR white wine vinegar
3 tablespoons salad oil

Combine beans, mushrooms and onion. Combine remaining ingredients; shake well. Pour over vegetables; toss. Chill at least 2 hours or overnight. Makes 6 to 8 servings.

Ensalada Esmeralda

Hints:
To make a tossed salad ahead of time, tear greens into pieces and place in bowl; cover with layer of paper towels. Prepare other vegetables, meats or cheeses but do not add items such as tomatoes (too moist), beets (will discolor), or avocados (will turn brown) until serving time. Place the cut vegetables, etc. over lettuce, cover with paper towels, then with plastic wrap and refrigerate.

A lovely, well-seasoned green salad tossed with zucchini and cream cheese.

1 zucchini, parboiled and thinly sliced
1/2 cup Lawry's Italian with Cheese Dressing
1 1/2 quarts torn romaine
1 red onion, thinly sliced
1 package (3 oz.) cream cheese, cubed
1 tablespoon Lawry's Bacon Onion Seasoning

Marinate zucchini in Italian with Cheese Dressing for several hours. Toss with remaining ingredients just before serving. Makes 6 servings.

Ensalada Esmeralda

Spring Asparagus Salad

1 package Lawry's Italian Salad Dressing Mix
1/4 cup water
1/4 cup lemon juice
1/3 cup salad oil
2 1/2 pounds fresh asparagus
2 cups water
1/2 teaspoon salt
1 jar (3 oz.) pimiento-stuffed green olives, drained and sliced
3/4 cup pepitas (toasted pumpkin seeds)
8 romaine leaves

Combine Italian Salad Dressing Mix, water and lemon juice in a jar; shake well. Add oil; shake again. Cut each asparagus stalk into 1/2-inch diagonal slices leaving tip whole; discard tough end. Bring water to a boil; add asparagus and salt. Cover and cook 3 minutes; drain. Add olives and dressing to asparagus. Chill 2 hours. Just before serving, drain asparagus mixture. Add pepitas; serve on bed of romaine leaves. Makes 8 servings.

Garbeano Salad

1 can (15 1/2 oz.) kidney beans, rinsed and drained
1 can (15 oz.) garbanzo beans, drained
1 package (9 oz.) Italian-cut green beans, cooked and drained
1/2 cup julienne carrots
1/2 cup julienne celery
1/2 cup julienne green bell pepper
1/2 cup slivered onion
2 tablespoons chopped parsley
2 tablespoons chopped pimiento
1 package Lawry's Italian with Cheese Salad Dressing Mix
1 clove garlic, crushed
1/2 teaspoon Lawry's Seasoned Salt
1/2 teaspoon Lawry's Seasoned Pepper

Hints:
Cut julienne vegetables 1 1/2-inches long.

Combine beans, carrots, celery, green pepper, onion, parsley and pimiento. Prepare Italian with Cheese Salad Dressing Mix according to package directions and add garlic, Seasoned Salt and Seasoned Pepper. Add to vegetables; toss. Marinate several hours or overnight. Makes 8 to 10 servings.

Jicama Salad

2 cups peeled, diced jicama
1 green OR red bell pepper, slivered
1 small onion, thinly sliced
1 cup sliced cucumber
1 recipe Lemon Garlic Dressing (see page 93)

Hints:
Jicama is in season from November to June. It can be cooked but is best served chilled and crisp.

Combine all ingredients and chill 2 to 3 hours. Makes 4 to 6 servings.

Tabbouleh

Tabbouleh

Hints:
Store parsley, watercress and mint in a tightly covered jar or container.

A Middle Eastern specialty, fresh-tasting and delicious.

1/2 cup uncooked long-grain brown rice
3/4 cup boiling water
2 large bunches parsley, chopped
1 bunch green onions, chopped
1 1/2 cups diced tomatoes
1/4 cup chopped fresh mint OR 1 tablespoon dried mint flakes, crushed
Juice of 1 lemon
1 recipe Lemon Garlic Dressing (see page 93)

Cook rice in boiling water, covered, for 5 minutes; drain. Combine all ingredients and refrigerate several hours or overnight before serving. Makes 10 servings.

Eva's Pea-Nut Salad

Hints:
Use regular or petite-size peas. Cooked crumbled bacon may be substituted for Bacon Onion Seasoning.

Peanuts add flavor and crunch to this bacon-flavored, do-ahead pea salad.

2 packages (10 oz. each) frozen peas, cooked and drained
1 cup diced celery
1 cup chopped green onions
1 cup dairy sour cream
3 tablespoons mayonnaise
1 tablespoon lemon juice
1 teaspoon Lawry's Seasoned Salt
1 cup unsalted, dry roasted peanuts
1/4 cup Lawry's Bacon Onion Seasoning

Combine peas, celery and green onions. Blend together sour cream, mayonnaise, lemon juice and Seasoned Salt. Mix with vegetables and chill several hours or overnight. Before serving, add peanuts and Bacon Onion Seasoning and mix well. Makes 6 to 8 servings.

Tomato and Mushroom Salad

2 large tomatoes, peeled and cut crosswise in thirds
Romaine leaves
1/3 pound fresh mushrooms, finely chopped
1/2 recipe French Vinaigrette Dressing (see page 94)

Arrange tomato slices on romaine leaves and top with mushrooms. Spoon French Vinaigrette Dressing over each serving. Makes 6 servings.

Hints:
Chill salad ingredients thoroughly before serving.

Salad Niçoise ———————————————— Classics

1 small head iceberg lettuce, torn in bite-size pieces
1 head butter lettuce, torn in bite-size pieces
2 cups cooked, cubed potatoes
1 package (9 oz.) French-cut green beans, cooked and drained
1 can (7 oz.) white tuna, drained and flaked
1/4 green bell pepper, cut in strips
2 hard-cooked eggs, sliced
16 pitted ripe olives
1 small onion, thinly sliced
1 medium tomato, cut in 8 wedges
1 tablespoon lemon juice
1 teaspoon Lawry's Seasoned Salt
1/2 teaspoon Lawry's Seasoned Pepper
1 bottle Lawry's San Francisco Dressing

Place lettuce in bottom of large salad bowl. Arrange potatoes, green beans, tuna, green pepper, eggs, olives, onion and tomato attractively on lettuce. When ready to serve salad, toss lightly with lemon juice, Seasoned Salt, Seasoned Pepper and San Francisco Dressing. Makes 6 to 8 servings.

Hints:
Choose from a variety of greens — iceberg, romaine, bibb or limestone, leaf, Boston, spinach, watercress, endive, escarole and cabbage.

Handle greens gently as they bruise easily.

To wash lettuce, remove core by tearing not cutting. Wash each leaf separately on those that are leafy and break apart easily (romaine, Boston, leaf, etc.).

Caesar Salad

A classic and beautiful salad.

1 clove garlic
2 medium heads romaine OR leaf lettuce
2 anchovy fillets
3/4 cup Lawry's Caesar Dressing
1 egg, coddled
1 tablespoon lemon juice
2 tablespoons grated Parmesan cheese
1 cup garlic-flavored croutons
Lawry's Seasoned Salt
Lawry's Seasoned Pepper

Rub a large wooden salad bowl with garlic and discard garlic. Tear lettuce into pieces; place in salad bowl. In a small bowl, combine anchovy fillets and 1 tablespoon prepared Caesar Dressing; mash thoroughly. Add remainder of dressing and coddled egg; blend thoroughly. Pour over greens; add lemon juice, Parmesan cheese and croutons. Sprinkle with Lawry's Seasoned Salt and Seasoned Pepper; toss. Makes 6 servings.

Hints:
Croutons add flavor and texture to salads. Homemade croutons are delicious and easy to prepare. See page 125 for directions.

Cobb Salad

Cobb Salad

Hints:

Salad may be made several hours ahead but do not add dressing. Cover with damp paper towel and plastic wrap and refrigerate. Chop all ingredients very fine so they are all about the same size. Quantities for greens are given in cup measurements since heads of various kinds of lettuce differ in size.

Cobb Salad was created by the president of the Brown Derby restaurant in Los Angeles.

2 quarts finely chopped iceberg and romaine lettuce
1 1/2 cups finely chopped, cooked chicken breast
6 green onions, finely chopped
2 hard-cooked eggs, finely chopped
2 medium tomatoes, peeled, seeded and finely chopped
6 bacon slices, cooked crisp and crumbled
1/2 cup crumbled blue cheese
2 avocados, peeled, seeds removed and minced
1 tablespoon lemon juice
1 recipe French Vinaigrette Dressing (see page 94)

Place lettuce in bottom of a large shallow salad bowl. Arrange minced chicken in narrow strip down center of salad. Arrange strips of green onion, egg and tomato on one side; arrange bacon, blue cheese and avocado (sprinkled with lemon juice) on the other. Add French Vinaigrette Dressing and toss. Makes 4 servings.

Mashed Potato Salad a la Mold ————————— Pasta and Potato

4 cups water
1 cup milk
6 tablespoons butter
1 1/2 teaspoons Lawry's Seasoned Salt
1 tablespoon Lawry's Lemon Pepper Seasoning
4 cups instant potato buds OR flakes
1/4 cup cider OR white wine vinegar
1 cup mayonnaise
6 hard-cooked eggs, coarsely chopped
1 cup chopped celery
3/4 cup chopped green bell pepper
1/2 cup chopped green onions (including tops)
1/4 cup chopped pimiento
Lettuce, to garnish
Tomato wedges, to garnish

Combine water, milk, butter, Seasoned Salt and Lemon Pepper Seasoning in a large saucepan; heat just to boiling. Remove from heat. Stir in instant potatoes, cover and let stand 5 minutes. Add remaining ingredients; mix well. Serve warm or chilled in lettuce cups. Or pack into a 6-cup ring mold, chill until firm and unmold on lettuce. Garnish with tomato wedges and sprinkle with additional Lemon Pepper Seasoning. Makes 12 servings.

Pasta Salad ————————————————————

5 ounces vermicelli
5 hard-cooked eggs, chopped
1 1/2 cups finely chopped celery
1 cup finely chopped sweet pickle
2 to 2 1/2 teaspoons Lawry's Garlic Salt
1 cup mayonnaise
Lettuce leaves
1 can (7 1/2 oz.) crabmeat, drained and flaked
Paprika

Hints:
Tuna, shrimp or lobster may be substituted. For an economical version, omit seafood. Pasta is best cooked to the "al dente" (firm to the bite) stage.

Drain lettuce thoroughly on paper towels or place in a salad basket or spinner and whirl dry.

Break vermicelli in pieces and cook according to package directions. Rinse and drain; cool. Add eggs, celery, pickle, Garlic Salt and mayonnaise. Mix lightly and chill. To serve, mound vermicelli mixture on bed of lettuce leaves. Top with crabmeat and sprinkle with paprika. Makes 6 to 8 servings.

Mary Alice's Macaroni Salad

Hints:

Use colorful garnishes that are complementary in color, flavor and texture.

May add more chopped celery, olives and pimiento, if desired.

A zesty macaroni salad that's different and delicious.

1 package (16 oz.) salad macaroni, cooked and drained
3 tablespoons vinegar
9 tablespoons olive oil
1 package Lawry's Italian Salad Dressing Mix
1 cup chopped celery
1 cup chopped green onion
1 can (4 oz.) sliced ripe olives, drained
1 can (2 oz.) sliced pimiento, drained
3/4 cup mayonnaise
Lawry's Seasoned Salt, to taste
Lawry's Seasoned Pepper, to taste
Avocado slices, tomato wedges and ripe olives for garnish

While macaroni is warm, add vinegar, oil and sprinkle Italian Dressing Mix over macaroni; mix well. Let stand until cool. Add remaining ingredients and mix well. Chill several hours before serving. Garnish with avocado slices, tomato wedges and ripe olives. Makes 10 servings.

Bohemian Potato Salad

6 new potatoes, cooked in their skins
1/4 cup cider vinegar
1/2 cup salad oil
2 teaspoons Lawry's Seasoned Salt
1 1/2 teaspoons Lawry's Pinch of Herbs
1/2 teaspoon dill weed
1 medium onion, thinly sliced

Remove potato skins and slice potatoes while still warm. Combine remaining ingredients except onion; mix well. Pour over potatoes; add onion and toss to coat potato slices. Serve warm or cold. Makes 6 servings.

Picnic Potato Salad

6 cups (6 medium) cooked, diced potatoes
6 hard-cooked eggs, diced
3/4 cup chopped celery
2 teaspoons Lawry's Seasoned Salt
1 package Lawry's Tartar Sauce Mix
2 tablespoons water
1 cup mayonnaise OR salad dressing
1 tablespoon prepared mustard

Combine potatoes, eggs and celery. Sprinkle with Seasoned Salt. Blend Tartar Sauce Mix and water. Add mayonnaise or salad dressing and mustard and stir thoroughly. Pour over potato mixture and toss to combine. Makes 6 servings.

_____ # Basque Salad

6 cups (6 medium) cooked, diced new potatoes
1 package (9 oz.) frozen whole green beans, cooked and drained
1 bottle Lawry's San Francisco Dressing
Lettuce leaves
1 teaspoon Lawry's Seasoned Salt
3 tablespoons minced green onion
1 tablespoon sliced ripe olives
1 tomato, cut in wedges
1 cup julienne ham OR 1 can (7 1/2 oz.) crabmeat, optional

Combine potatoes and green beans (while warm) in shallow dish. Add San Francisco Dressing; cover and marinate overnight in refrigerator. Line a salad bowl with lettuce leaves; arrange potato-bean mixture over greens and sprinkle with Seasoned Salt. Add green onions and ripe olives; garnish with tomato wedges. Add ham or crabmeat if desired. Toss before serving. Makes 8 servings.

Summer Beef Salad

Hints:
May use leftover roasts, pot roasts or steaks for beef strips.

4 carrots, pared and diagonally sliced 1/4 to 1/2-inch thick
1 small cauliflower, broken into flowerets
1 cucumber, peeled, seeded and coarsely grated
1/4 cup sliced green bell pepper
1 pound cooked roast beef, cut in thin strips
1/2 cup Lawry's Green Onion Dressing

Cook carrots and cauliflower until tender-crisp; chill. Combine chilled vegetables, cucumber, bell pepper, beef and Green Onion Dressing. Toss lightly but thoroughly before serving. Makes 6 to 8 servings.

Turkey Salad Supreme

Hints:
Use almonds or cashews in place of pecans.

Always tear greens into pieces. Tearing gives more interesting shapes and is more gentle on the lettuce than cutting. Cutting can also cause discoloration.

4 cups diced cooked turkey
1/4 cup chopped celery
1 1/2 cups seedless green grapes, halved
1 cup chopped pecans
2 heads butter lettuce, torn in bite-size pieces
1 bottle Lawry's Famous French Dressing

Combine first 5 ingredients; add dressing. Toss lightly. Makes 6 servings.

Basque Salad

Crunchy Turkey Salad

2 1/2 cups cubed cooked turkey OR chicken
1 recipe Tangy Hawaiian Dressing (see page 96)
1/2 cup sliced celery
1/4 cup sliced water chestnuts
1/2 cup pineapple chunks
1/4 teaspoon Lawry's Seasoned Salt
1/8 teaspoon ground ginger
1/2 teaspoon sugar
3 cups crisp chow mein noodles
Poppy seeds and watercress sprigs, to garnish

Marinate cubed turkey in refrigerator overnight in Tangy Hawaiian Dressing. Drain and reserve 1/4 cup of dressing. In a large bowl, toss marinated turkey, reserved 1/4 cup dressing and all remaining ingredients except noodles, poppy seeds and watercress. Serve over crisp noodles; garnish with poppy seeds and watercress. Makes 4 servings.

Chicken Piquant Salad

1 cup uncooked long-grain brown rice
1 cup chicken broth
1 package (10 oz.) frozen peas, cooked and drained
2 cups cooked, shredded chicken
2 cans (11 oz. each) Mandarin oranges, drained
1 cup diced celery
1 cup chopped green onions
1 can (6 oz.) salted cashew nuts, chopped
1 cup dairy sour cream
1 bottle Lawry's Famous French Dressing
2 to 3 tablespoons finely chopped candied ginger

Hints:
Recipe can easily be cut in half.

Cook rice according to package directions, substituting 1 cup chicken broth for 1 cup water. Chill rice and peas. In a large bowl, combine chicken, oranges, celery, green onion, cashews, rice and peas. Combine sour cream, Famous French Dressing and ginger. Gently mix dressing and chicken mixture. Refrigerate until ready to serve. Makes 15 servings.

Crab-Cado

1 package Lawry's Italian with Cheese Salad Dressing Mix
1 can (10 oz.) white sauce
1 can (6 1/2 oz.) crabmeat
4 avocados, halved
Paprika

Hints:
Use cooked shrimp or lobster in place of crab. Homemade medium white sauce may be substituted for canned.

Combine Italian with Cheese Salad Dressing Mix, white sauce and crabmeat. Cook, stirring constantly, until well blended. Spoon into avocado halves. Sprinkle with paprika; place under broiler until heated. Makes 8 servings.

Chicken Piquant Salad

Karen's Spaghetti Squash Salad

All your friends will want this recipe.

1/2 spaghetti squash, cooked
1 cup cooked bay shrimp
1/2 cup chopped celery
2 tablespoons salad oil
2 tablespoons cider vinegar
Juice of 1 lemon
Lawry's Seasoned Salt
Lawry's Seasoned Pepper

Remove "spaghetti strands" from squash shell using 2 forks. Add shrimp and celery. Combine oil, vinegar and lemon juice; mix well. Pour over squash and add Seasoned Salt and Seasoned Pepper to taste. Chill several hours before serving. Makes 4 to 6 servings.

Hints:
Recipe may easily be doubled for a larger gathering.
Add a shake or two of Lawry's Seasoned Salt and Lawry's Seasoned Pepper to salads before tossing.

Oriental Tuna Salad

2 cans (6 1/2 to 7 oz. each) white albacore tuna (water packed),
    drained and flaked
3 cups shredded Chinese cabbage
1 1/2 cups sliced fresh mushrooms
1 1/2 cups fresh bean sprouts, washed and drained
3/4 cup sliced radishes
1/2 cup sliced green onions
1 recipe Peanut Dressing (see page 93)

In a large salad bowl, toss all salad ingredients. Pour Peanut Dressing over salad and toss again. Cover and refrigerate about 1/2 hour before serving. Makes 4 main dish servings.

Hints:
Use fresh sliced mushrooms, uncooked, or canned marinated mushrooms in salads.

Cathy's Coleslaw Relish Mold ————————— Molded

A fancy version of an old favorite.

1 package (3 oz.) lemon-flavored gelatin
2/3 cup boiling water
1/2 cup cold water
1/2 cup mayonnaise
1/2 cup dairy sour cream
1 tablespoon prepared mustard
1 package Lawry's Italian Salad Dressing Mix
2 tablespoons vinegar
3 cups finely chopped cabbage
1 tablespoon chopped parsley
1 jar (2 oz.) pimiento, drained and chopped
1/4 cup finely chopped green OR red bell pepper

Dissolve gelatin in boiling water; add cold water, mayonnaise, sour cream and mustard. Combine Italian Salad Dressing Mix and vinegar; add to gelatin mixture. Chill until syrupy. Add remaining ingredients. Lightly oil and drain a 1-quart mold. Pour in gelatin mixture. Chill until firm. Makes 8 servings.

Hints:
Chop cabbage very fine. To speed up chilling (before adding vegetables) set gelatin mixture in a large bowl of ice water. Stir frequently and watch carefully so gelatin doesn't get too firm.
Lightly oil salad molds with unflavored oil to ensure easy removal. Turn upside down on paper towels to drain before adding gelatin mixture.

Cucumber Sour Cream Mousse ————————

1 package (3 oz.) lemon-flavored gelatin
1 1/2 cups boiling water
1 package Lawry's Tartar Sauce Mix
3 tablespoons white wine vinegar
2 large cucumbers
1 cup dairy sour cream

Dissolve gelatin in boiling water; cool slightly. Add Tartar Sauce Mix and vinegar; stir. Refrigerate until consistency of unbeaten egg white. Meanwhile, peel and coarsely grate cucumbers. Drain thoroughly and place in sieve or colander. Press out juice with back of spoon and hand-squeeze. Add cucumbers and sour cream to gelatin mixture. Lightly oil and drain a 1-quart mold. Pour in gelatin mixture. Refrigerate until firm. Makes 6 servings.

Lemon Garlic Dressing

Hints:
Use 2/3 cup buttermilk in place of salad oil for a creamy lower calorie version.

3 tablespoons lemon juice
3 tablespoons water
1 tablespoon finely minced parsley
1/2 teaspoon grated lemon peel
1/2 teaspoon dry mustard
1/2 teaspoon sugar
1/2 teaspoon Lawry's Seasoned Salt
1/2 teaspoon Lawry's Garlic Powder with Parsley
1/4 teaspoon turmeric
Dash Lawry's Seasoned Pepper
2/3 cup salad oil

Combine all ingredients except oil in a jar; shake well. Add oil and shake again for 30 seconds. For best flavor refrigerate several hours before serving. Makes about 1 cup.

Peanut Dressing

1/4 cup warm water
3 tablespoons creamy peanut butter
4 teaspoons white vinegar
4 teaspoons Lawry's Teriyaki Barbecue Marinade
1/2 teaspoon Lawry's Seasoned Salt
1/4 teaspoon Lawry's Garlic Powder with Parsley
1/4 cup salad oil

In small bowl, blend together water and peanut butter. Stir in remaining ingredients, except oil. When thoroughly blended, mix in oil. Cover and let stand for 1/2 hour. Makes 3/4 cup.

Roquefort Romaine Dressing

Hints:
Toss dressing with greens carefully and gently but thoroughly, just before serving.

2 packages Lawry's Caesar Salad Dressing Mix
1/4 cup wine vinegar
1 tablespoon lemon juice
3/4 cup salad oil
2 tablespoons sugar
3/4 cup dairy sour cream
1/4 cup buttermilk
1/2 pound Roquefort cheese, crumbled

Combine Caesar Salad Dressing Mix, vinegar and lemon juice in a large jar; shake well. Add salad oil; shake again. Blend in sugar, sour cream and buttermilk. Add cheese. Chill at least 2 hours. Makes about 1 pint.

French Vinaigrette Dressing

1/4 cup red wine vinegar
1 tablespoon water
1 tablespoon lemon juice
1 teaspoon sugar
1/2 teaspoon paprika
1/2 teaspoon dry mustard
1/2 teaspoon tarragon
1/2 teaspoon celery seed
1/2 teaspoon Lawry's Seasoned Salt
1/2 teaspoon Lawry's Garlic Salt
2/3 cup salad oil

Hints:
Shake separating (oil & vinegar type) dressings vigorously before serving to make sure all ingredients are well mixed.

Combine all ingredients except oil in a jar; shake well. Add oil and shake again. Chill several hours before serving. Makes about 1 cup.

Avocado Dressing Deluxe

1 avocado, mashed
1 tablespoon lemon juice
1/2 cup dairy sour cream
2 tablespoons minced parsley
2 tablespoons minced green onion tops
1 teaspoon Lawry's Seasoned Salt
1 teaspoon Lawry's Seasoned Pepper
1 tablespoon vinegar
1 tablespoon salad oil

Hints:
Dressing should be made and served the same day.

Combine all ingredients and blend well. Keep dressing tightly covered until ready to serve. Makes 3/4 cup.

Creamy Lemon Lime

1 cup dairy sour cream
1/2 cup mayonnaise
1/2 cup milk
1 tablespoon grated lemon peel
1 tablespoon grated lime peel
1 teaspoon lime juice
1 teaspoon Lawry's Minced Onion with Green Onion Flakes
1/2 teaspoon lemon juice
1/2 teaspoon Lawry's Seasoned Salt

Hints:
Excellent dressing over fruit. One average-size lemon gives about 1 tablespoon grated peel. Use 1 large lime or 2 small ones for 1 tablespoon peel.

In medium bowl, combine all ingredients. Use wire whisk to blend. Chill several hours or overnight before serving. Makes 2 cups.

Hints:

Make dressings ahead and chill several hours before serving to blend flavors.

3/4 cup dairy sour cream
1/3 cup mayonnaise
1/3 cup buttermilk
1 tablespoon lemon juice
1 tablespoon water
1/2 teaspoon Lawry's Seasoned Salt
1/8 teaspoon Lawry's Garlic Powder with Parsley
1/8 teaspoon oregano
1/4 teaspoon basil
1/4 teaspoon dry mustard
1/4 teaspoon Lawry's Seasoned Pepper

Avocado Dressing Deluxe
Creamy Lemon Lime
French Vinaigrette Dressing

Combine all ingredients with a whisk or fork; blend thoroughly. Chill several hours or overnight. Makes about 1 1/2 cups.

Onion Sour Cream Dressing

1 cup dairy sour cream
1/2 cup mayonnaise
1/4 cup salad oil
1/4 cup water
1 tablespoon cider vinegar
1 1/2 teaspoons Lawry's Minced Onion with Green Onion Flakes
1 teaspoon minced parsley
1/4 teaspoon Lawry's Lemon Pepper Seasoning

Hints:
Greens and other vegetables must be free of moisture so the dressing will cling.

Combine all ingredients and blend thoroughly with wire whisk. Chill several hours or overnight before serving. Makes 2 cups.

Honey Lime Fruit Dressing

1/3 cup lime juice
1/3 cup salad oil
2 tablespoons honey

Combine ingredients in a jar; shake well. Makes about 3/4 cup.

Fresh Mint Dressing

1 cup dairy sour cream
1/2 cup mayonnaise
1 tablespoon lemon juice
1/2 teaspoon Lawry's Garlic Salt
1/4 cup water
1/4 cup salad oil
1/4 cup minced fresh mint

Hints:
May use 1 tablespoon of dried mint leaves instead of fresh.

Combine all ingredients; blend thoroughly. Chill several hours or overnight before serving. Makes about 2 cups.

Tangy Hawaiian Dressing

3 tablespoons red wine vinegar
3 tablespoons lemon juice
3 tablespoons water
2 tablespoons pineapple juice
1/4 cup honey
1/2 teaspoon paprika
1/4 teaspoon Worcestershire sauce
1/4 teaspoon celery seed
1/4 teaspoon Lawry's Seasoned Salt
Dash Lawry's Garlic Powder with Parsley
1/3 cup salad oil

Combine all ingredients except oil in a jar and shake well. Add oil and shake again for at least 30 seconds. For best flavor, refrigerate several hours or overnight before serving. Makes 1 cup.

Mary Alice's Salad Dressing

Hints:
Use dressing sparingly to avoid sogginess. You can always add more if needed.

1 large clove garlic, crushed
1 teaspoon Lawry's Seasoned Salt
1 teaspoon Lawry's Seasoned Pepper
1 teaspoon Lawry's Pinch of Herbs
1 teaspoon dry mustard
1/3 cup red OR white wine vinegar
1 cup salad OR olive oil

Combine all ingredients, except oil, in a jar. Shake well. Let stand 20 minutes. Add oil. Shake again. Makes 1 1/3 cups.

Creamy Caesar Dressing

1 package Lawry's Caesar Salad Dressing Mix
2 tablespoons water
1/4 cup cider vinegar
1 egg
2/3 cup dairy sour cream
2 teaspoons prepared mustard

Blend Caesar Salad Dressing Mix with water. Add vinegar and egg and beat throughly. Add sour cream and mustard; blend well. Makes about 1 cup.

Homemade Bacon Dressing

1/3 cup red wine vinegar
3 tablespoons lemon juice
2 tablespoons Lawry's Bacon Onion Seasoning
1 tablespoon grated Parmesan OR Romano cheese
1/4 teaspoon Lawry's Garlic Powder with Parsley
2/3 cup salad oil

Combine all ingredients except oil in a jar; shake well. Add oil and shake again. Chill several hours before serving. Makes about 1 cup.

Claudia's Creamy Pepper Dressing

Hints:
Keeps 2 to 3 weeks in refrigerator.

1 cup mayonnaise
2 tablespoons water
1 tablespoon Lawry's Seasoned Pepper
1 tablespoon grated Parmesan cheese
1/2 teaspoon Lawry's Seasoned Salt
1/2 teaspoon lemon juice
1/4 teaspoon Lawry's Garlic Powder with Parsley
1/4 teaspoon Worcestershire sauce
1/4 teaspoon dry mustard
1/4 teaspoon sugar

Blend together all ingredients; refrigerate several hours before serving. Makes 1 cup.

CALIFORNIA'S VEGETABLE BOUNTY

The variety of foods grown in California is vast, and one of the many advantages of living in the "Golden State" is the abundance of fresh produce. A trip to the Farmers Market in Los Angeles is a must for visitors, who are awed by the array of produce so beautifully displayed.

While vegetables now occupy a place of prominence in our meals, this was not always the case. And no wonder, since the recommended method for cooking in days past was to boil vegetables almost to death.

Thanks to the Far East, our tastes have been re-educated to relish tender-crisp vegetables with simple seasonings. Steaming or stir-frying makes vegetables taste better and look better.

The recipes in this chapter include some simple, quick and tasty ways to season vegetables and ideas for more involved dishes. There are vegetables to stuff and bake, vegetables to prepare Oriental-style and combination dishes for heartier fare. Since so many soups include vegetables, recipes for light soups are also found in this chapter. These are great for summertime eating or as a first course for a more formal meal.

Stuffed Artichokes

Stuffed Artichokes

Hints:

Artichokes are in season from October to May. Choose green tightly closed heads of small to medium size. Trim just before cooking to prevent discoloration.

4 artichokes
2 tablespoons Lawry's Minced Onion with Green Onion Flakes
2 tablespoons grated Parmesan cheese
1 tablespoon capers, drained and minced
1 tablespoon minced parsley
1/2 teaspoon Lawry's Seasoned Salt
1/4 teaspoon Lawry's Seasoned Pepper
1/4 teaspoon Lawry's Garlic Powder with Parsley
1 cup fine dry bread crumbs
3/4 pound bay shrimp, optional
1/2 cup dry white wine OR chicken stock
1 package Lawry's Italian Salad Dressing Mix, prepared according to package directions

Cut off stems and sharp tips of leaves. Set artichokes in boiling water to cover. Bring to a boil, reduce heat, cover and simmer 20 minutes. Drain thoroughly. Spread leaves apart carefully, reach inside with a small spoon and scrape out the furry, inedible part. Combine remaining ingredients except wine or stock and Italian Salad Dressing. Divide mixture among artichokes, spooning into center and between leaves. Place artichokes in roasting pan to fit tightly. Sprinkle 2 tablespoons wine or stock into each artichoke center. Pour Italian Salad Dressing over artichokes. Cover and bake in 350°F. oven 1 hour; baste with pan juices several times. Makes 4 servings.

Hattie's Five Bean Bake

Hints:

Assemble the night before and refrigerate. Or, divide recipe between two smaller casserole dishes and bake one for 1 hour and freeze. To serve, continue baking directly from freezer for remaining time.

There are several versions of this favorite which orginally came from the Midwest.

1 can (1 lb. 15 oz.) pork 'n beans
1 can (15 oz.) butter beans
1 can (15 1/4 oz.) kidney OR pinto beans
1 can (15 oz.) white beans
1 can (15 3/4 oz.) barbecued beans
1 pound bacon, cut in 1-inch pieces
3/4 cup brown sugar
1/4 to 1/2 cup white vinegar
1/4 cup Lawry's Minced Onion with Green Onion Flakes
1 teaspoon dry mustard
1 teaspoon Lawry's Garlic Salt

Combine all ingredients (do not drain beans) in a 3 1/2-quart casserole. Bake, uncovered, in 350°F. oven 2 1/2 to 3 hours. Makes 20 servings.

Lemon Broccoletti

Serve as a vegetable while still slightly warm or chill and serve as a salad.

2 packages (10 oz. each) frozen broccoli spears
1 package Lawry's Italian with Cheese Salad Dressing Mix
2 tablespoons water
1/4 cup fresh lemon juice
2/3 cup salad oil
Grated lemon peel and lemon wedges
Lawry's Garlic Salt, optional

Cook broccoli in unsalted water according to package directions; drain and arrange in shallow serving dish. Combine Italian with Cheese Salad Dressing Mix and water in a jar; shake well. Add lemon juice and shake. Add salad oil and shake again. While broccoli is still warm, add dressing. Garnish with lemon peel and lemon wedges. Add Garlic Salt to taste. Makes 6 to 8 servings.

Gingered Carrots

Ginger and coconut are a wonderful complement to carrots.

1 pound carrots, pared and thinly sliced
2 tablespoons butter, melted
3/4 teaspoon finely chopped candied ginger
Lawry's Garlic Salt, to taste
2 to 3 tablespoons shredded coconut, toasted

Cook carrots until tender; drain. Add butter, ginger and Garlic Salt; mix well. Sprinkle coconut over carrots. Makes 4 servings.

Hints:
To chop candied ginger, use kitchen scissors and snip; dip scissors in hot water frequently for easier cutting.

Deviled Cauliflower

1 medium-size head cauliflower, trimmed
1/3 cup butter
1 tablespoon prepared mustard
1 teaspoon Worcestershire sauce
1/2 teaspoon Lawry's Seasoned Salt
Dash Lawry's Seasoned Pepper

Cut or break cauliflower into flowerets; cook and drain. Add remaining ingredients and heat just until butter melts. Makes 4 servings.

Hints:
Use Brussels sprouts instead of cauliflower.

Gingered Carrots   Lemon Broccoletti
Deviled Cauliflower

Eggplant Cheese Casserole

Hints:

Eggplant absorbs oil quickly. Be sure to brown quickly over high heat and drain well. Eggplant is also delicious cut in half and stuffed with a seasoned ground beef mixture and topped with cheese.

1 package (1 1/2 oz.) Lawry's Spaghetti Sauce Mix with Imported Mushrooms
1 can (8 oz.) tomato sauce
1 1/2 cups water
1 teaspoon Lawry's Seasoned Salt
1/2 cup finely chopped onion
1 large eggplant
1/2 to 3/4 cup salad oil
1/2 pound Mozzarella cheese, thinly sliced
1/4 cup grated Parmesan cheese

Combine Spaghetti Sauce Mix, tomato sauce, water, Seasoned Salt and onion. Bring to a boil, reduce heat and simmer, uncovered, 20 minutes. Peel eggplant; cut in 1/4-inch slices. Sauté in hot oil in skillet until brown, adding oil as needed. Drain well on paper towels. Pour 1/3 of sauce into 8-inch square baking dish. Cover sauce with 1/2 of eggplant and Mozzarella slices. Repeat layers, ending with sauce and top with Parmesan cheese. Bake, uncovered, in 350°F. oven about 20 minutes. Makes 6 servings.

Zesty Green Beans

Use fresh green beans in season.

2 cups cut green beans, cooked and drained
1/2 cup Lawry's Chunky Taco Sauce
1 teaspoon lemon juice

Combine ingredients; heat. Makes 4 servings.

Roasted Onions

Great with roasts, steaks or barbecued meats.

2 packages (20 oz. each) frozen baby onions
4 teaspoons brown sugar
1 teaspoon Lawry's Seasoned Salt
Dash Lawry's Seasoned Pepper
2 tablespoons Lawry's Au Jus Gravy Mix
1/2 cup water
1/2 cup white wine
3 tablespoons butter
2 tablespoons lemon juice
2 tablespoons chopped parsley

Hints:
To chop a small quantity of parsley, place in 1 cup glass measuring cup or glass of equivalent size and snip parsley with kitchen shears.

Combine all ingredients except butter, lemon juice and parsley in 2-quart baking dish. Mix well; dot with butter. Cover and bake in 375°F. oven 45 minutes; uncover and continue baking 15 to 20 minutes until top is glazed. Add lemon juice and parsley. Makes 8 servings.

Sally's Baked Potato Casserole

5 medium-size baking potatoes, baked
1/4 cup chopped green onion
1 cup dairy sour cream
1 teaspoon caraway seeds
1 cup grated Tillamook cheese
1/2 cup milk
Lawry's Seasoned Salt, to taste
Lawry's Seasoned Pepper, to taste

Hints:
Freeze the potato skins and use to prepare Crispy Potato Skins (see page 23). Casserole freezes well; don't add the extra cheese topping until just before baking.

While warm, cut potatoes in half lengthwise; scoop out potato, leaving shells intact. Combine potato with remaining ingredients reserving 1/4 cup cheese. Mix thoroughly and place in buttered 1 1/2 to 2-quart shallow casserole. Top with 1/4 cup cheese. Bake, uncovered, in 350°F. oven 20 to 30 minutes, until heated and slightly browned on top. Makes 8 servings.

Stuffed Mushrooms on a Skewer

Hints:
Make ahead and broil just before serving.

A delicious way to prepare whole mushrooms.

1/4 cup dry white wine
1 chicken bouillon cube
20 large mushrooms, stems removed and reserved
1/4 cup finely chopped onion
2 tablespoons butter
1/2 cup fine dry bread crumbs
1/2 teaspoon Lawry's Pinch of Herbs
Melted butter

Combine wine and bouillon; heat until cube dissolves. Finely chop mushroom stems; sauté with onions in butter. Remove from heat; add wine liquid, bread crumbs and Pinch of Herbs. Mix thoroughly. Fit two mushroom caps together with 1 tablespoon stuffing between them. Place 2 or 3 on a skewer. Broil 3 to 5 minutes, brushing with additional butter. Makes 10 double mushrooms.

Lila's Creamy Spaghetti Squash

Hints:
To cook spaghetti squash cut in half lengthwise and remove seeds. Bake in 350°F. oven 25 to 30 minutes, cut side down, on baking sheet; or boil, cut side down, in 2-inches of water for 20 minutes (covered). To microwave, place squash, cut side up, in dish with 1/4 cup water. Cover with plastic wrap and cook on High about 8 minutes. Use remaining half of squash for Karen's Spaghetti Squash Salad (see page 91).

Spaghetti squash, once cooked, looks just like golden strands of spaghetti, yet tastes like squash.

1/2 spaghetti squash, cooked
1 1/2 cups dairy sour cream
1 tablespoon ground ginger
1 teaspoon Lawry's Seasoned Salt
1/2 teaspoon Lawry's Seasoned Pepper
Freshly grated nutmeg OR ground nutmeg
1/2 cup freshly grated Parmesan cheese

Remove "spaghetti strands" from squash shell using 2 forks. Place in shallow dish. Combine all ingredients except nutmeg and cheese; mix with squash. Top generously with nutmeg, then cheese. Broil until cheese melts and begins to brown slightly. Makes 4 to 6 servings.

Potatoes Au Gratin

Hints:
Assemble ahead and bake just before serving. Fresh shredded potatoes may be used instead of frozen if desired.

1 package (12 oz.) frozen hash brown potatoes, thawed
1 cup milk
2 tablespoons butter, melted
1 teaspoon Lawry's Seasoned Salt
1/2 teaspoon Lawry's Seasoned Pepper
1/4 cup sliced green onion
1 1/2 cups grated Cheddar cheese

Spread potatoes evenly in shallow casserole. Combine milk with butter, Seasoned Salt and Seasoned Pepper. Sprinkle onions and cheese over potatoes; add milk. Bake, covered, in 350°F. oven 25 to 30 minutes. Makes 4 servings.

Open Face Pattypan Squash

Pattypan squash (summer squash) are round with a scalloped edge, light green and fairly flat.

8 pattypan squash, cut in half crosswise
2 tablespoons butter, melted
1 teaspoon Lawry's Seasoned Salt OR Lawry's Lemon Pepper
    Seasoning
1/2 cup grated Cheddar cheese
Lawry's Seasoned Pepper

Steam squash about 10 minutes. Arrange, cut side up, in 13 x 9 x 2-inch baking dish. Pierce centers of squash. Combine melted butter and Seasoned Salt or Lemon Pepper Seasoning; pour over squash. Cover and bake in 350°F. oven 20 minutes. Uncover, top with cheese and continue baking about 10 minutes or until cheese melts. Sprinkle with Seasoned Pepper. Makes 6 to 8 servings.

Hints:
Steam squash in advance and refrigerate. Complete dish and bake just before serving.

Festive Brandied Yams

Yams are plentiful in the fall and winter.

1 can (1 lb. 4 oz.) pineapple slices in natural juice, drained
6 medium yams, cooked, peeled and sliced
1/4 cup brandy
2 tablespoons grated orange peel
1/2 cup brown sugar
1 teaspoon cinnamon
1/2 teaspoon cloves
2 tablespoons butter

In a buttered 2-quart shallow casserole, layer 1/2 of pineapple slices and 1/2 of yam slices. Top with 2 tablespoons brandy. Mix together orange peel, brown sugar, cinnamon and cloves; top yams with 1/2 of this mixture. Repeat layers, using all ingredients except butter. Dot top with butter. Bake, uncovered, in 350°F. oven 30 to 40 minutes or until top is crusty. Makes 8 servings.

Hints:
Bake yams or sweet potatoes whole. Be sure to prick skin in several places and either wrap in aluminum foil or place a piece of foil under them in the oven to catch the syrupy drippings.

Zucchini Custard

Use carrots instead of zucchini for a change-of-pace.

1 medium onion, sliced
2 tablespoons butter
1 pound zucchini, cut in 1/2-inch slices
2 teaspoons Lawry's Seasoned Salt
1/2 teaspoon Lawry's Seasoned Pepper
6 eggs
1 cup milk
1/2 pound Mozzarella cheese, sliced

Sauté onions in butter. Add zucchini, Seasoned Salt and Seasoned Pepper to onions and sauté for about 5 minutes. Beat eggs slightly. Stir in milk and vegetable mixture. Pour into buttered 2-quart oblong baking dish. Set dish in pan of hot water. Bake, uncovered, in 300°F. oven 25 minutes. Top with Mozzarella cheese slices. Bake an additional 25 minutes or until custard is firm. Makes 6 to 8 servings.

Hints:
May be made ahead and reheated before serving.

Oriental Vegetables

Oriental Vegetables

Hints:

To stir-fry, make sure the oil is hot and quickly move food around in the wok or skillet.

3 tablespoons salad oil
1/4 pound mushrooms, sliced
2 stalks broccoli, cut in bite-size pieces
1/2 head cauliflower, separated into flowerets
2 green onions, diagonally sliced
2 celery stalks, diagonally sliced
1 carrot, diagonally sliced
1 small zucchini, cut in 1/4-inch slices
1 tablespoon cornstarch
1/2 cup Lawry's Teriyaki Barbecue Marinade

Heat oil in wok or large skillet. Add vegetables and stir-fry. Add about 1 to 2 tablespoons water, cover and steam until vegetables are tender but still crisp. Combine cornstarch and Teriyaki Barbecue Marinade, pour over vegetables and stir until vegetables are coated. Serve immediately. Makes 4 to 6 servings.

Minted Peas

Cook peas with a sprig of fresh mint, if available, and omit dried mint.

1/4 cup butter, melted
1 teaspoon dried mint, crushed
1/4 teaspoon Lawry's Pinch of Herbs
1 package (10 oz.) frozen peas, cooked and drained

Combine all ingredients; mix well. Makes 4 servings.

Hints:
Peas are one of the most versatile vegetables to add color to soups, stews, casseroles and salads.

Ratatouille

A classic vegetable dish.

1 large onion, sliced
1/2 cup olive oil
1/2 teaspoon Lawry's Garlic Powder with Parsley
2 zucchini, sliced crosswise
1 small eggplant, peeled and diced
2 green bell peppers, cut in strips
5 tomatoes, peeled, seeded and chopped
Lawry's Seasoned Salt
Lawry's Seasoned Pepper
1 tablespoon capers, optional

Hints:
This can be baked in a 350°F oven 45 minutes to 1 hour (or slightly less for crisper vegetables).

In large skillet, sauté onion in oil. Add Garlic Powder with Parsley, zucchini and eggplant; sauté 4 to 5 minutes. Add green pepper. Bring to a boil, reduce heat and simmer, covered, about 15 minutes. Add tomatoes and seasonings; simmer, covered, an additional 15 minutes. Before serving, add capers if desired. Serve hot or cold. Makes 6 to 8 servings.

Napa Valley Corn Chowder

A soup you can prepare in just minutes.

2 tablespoons butter
1/2 cup chopped onion
1 1/2 teaspoons Lawry's Seasoned Salt
1/4 teaspoon Lawry's Seasoned Pepper
1 medium potato, peeled and diced
1 cup water
1 can (8 oz.) whole kernel corn, drained
1 1/2 cups milk
1/4 cup dry white wine
1 tablespoon chopped parsley

Hints:
Prepare ahead and reheat before serving. Serve in warmed bowls to help keep the soup hot.

Melt butter in a saucepan. Add onions and sauté about 5 minutes. Add Seasoned Salt and Seasoned Pepper. Stir to combine. Add potato and water. Bring to a boil, reduce heat, cover and simmer about 10 minutes or until potato is tender. Add corn, milk, wine and parsley. Heat just to boiling. Makes about 4 cups.

Spiked Tomato-Beef Consomme

Hints:
Chopped cilantro may be used instead of parsley. Very thin lemon slices would also be appropriate as a garnish, alone or in combination with parsley or cilantro.

An elegant but easy, light soup.

2 cups tomato juice
1 can (10 1/2 oz.) beef consomme
2 lemon slices
6 whole cloves
1/2 teaspoon Lawry's Seasoned Salt
1/4 teaspoon Lawry's Seasoned Pepper
1/2 cup dry sherry
Finely chopped parsley

Mix tomato juice and consomme in 3-quart saucepan. Add lemon, cloves, Seasoned Salt and Seasoned Pepper. Bring to a boil, reduce heat, cover and simmer 15 minutes. Strain; add sherry. Heat thoroughly. Top with parsley. Makes 6 servings.

Cream of Spinach Soup

Hints:
Use 1 bunch fresh spinach, finely chopped and cooked in place of frozen if desired.

This delicately seasoned soup is a wonderful first course.

2 bacon slices, finely chopped
1/2 cup finely chopped onion
1 package (10 oz.) frozen chopped spinach, thawed and drained
2 tablespoons flour
1 1/2 teaspoons Lawry's Seasoned Salt
1/2 teaspoon Lawry's Seasoned Pepper
1/4 teaspoon Lawry's Garlic Powder with Parsley
1 teaspoon Worcestershire sauce
2 1/2 cups milk
1 1/2 cups chicken broth
Dash nutmeg

In large skillet or Dutch oven, fry bacon and onions together until onions are tender, about 10 minutes; drain fat. Place bacon, onions and spinach in food processor with steel blade or in blender; puree. Return pureed spinach-bacon mixture to skillet or Dutch oven; mix in flour and seasonings. Heat thoroughly and slowly blend in milk and chicken broth. Cook over low heat, stirring until thickened. Garnish with dash of nutmeg. Makes 6 to 8 servings.

Ginger Avocado Soup

The ginger and orange flavors are a refreshing combination in this cold soup.

3 tablespoons butter
3 tablespoons flour
1 can (14 1/2 oz.) chicken broth
Milk
1/4 teaspoon powdered ginger
4 1/2 teaspoons grated orange peel
2 avocados, pureed
2 tablespoons lemon juice
Dairy sour cream
Finely chopped candied ginger

Melt butter; stir in flour and cook until bubbly. Combine chicken broth and milk to total 3 cups. Gradually add to butter-flour mixture, stirring constantly until thickened. Add ginger, orange peel, avocado and lemon juice. Mix well. Chill thoroughly and serve garnished with dollop of sour cream and a sprinkling of candied ginger. Makes 6 to 8 servings.

Hints:

Serve this soup in chilled cups or bowls. It's rich, so portions should be small if served as a first course for a meal.

Ginger Avocado Soup
Cream of Romaine Soup
Creamy Peanut Soup

Cream of Romaine Soup

Hints:
If made in advance, reheat soup gently and do not boil.

Lettuce is not usually a soup ingredient but here it's the star.

1 small onion, minced
2 tablespoons butter
1 quart chicken broth
1/2 teaspoon Lawry's Pinch of Herbs
1/4 teaspoon Lawry's Seasoned Salt
1/4 teaspoon Lawry's Seasoned Pepper
2 quarts chopped romaine
4 egg yolks
1 cup heavy cream

In a large saucepan, sauté onions in butter until tender. Add chicken broth, Pinch of Herbs, Seasoned Salt and Seasoned Pepper; bring to a boil. Add romaine, reduce heat, cover and simmer 10 minutes or until romaine is wilted. Beat together eggs and cream; stir into soup mixture. Cook over low heat, stirring constantly until soup begins to thicken. Do not boil. Makes 8 to 10 servings.

Creamy Peanut Soup

Hints:
If coconut milk is available, use 1 cup in place of 1 cup of light cream and omit coconut extract.

A dramatically unusual chilled soup to serve as a first course.

2 cups beef broth
3 medium onions, finely chopped
2 cups light cream
2 teaspoons coconut extract
Dash cayenne pepper
2 tablespoons creamy peanut butter
1/4 cup fresh lime juice
Finely chopped dry-roasted peanuts

Combine broth and onions in large saucepan. Bring to a boil, reduce heat and simmer, uncovered, 30 minutes or until liquid is reduced. Strain liquid through sieve, pressing firmly to extract broth; discard onions. Add light cream, coconut extract, cayenne and peanut butter. Heat and stir with wire whisk to blend peanut butter; chill. Add lime juice just before serving. Top each serving with chopped peanuts. Makes about 3 cups.

OUTDOOR COOKING...AND INDOORS, TOO

In a book from California, one would surely expect to find a section on barbecuing. Some people think that Californians only cook on a barbecue grill. While not exactly true, with sunny skies and temperate weather almost year 'round, cooking and eating out-of-doors is definitely a major part of the California lifestyle.

Historically, the name "barbecue" either comes from the Spanish word "barbacoa," a wooden grid on which meat is roasted or the French "barbe a queue" meaning a way of cooking meat in ancient times.

The term "barbecue" needs further clarification as it means something quite different to people in various parts of the country. In Texas, a barbecue, in addition to being a social event, is a method of roasting meats (usually a whole calf or pig) over a slow wood fire. The type of wood, the cooking time and the sauce are the key ingredients.

To most of the rest of the country, barbecuing means lighting the charcoal fire and cooking meats, poultry, fish and possibly vegetables and fruit on a grill over coals. Today there are many types of barbecue appliances and aids on the market to make the job easier and more convenient.

While "barbecue" often connotes the use of sauce, not all foods cooked on a barbecue grill are coated or basted with a barbecue sauce. However, the majority of recipes for meat, poultry and fish involve some type of marinade or sauce for added flavor. Most barbecue recipes may also be prepared in the oven or broiler as well as on the grill. While the flavor will be excellent either way, food cooked on a barbecue grill does have extra special appeal.

No matter whether you live in an apartment or condominium with a balcony, or you have an entire backyard for your endeavors, barbecue cooking is fun. And though times have changed where the kitchen is no longer a woman's exclusive domain, barbecuing traditionally has been a man's job. Perhaps you'd prefer to keep it that way. Perhaps not! No matter who does it, barbecuing foods is a relaxed and social way to cook for family and friends.

Marinated Family Steak

Marinated Family Steak

Serving Suggestions:

Grilled Lemon Potatoes, Marinated Summer Salad.

Hints:

For best results, a round or chuck roast for barbecuing or broiling should be at least 1 1/2 to 2-inches thick and cooked no more than medium. Also may use a round or flank steak.

Less tender meat cuts, properly treated, can be barbecued with great success.

1 package Lawry's Tenderizing Beef Marinade
2/3 cup cold water
1 1/2 pounds boneless chuck roast
Lawry's Seasoned Salt
Lawry's Seasoned Pepper
Lawry's Lemon Pepper Seasoning

Prepare marinade according to package directions; place meat in marinade for recommended length of time and no longer. Remove from marinade, sprinkle generously with Seasoned Salt, Seasoned Pepper and Lemon Pepper Seasoning. Grill or broil immediately. To serve, slice on the diagonal. Makes 6 servings.

Lemon Lamb Shish Kabobs

Serving Suggestions:

Lima-Mushroom Vinaigrette, Lawry's Garlic Bread.

Hints:

Vegetables cook faster than meat. If you cook meat to the rare stage, the vegetables will not overcook. If you want well done meat, place vegetables on separate skewers and cook less.

Lamb is traditional for shish kabobs, though beef or chicken may be used.

2 pounds lamb, cut in 1 1/2-inch cubes
Lemon Marinade for Lamb
1 box cherry tomatoes
1/2 pound fresh mushrooms
2 green bell peppers, cut in 2-inch squares
3 onions, cut in six wedges
Bamboo skewers, soaked in water for 2 hours

Place meat in Lemon Marinade for Lamb for at least 6 hours or overnight in refrigerator. Turn occasionally. Skewer lamb, alternating with a tomato, mushroom, green pepper and onion. Grill over ash grey coals, about 10 to 20 minutes, turning frequently. Makes 10 to 12 servings.

Lemon Marinade for Lamb

1 onion, thinly sliced
1/4 cup finely chopped parsley
2 tablespoons vinegar
Juice of 1 lemon, about 1/4 cup
1/2 cup olive oil
1 teaspoon Lawry's Seasoned Salt
1/2 teaspoon Lawry's Seasoned Pepper
1 1/2 teaspoons Lawry's Pinch of Herbs

In a large bowl, combine all ingredients. Marinate lamb at least 6 hours or overnight in refrigerator. Turn occasionally.

Halibut Kabobs

Fish absorbs a marinade flavor quickly so the marinating time is short.

1/4 cup salad oil
1/4 cup dry vermouth OR white wine
1/4 cup fresh lemon juice
1 teaspoon Lawry's Seasoned Salt
1/4 teaspoon Lawry's Garlic Salt
1/2 teaspoon oregano, crushed
1 pound fresh or frozen and thawed halibut steaks, cut in 1-inch cubes
6 mushroom caps
1 green bell pepper, cut in 1-inch squares
12 cherry tomatoes
4 bamboo skewers, soaked in water 2 hours

Combine first six ingredients in a shallow glass or ceramic dish. Marinate halibut cubes for 1 hour at room temperature. Drain and reserve marinade. On skewers alternate fish, green pepper, tomato and end with mushroom. Grill the kabobs over medium coals for 8 to 10 minutes, turning and basting frequently with reserved marinade. Makes 4 servings.

Serving Suggestions:
Eggplant Cheese Casserole, Wilted Spinach Salad.

Hints:
Use any firm-fleshed thick whitefish, such as swordfish. Generously brush the grid of the grill with vegetable oil to prevent sticking.

Lemon Lamb Shish Kabobs
Halibut Kabobs

Fiesta Kabobs

Serving Suggestions:
Roasted Corn on the Cob, Lawry's Garlic Bread, Eva's Pea-Nut Salad.

Hints:
Turn kabobs frequently while cooking. The tomato-based marinade will tend to char more quickly than the meat cooks. A low fire is also a good idea.

Use any combination of favorite vegetables or fruit for kabobs.

1 package Lawry's Enchilada Sauce Mix
1 can (8 oz.) tomato sauce
3 cups water
3 pounds boneless chuck steak, cut in 1 1/2-inch cubes
Mushroom caps
Cherry tomatoes
Green chili pepper OR green bell peppers
Small boiling onions OR onion wedges
6 large skewers

Combine Enchilada Sauce Mix, tomato sauce and water. Bring to a boil, reduce heat and simmer uncovered, 15 minutes. Cool slightly. Combine sauce and beef cubes in a shallow dish. Cover; marinate overnight in refrigerator. Remove meat and drain slightly. Alternate beef, mushrooms, tomatoes, peppers and onions on skewers. Grill or broil until done as desired. Baste with remaining marinade while cooking. Makes 6 servings.

Butterfly Leg of Lamb

Serving Suggestions:
Sour Cream Tortilla Casserole, Tabbouleh.

Hints:
Leftover lamb may be wrapped in aluminum foil and reheated, or heated in a microwave. A butterflied leg of lamb may also be stuffed, rolled and roasted.

Lamb is best cooked medium rare.

5 to 6 pound leg of lamb
1 package Lawry's Italian Salad Dressing Mix
2 tablespoons water
1/4 cup vinegar OR 1/2 cup dry white wine
2/3 cup salad oil
Lawry's Seasoned Salt

Have lamb boned and cut open butterfly fashion. Combine Italian Salad Dressing Mix and water in a jar. Shake well. Add vinegar or wine and salad oil. Shake again about 30 seconds. Pour over lamb in a shallow pan and marinate overnight. Sprinkle generously with Seasoned Salt before broiling. Place lamb, fat side up, on grill over hot coals. Grill 40 to 50 minutes, turning about every 10 minutes and basting with remaining marinade. Remove from grill and cut across grain into thick slices. Serve immediately. Makes 8 to 12 servings.

Mini Beef Rolls Madrid

Keep the sauce warm on the grill and use to baste the meat.

1 1/2 pounds lean ground beef
2 cups soft bread crumbs
1/2 cup evaporated milk
1 medium onion, chopped
1 cup pimiento-stuffed green olives, chopped
1 clove garlic, minced
2 eggs
1 1/2 teaspoons Lawry's Seasoned Salt
1/4 teaspoon Lawry's Seasoned Pepper
1/2 cup Lawry's Sweet 'N Sour Barbecue Sauce

Combine all ingredients except Barbecue Sauce; mix thoroughly. Shape meat into "sausages" about 5-inches long and 1 1/2-inches in diameter. Refrigerate until ready to use. Grill to desired degree of doneness. Brush with Sweet 'N Sour Barbecue Sauce while meat cooks. Serve in hot dog buns with assorted relishes. Makes 12 servings.

Serving Suggestions:
Mary Alice's Macaroni Salad, Pineapple on a Spit.

Hints:
Brush the meat close to the end of the cooking time so that the barbecue sauce, which contains sugar, doesn't burn.

Stuffed Grilled Hamburgers

Use your imagination for other stuffing combinations.

1 1/2 pounds lean ground beef
1 1/2 teaspoons Lawry's Seasoned Salt

Combine ground beef and Seasoned Salt. Make 10 thin patties with this mixture. Stuff with any of the following mixtures:

Stuffings

1 cup of any combination of grated cheeses

1 cup grated Monterey Jack cheese and 2 ounces chopped green chiles

3/4 cup grated Cheddar OR Mozzarella cheese
3 tablespoons chili sauce
3 tablespoons sweet pickle relish, drained

1 cup mashed blue cheese

Swiss cheese slices and crisp bacon, crumbled

Place stuffing mixture on 5 patties; top with remaining patties. Seal the edges securely by pressing edges together. Grill over hot coals. Makes 5 patties.

Serving Suggestions:
Hattie's Five Bean Bake, California Vegetable Kabobs.

Hints:
To create wonderful outdoor aromas while barbecuing, toss in an herb such as Pinch of Herbs, Seasoned Salt, bay leaf, thyme, fennel, dill or marjoram toward the end of the cooking time.

Serving Suggestions:

Bohemian Potato Salad, Apple Valley Salad.

Hints:

Buy fresh fish if possible. Whole trout are excellent barbecued. The more you brush or baste fish with a marinade, the more flavorful and juicy the fish will be.

A wire grill basket is handy for barbecuing fish. Brush grill basket generously with oil, and fish with marinade, to prevent sticking.

1 1/2 pounds fresh or frozen fish fillets OR steaks
1/2 cup salad oil
1 tablespoon Worcestershire sauce
1/2 teaspoon Lawry's Garlic Salt
1/2 teaspoon Lawry's Seasoned Pepper
Lemon wedges

Thaw fish if frozen. Combine oil, Worcestershire sauce, Garlic Salt and Seasoned Pepper; mix well. Brush fish with oil mixture. Place in well-oiled wire grill basket. Grill for 5 to 8 minutes. Turn basket over and brush fish again (through basket) with oil mixture. Grill until fish flakes easily when tested with a fork, 5 to 8 minutes more. Serve with lemon wedges. Makes 4 servings.

Barbecued Fish

Grilled Lemon Potatoes

Lemon adds a delightful flavor to these potatoes.

3 large baking potatoes
1/2 cup butter OR margarine
1/2 teaspoon Lawry's Garlic Salt
1 tablespoon Lawry's Seasoned Salt
1 1/4 teaspoons Lawry's Lemon Pepper Seasoning
1 tablespoon lemon juice

Cut potatoes in half lengthwise; deeply score cut surfaces. Cover skin side with aluminum foil. Melt butter; add remaining ingredients. Generously brush cut side of potatoes with butter sauce. Place potatoes, foil side down, on grill. Cook until tender, about 45 minutes. Turn cut side down occasionally during cooking. Makes 6 servings.

Lawry's Garlic Bread and Variations

Garlic bread has long been a popular favorite. Garlic Spread Concentrate makes delicious bread and is a wonderful garlic seasoning for many kinds of dishes.

Lawry's Garlic Bread

1 jar Lawry's Garlic Spread Concentrate
1/2 cup butter OR margarine
1 loaf (1 lb.) regular OR sourdough French bread, unsliced
1/4 cup grated Parmesan cheese.

Melt Garlic Spread Concentrate and butter or margarine in a long, shallow baking dish. Cut bread in half crosswise; then cut each half lengthwise. Score each quarter into 5 sections; do not cut through bottom crust. Dip cut sides of bread into garlic-butter mixture until well saturated. (Use all of mixture.) Sprinkle with Parmesan cheese. Broil until golden brown or wrap in foil and place on grill until heated through. Makes 20 slices.

Garlic Bread Variations

Garlic Sticks

Separate 12 wiener buns and cut in half lengthwise again to make sticks. Brush cut sides with garlic-butter. Sprinkle with Parmesan cheese, poppy and/or sesame seeds. Bake in 450°F. oven for 8 minutes.

Garlic Rye Bread

Use 1 uncut loaf rye bread instead of French bread.

Dinner Rolls

Brush cut sides of favorite dinner rolls with some garlic-butter. Broil until golden.

Hamburger Buns

Brush cut sides of hamburger buns with some garlic-butter. Broil until golden. Serve with broiled or barbecued meat patties.

Garlic Croutons

Cut 6 white or rye bread slices into 3/4-inch cubes. Toast cubes in 300°F. oven 30 to 45 minutes, stirring occasionally. While hot, sprinkle with Lawry's Seasoned Salt and brush with 1/4 cup Lawry's Garlic Spread Concentrate, melted. Toss and use for salads.

English Muffins

Split muffins in half. Toast until slightly browned. Spread each muffin half with garlic-butter. Sprinkle lightly with some grated Parmesan cheese or sesame seeds. Broil until golden brown.

Lawry's Herb Bread and Variations

Pinch of Herbs, wonderfully versatile as an herb seasoning, makes an herb bread that is out of this world.

Lawry's Herb Butter for Bread

1/2 cup melted butter
2 teaspoons Lawry's Pinch of Herbs
1 loaf (1 lb.) regular OR sourdough French bread, unsliced
1/4 cup grated Parmesan cheese
Sesame seeds, optional

Blend together butter and Pinch of Herbs. Cut bread in half lengthwise. Brush cut sides of bread with herb butter. Sprinkle with cheese and/or sesame seeds. Broil until golden brown or wrap in foil and place on grill until heated through.

Herb Bread Variations

Monkey Bread

Separate 1 package (10 oz.) refrigerated flaky buttermilk biscuits; cut each biscuit in half. Use 1/2 of the above herb butter recipe. Dip each biscuit half in butter; stand on flat end, side by side and slightly overlapping, in loaf pan. Pour remaining butter over biscuits. Bake in 375°F. oven 20 to 25 minutes. Let stand about 20 minutes before serving for butter to absorb.

Herb Butter Crescent Rolls

Remove dough from 2 packages (8 oz. each) refrigerated crescent rolls. Unroll and separate into triangles. Brush with herb butter, roll and bake according to package directions.

Fancy Herb Sticks

Thaw 1 package (10 oz.) frozen patty shells. Overlap shells and roll out to about 1/4-inch thick. Cut strips 4 to 6-inches long and 1/2-inch wide. Twist into a spiral shape, brush with herb butter. If desired, sprinkle with sesame or poppy seeds.

Herb Sticks

Separate 6 wiener buns and cut in half lengthwise. Cut each half lengthwise again to make sticks. Brush with herb butter and sprinkle with Lawry's Seasoned Salt and grated Parmesan cheese. Bake in 450°F. oven about 7 minutes. Serve hot.

Pineapple on a Spit

Cooked pineapple is delicious as a meat accompaniment or as a dessert.

1/4 cup brown sugar
1/4 cup orange-flavored liqueur
1/4 cup corn syrup
1 pineapple
15 to 20 whole cloves

Mix together brown sugar, orange-flavored liqueur and corn syrup; set aside. Cut away pineapple skin, leaving the crown; trim "eyes" from pineapple. Stud pineapple with cloves. Insert skewer, lengthwise from base through crown. Cover crown with foil. Rotate over hot coals 45 to 60 minutes, basting occasionally with sauce.
To prepare in oven: Place in roasting pan and bake in 300°F. oven for 1 hour. Baste occasionally with sauce. To serve, cut crosswise.

Hints:
If you don't have a rotisserie, slice the pineapple crosswise and grill. Or, bake whole, in a 300°F. oven for 1 hour, turning and basting occasionally.

Steamed Mushrooms

An easy way to prepare fresh vegetables on the grill.

1 pound medium-size mushrooms, washed and trimmed
1 teaspoon Lawry's Seasoned Salt
Dash Lawry's Seasoned Pepper
1/4 teaspoon paprika
1/4 cup butter OR margarine
2 tablespoons dry sherry
1/4 cup chopped parsley

Place mushrooms in center of 24 x 18-inch piece of heavy duty aluminum foil. Sprinkle with Seasoned Salt, Seasoned Pepper and paprika. Dot with butter and sprinkle sherry over all. Fold foil securely, leaving room for steam expansion. Place on grill and cook until done, about 30 minutes. Sprinkle with parsley before serving. Makes 4 to 6 servings.

Hints:
May be baked in 400°F. oven 20 minutes.

California Vegetable Kabobs

Use any combination of zucchini, crookneck or pattypan squash.

2 medium zucchini, cut in 1/2-inch chunks
2 yellow crookneck squash, cut in 1/2-inch chunks
1/2 pound medium mushrooms, stems removed
Cherry tomatoes
1 bottle Lawry's California Herb and Cheese Dressing
Bamboo skewers, soaked in water 2 hours

Place vegetables, except tomatoes, in plastic bag; add California Herb and Cheese Dressing. Close bag securely and marinate in refrigerator overnight, turning occasionally. Thread vegetables (with tomatoes) onto skewers. Broil or grill, turning skewers once, until vegetables are slightly tender. Serve immediately. Makes 4 to 6 servings.

Hints:
May use your favorite oil and vinegar dressing (with grated Parmesan cheese added) in place of California Herb and Cheese Dressing.

Roasted Corn on the Cob

Serving Suggestions:
Have extra seasoned butter to pass with hot corn.

Hints:
The corn can be husked, seasoned, wrapped in aluminum foil and roasted the same way. However, leaving the husks on adds flavor and a feeling of freshness. Gloves are needed in order to husk the corn once roasted.

Roasted Corn on the Cob
Steamed Mushrooms
California Vegetable Kabobs

The most flavorful corn is picked at dawn and eaten the same day. If you grow your own, that's no problem. If not, there are outdoor markets specializing in freshly-picked corn.

8 ears corn (with husks)
1/2 cup butter, softened
1 tablespoon Lawry's Seasoned Salt
1 teaspoon Lawry's Seasoned Pepper

Peel husks back carefully and remove silk. Combine softened butter, Seasoned Salt and Seasoned Pepper. Spread each ear with seasoned butter. Smooth husks over corn and tie ends together with string. Arrange corn over medium hot coals. Roast about 20 minutes turning every 5 minutes. Makes 8 ears.

Marinades and Basting Sauces

Barbecued meats and poultry are often marinated and/or basted with a sauce. Here are several excellent choices.

California Poultry Marinade

1/2 cup soy sauce
1/2 cup salad oil
1/2 cup dry white wine
1/4 cup lemon juice
1 teaspoon Lawry's Minced Onion with Green Onion Flakes
1/4 teaspoon ground ginger
1/2 teaspoon Lawry's Garlic Powder with Parsley
Dash Lawry's Seasoned Pepper

Hints:
Marinating may be done in a plastic bag. Just be sure the bag is sturdy and, to be on the safe side, place bag and contents in a dish or pan in the refrigerator. If marinating in a shallow pan or bowl always use glass or ceramic, not metal.

In large, leak-proof plastic bag, combine all ingredients. Place up to 5 pounds of turkey or chicken in marinade. Marinate in refrigerator for 6 to 8 hours or overnight, turning occasionally. Remove poultry, reserving marinade, and grill or bake. Baste frequently with reserved marinade. Makes 1 3/4 cups.

Savory Fruit Basting Sauce

1/2 cup white vinegar
1/4 cup salad oil
1/4 cup honey
1 can (12 oz.) peach OR apricot nectar
2 tablespoons Worcestershire sauce
2 teaspoons Lawry's Minced Onion with Green Onion Flakes
1 teaspoon prepared mustard
3/4 teaspoon Lawry's Seasoned Salt
1/2 teaspoon thyme
1/4 teaspoon crushed rosemary
1/4 teaspoon Lawry's Garlic Powder with Parsley
Dash Lawry's Seasoned Pepper

In medium saucepan, combine all ingredients. Bring to a boil, reduce heat and simmer, uncovered, 5 minutes. Use as basting sauce for baked or grilled turkey, chicken or pork. Makes 2 1/2 cups.

Steak Bora Bora Marinade

1 bottle (8 oz.) Lawry's Teriyaki Barbecue Marinade
4 medium cloves garlic, crushed
1/4 teaspoon Lawry's Seasoned Pepper
1 tablespoon finely grated ginger root OR 3/4 teaspoon ground ginger

Combine all ingredients thoroughly. Marinate beef steaks 2 to 3 hours before grilling or broiling. Makes 1 cup—enough for 3 pounds steak.

Barbecue Sauce for Poultry and Pork

Hints:

When using a marinade or sauce that contains sugar, baste near the end of the cooking period. If either is brushed on at the beginning, the meat or poultry may become too charred.

1/2 cup salad oil
1/4 cup cider vinegar
1/4 cup Worcestershire sauce
1 can (8 oz.) tomato sauce
2 1/2 tablespoons Lawry's Minced Onion with Green Onion Flakes
2 tablespoons firmly packed brown sugar
1 tablespoon chili powder
1 teaspoon sugar
1/2 teaspoon Lawry's Seasoned Salt
1/4 teaspoon Lawry's Garlic Powder with Parsley
Dash Lawry's Seasoned Pepper

In a small bowl, combine all ingredients; let stand 5 minutes. Generously baste chicken, turkey or pork during the last 15 minutes of grilling. Heat remaining sauce and serve. Makes 2 cups.

Quick and Easy Barbecue Ideas

Accompaniments for favorite grilled entrees.

Eggplant: Cut large eggplant in thick, crosswise slices. Brush with vegetable oil OR butter and sprinkle with Lawry's Seasoned Salt and Lawry's Seasoned Pepper. Grill until done.

Green Onions: Clean and trim several bunches of green onions. Brush white part lightly with vegetable oil. Grill. Serve sprinkled generously with fresh lime juice and Lawry's Seasoned Salt.

Vegetables in Foil: Cut fresh vegetables such as carrots, zucchini, celery, green beans, broccoli and green pepper in fairly small pieces. Season with butter and your choice of Lawry's Seasonings. Wrap in foil and place on grill until vegetables are tender. Timing will vary depending upon the vegetable used.

Fruit on the Grill: Bananas, either whole or in chunks, can be placed on skewers, brushed with melted butter and cinnamon and grilled. Pineapple slices or chunks (skewer if chunks) also work well.

EASY RECIPES FOR YOUNG PEOPLE AND BEGINNING COOKS

Learning any new skill is usually a combination of feelings—excitement about the new adventure and frustration with one's initial lack of skill and ability. Just as a painter begins to learn by exploring color, texture and design, so a cook begins with simple recipes and gradually progresses to more complex procedures.

Lawry's Chunky Taco Sauce   Fiesta Rice   Burritos
Enchiladas   Taco Joe   Tostada
Spicy Refried Beans   Supper Nachos   Tacos
Tostada

Cooking is a creative art, a means of self expression and relaxation for many people. Cooking is a hobby that can be done with others while some prefer the solitude of cooking alone. Whatever your preference, you must first learn some of the basic cooking techniques and then practice. No one has ever learned to do anything instantly.

The wonderful thing about cooking is that the results can be shared and experienced with others. Cook for yourself, your friends, neighbors and family. Read cookbooks and magazines; attend cooking classes and see how the experts do it. As you cook you will begin to develop a style of your own. You will put a part of yourself into the flavor or the presentation of the dish or meal. You will begin to develop your own tastes and imagination. You will be able to change a recipe to better suit your taste. You will develop a sense of style—a flair, if you will.

Experts give the following important advice to beginning cooks. First, always read the entire recipe. Do so completely and thoroughly. You will begin to familiarize yourself with what you are going to prepare so that there will be no surprises. As you read, visualize the various steps and procedures as well as the finished dish.

Second, assemble all ingredients and utensils needed. Measure out the proper amounts of all ingredients before you begin to prepare the dish. Use custard cups or paper containers for small amounts. As you measure, combine those ingredients that go into the recipe together. This step is insurance against forgetting something.

A brief word about "failures." In cooking there is rarely such a thing as an honest-to-goodness failure, unless you have burned a dish beyond recognition or overly seasoned a dish beyond repair. Failures can almost always be "fixed" with a little imagination and creativity and turned into presentable, edible dishes. For example, if the omelet fails, it can become scrambled eggs served with a flourish. If the molded jello falls apart, spoon into glass dishes, garnish and serve in style. Most of all, don't explain and don't apologize. Act as if you had planned it all along. While some of this know-how does come with experience, turning a negative into a positive is something anyone can do.

So no matter what your age, if you are venturing into the kitchen for the first time, use this collection of recipes as a beginning. Then as you gain experience, try recipes in other chapters. There are also many hints about cooking procedures, substitutions and information about buying and preparing ingredients. Use them all and begin your love affair with food. It could easily last a lifetime!

Here are some favorite Mexican foods that you can prepare quickly and easily. Start with a package of Lawry's Seasoning Mix, pre-blended with just the right flavor combinations, and follow the package directions. Lawry's makes Mexican favorites easy!

Tacos

1. Prepare taco filling using 1 package Lawry's Taco Seasoning Mix or 1 package Lawry's Chicken Taco Seasoning Mix. Follow package directions.
2. Prepare taco toppings according to package directions.
3. Heat Lawry's Taco Shells in 350°F. oven for 3 to 5 minutes.
4. Fill each taco shell and serve.

Tostadas

Tostadas are open-face tacos, so follow the above directions except use 1 package Lawry's Tostada Shells and 1 can refried beans, heated. To serve, spread warmed Tostada Shells with layer of refried beans, your choice of taco filling and garnishes.

Burritos

Prepare burrito filling using 1 package Lawry's Burrito Seasoning Mix. Follow package directions to prepare and assemble.

Taco Joe

Taco Joe is like a tostada but with a different flavored ground beef filling. Served over corn chips, this delicious dish is great for parties. Prepare according to package directions using 1 package Lawry's Taco Joe Seasoning Mix.

Spicy Refried Beans

Serving Suggestions:
Good as a burrito, taco or enchilada filling.

Hints:
Assemble this quick and easy dish ahead and bake just before serving.

An accompaniment to Mexican dishes.

2 cans (17 oz. each) refried beans
1 package (1 1/4 oz.) Lawry's Taco Seasoning Mix
2 cups grated Cheddar cheese
1 tablespoon Lawry's Minced Onion with Green Onion Flakes

Combine all ingredients in 2 1/2-quart casserole dish. Cover and bake in 350°F. oven 25 minutes. Makes about 4 cups.

Fiesta Rice

This is a popular accompaniment to Mexican dishes as well as a nice change-of-pace way to season rice.

1 cup uncooked long-grain white rice
2 tablespoons salad oil
1 3/4 cups water
1 package Lawry's Mexican Rice Seasoning Mix
1/2 cup grated Cheddar cheese
2 tablespoons chopped green onion
1 tablespoon chopped pimiento
2 tablespoons sliced ripe olives

In 2-quart saucepan, brown rice in hot oil until golden; stir often. Remove from heat. Stir in water and Mexican Rice Seasoning Mix; blend thoroughly. Bring to a boil, reduce heat, cover and simmer 20 minutes. Gently stir in remaining ingredients; cover and heat thoroughly for 3 to 5 minutes. Makes about 3 1/4 cups.

Serving Suggestions:
Good with almost all Mexican food.

Hints:
Use 2 cups instant rice and 1 cup water in place of the long-grain rice. Instant rice has a different texture and a slightly different flavor but is quite acceptable.

Beef & Vegetable Soup

When browning, keep the meat in small chunks for added texture.

1 pound ground beef
1 medium onion, halved and sliced
1 package Lawry's Au Jus Gravy Mix
2 1/2 cups water
1 can (1 lb.) tomatoes
4 medium carrots, pared and cut in 1/2-inch pieces
2 stalks celery, including tops, chopped
1 teaspoon Lawry's Seasoned Salt
1 teaspoon Lawry's Seasoned Pepper
2 teaspoons Worcestershire sauce

Brown meat and onions; drain fat. Add Au Jus Gravy Mix and blend thoroughly. Add water and remaining ingredients; mix together. Bring to a boil, reduce heat, cover and simmer 45 minutes. Makes 6 servings.

Serving Suggestions:
Lawry's Herb or *Garlic Bread.*

Hints:
Use any combination of vegetables and add more than the recipe calls for if you wish. Some suggestions are zucchini, shredded cabbage or cubed potatoes. Or, add about 1/2 cup long-grain rice or 1/2 to 3/4 cup elbow macaroni for a heartier version.

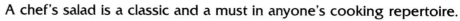

A chef's salad is a classic and a must in anyone's cooking repertoire.

1 quart torn romaine
2 medium heads butter lettuce, torn in bite-size pieces
Cucumber slices
Julienne strips of chicken OR turkey and ham
Crisp crumbled bacon
Julienne strips of Swiss cheese
Artichoke halves or quarters, cooked and cooled
Sliced fresh mushrooms
Asparagus tips, cooked and cooled
Chopped hard-cooked eggs
Croutons
1 teaspoon Lawry's Seasoned Salt
1/2 teaspoon Lawry's Seasoned Pepper
Use 8 oz. of your favorite Lawry's Salad Dressing

Combine romaine and butter lettuce in large bowl. Choose any or all of the first 9 ingredients and arrange them over lettuce. Sprinkle with Seasoned Salt and Seasoned Pepper. Add your favorite dressing and toss. Makes about 8 servings.

Chef's Salad Pacifica

Cut julienne strips evenly as shown. Julienne size may vary in length and thickness, but cut all of the same food the same size.

To score cucumber, hold table fork as shown. Draw fork tines (exert pressure to penetrate skin) lengthwise over skin. Slice thinly, either straight down or on the diagonal.

To make bread croutons, cut into uniform cubes. Sauté in butter and season with your favorite Lawry's seasoning—Seasoned Salt, Seasoned Pepper, Pinch of Herbs or Garlic Salt. Or, bake cubes in 375°F. oven until brown. Toss with melted butter and seasonings.

To make tortilla strips, cut corn tortillas into strips as shown. Deep fry at 375°F. until brown and crisp; drain thoroughly.

Mariachi Chicken

The flavor and texture of fried chicken done in the oven.

2 tablespoons butter
4 cups plain tortilla chips, crushed
1 package (1 1/4 oz.) Lawry's Taco Seasoning Mix
2 to 3 pounds chicken legs and wings
1 bottle Lawry's Chunky Taco Sauce, optional

In 350°F. oven, melt butter in jelly-roll or shallow baking pan. Combine crushed tortilla chips and Taco Seasoning Mix in a large plastic bag. Moisten chicken pieces with water and shake off excess. Place a few at a time in plastic bag; shake to coat thoroughly. Place coated chicken on pan with butter. Bake, uncovered, 30 to 45 minutes, until crispy and done. Serve with bowl of Chunky Taco Sauce for dipping, if desired. Makes 4 to 6 servings.

Serving Suggestions:
Chilaquiles, Jellied Gazpacho Salad.

Hints:
Use any favorite combination of chicken pieces. Crush tortilla chips in plastic bag, first with your hands, then with a rolling pin to make finer crumbs.

Taco Pizza

Another distinctively different pizza with a Mexican flavor.

1 pound ground beef
1 package (1 1/4 oz.) Lawry's Taco Seasoning Mix
1 cup water
1 package (13 1/4 oz.) hot roll mix
Salad oil, as needed
1 can (8 oz.) tomato sauce
2 cups grated Cheddar cheese

Brown ground beef until crumbly; drain fat. Add Taco Seasoning Mix and water; stir. Bring to a boil, reduce heat and simmer, uncovered, 15 to 20 minutes, stirring occasionally. Meanwhile, prepare hot roll mix according to package directions, but do not wait for dough to rise. Roll dough to fit a greased 17 x 12-inch cookie sheet. Build up sides of dough slightly to form a rim. Brush lightly with oil. Spread taco meat over dough. Then spread tomato sauce over meat. Top with cheese. Bake in 400°F. oven on bottom shelf 15 to 20 minutes. Makes 4 servings.

Serving Suggestions:
Tossed green salad.

Hints:
Frozen bread dough, thawed, may be used in place of hot roll mix. Add other pizza toppings if desired. When browning ground beef, use a fork to break up the meat. For some recipes, larger, chunkier pieces of the browned beef are desirable but for this recipe, the meat should be quite fine.

Easy Mini-Pizzas

The easiest pizza ever. And tasty, too.

4 English muffins
1 package Lawry's Extra Rich & Thick Spaghetti Sauce Mix
1 can (1 lb.) tomatoes, cut up
1 clove garlic, crushed OR 1/4 teaspoon Lawry's Garlic Powder with Parsley
1/2 cup grated Cheddar OR Parmesan cheese
Favorite pizza toppings

Split the muffins in half using fork. Broil until light brown. Meanwhile in a medium-sized saucepan, combine the Extra Rich & Thick Spaghetti Sauce Mix, tomatoes and crushed garlic; stir thoroughly. Bring to a boil, reduce heat, cover and simmer 20 minutes, stirring occasionally. Place 2 tablespoons sauce on each muffin half. Sprinkle with cheese and desired toppings. Broil until bubbling and brown. Makes 8 small pizzas.

Serving Suggestions:
Serve as a snack or as a party appetizer.

Hints:
When using garlic, remove outer skin and place in a garlic press. Crush and scrape off the garlic that comes through the press with a knife. Repeat one or two more times to get as much from the clove as possible. If you don't have a garlic press, mince very fine.
Use any favorite pizza toppings such as sliced pepperoni, salami, sliced olives, green pepper strips, browned and crumbled ground beef or pork sausage or anchovy fillets. Leftover spaghetti sauce may be frozen.

Serving Suggestions:

As an entree with *Garbeano Salad* or as a party appetizer.

Hints:

To roll dough, lightly flour a large bread board and the rolling pin, unless it is the non-stick variety. Pat dough into a rectangular shape and roll from the center out in all directions. If the dough is obstinate and won't roll easily, let it "rest" for about 10 to 15 minutes and then roll. To fit it into pan, fold the dough in quarters and lift into pan.

The frozen bread dough makes the crust, which is nice and thick, a snap to prepare.

1 loaf frozen bread dough
1 1/4 cups Lawry's Extra Rich & Thick Spaghetti Sauce, prepared from Mix according to package directions
1/2 teaspoon leaf oregano, crushed
12 ounces Mozzarella cheese, grated
6 ounces Provolone cheese, grated
2 ounces pepperoni, sliced
1 can (2 1/2 oz.) sliced ripe olives
1 cup sliced mushrooms
1 green bell pepper, cut in strips
Optional additions and/or substitutions; sausage, green chiles, anchovies, Canadian bacon

Let dough thaw and rise once; punch down. Roll to fit a 15 1/2 x 11-inch jelly-roll pan or round pizza pan. Arrange dough in pan and build up edge slightly. Spread sauce over dough; sprinkle with crushed oregano. Cover with grated cheeses. Arrange the remaining ingredients (and optional additions and/or substitutions) on cheese. Bake in 400°F. oven, on the lowest oven shelf, 30 minutes. Makes 6 to 8 servings or approximately 24 appetizer portions.

Deep Dish Pizza
Taco Pizza
Easy Mini-Pizzas

Chicken Breasts in Wine

Simple and elegant to serve for family and friends.

1/2 cup flour
1 teaspoon Lawry's Seasoned Salt
1/2 teaspoon Lawry's Seasoned Pepper
3 whole chicken breasts, halved
1/4 cup salad oil
1/4 cup butter
1/2 cup dry sherry
Rosemary, crushed

Combine flour, Seasoned Salt and Seasoned Pepper. Coat chicken breasts with seasoned flour. Heat salad oil and butter and fry chicken slowly until golden brown. Remove from skillet and place in a single layer in shallow baking pan. Pour sherry over chicken and sprinkle a pinch of crushed rosemary over each chicken breast. Cover and bake in 350°F. oven 45 to 50 minutes or until tender. Makes 6 servings.

Serving Suggestions:
Buttered rice, *Minted Peas, Peach Pudding Cake.*

Hints:
This recipe, easily increased for large groups, is good for buffet service. Boning the chicken breasts makes eating easier. A good boning knife and a little practice is all that's needed to do this task at home. Dry white wine may be used in place of sherry.

Jellied Gazpacho Salad

Probably one of the first things we all learned to make was jello. Here's a more sophisticated version.

2 envelopes unflavored gelatin
3 1/2 cups tomato juice
2 tablespoons lemon juice
2 tablespoons vinegar
1 package Lawry's Italian Salad Dressing Mix
1 cup finely chopped cucumber, well drained
1 cup finely chopped tomato, well drained
1/2 cup minced green bell pepper
Parsley OR lettuce
1 recipe Salad Dressing, optional

In a medium-sized saucepan, sprinkle gelatin over 2 cups tomato juice. Place over low heat and stir constantly until dissolved, about 3 minutes. Remove from heat and add remaining 1 1/2 cups tomato juice, lemon juice and vinegar. Stir gently. Add Italian Salad Dressing Mix and blend. Cool and refrigerate until slightly thickened. Add vegetables (well drained) to tomato mixture and stir gently. Turn into a 6-cup ring mold. Chill until set, preferably overnight. Unmold and garnish with parsley or lettuce. Serve with Salad Dressing, if desired. Makes 12 servings.

Serving Suggestions:
This salad may also be molded in 12 (1/2 cup) individual molds.

Hints:
Here's a way to make certain the gelatin will unmold easily. Brush the mold lightly with vegetable oil or coat with vegetable spray; turn mold upside down to drain any excess oil. Add the gelatin mixture and chill until firm. To unmold, carefully loosen the edges of the gelatin mixture with a rubber spatula or knife. Then shake the mold gently so that the gelatin pulls away from the sides and air gets underneath. Place the serving platter on top of the mold, turn over and shake a couple of times. The molded salad will slip right out. If, by chance, it doesn't, turn the mold over and repeat the above process. Dipping the mold in hot water isn't recommended as the heat tends to melt the gelatin.

Salad Dressing
1/2 cup mayonnaise
1/2 cup dairy sour cream
Lemon juice

Combine mayonnaise and sour cream; thin with lemon juice if needed. Makes 1 cup.

Chili Cheese Dogs

Serving Suggestions:

Serve chili sauce over avocado halves or baked potatoes for a different and tasty entree. Great over hamburgers, too.

Hints:

Make the chili ahead. Add chopped onion to the finished chili dog if desired.

Hot dogs are an American institution. Here's a way to make the best chili dogs in town.

1/2 pound ground beef
1 package Lawry's Chili Seasoning Mix
1 can (6 oz.) tomato paste
1 cup water
1 can (15 1/2 oz.) kidney OR pinto beans, drained
1 teaspoon prepared mustard
12 frankfurters
12 frankfurter buns
3/4 cup grated Cheddar cheese

Brown ground beef until crumbly; drain fat. Add Chili Seasoning Mix, tomato paste and water; mix well. Add kidney beans and mustard; bring to a boil, reduce heat and simmer, uncovered, 10 minutes, stirring frequently. Place frankfurters in buns, top with 1/4 cup of chili meat sauce and 1 tablespoon of cheese. Wrap each Chili Cheese Dog securely in aluminum foil. Heat in 400°F. oven 15 minutes. Makes 6 servings of 2 each.

Beef Tomato

Serving Suggestions:

Cooked rice, *Tangy Bean Sprout Toss.*

Hints:

The secret of stir fry cooking is high heat and keeping the food in motion. Stirring food in a wok is most efficient when done with chopsticks. If you don't have a wok, use a large skillet or Dutch oven. Partially freeze flank steak for easier slicing. Always slice diagonally across the grain. For best results use a very sharp knife.

A good stir fry dish for beginners.

1/3 cup Lawry's Teriyaki Barbecue Marinade
1 tablespoon cornstarch
1 flank steak (1 lb.), diagonally sliced paper thin
1/4 cup salad oil
1 clove garlic
1 medium green bell pepper, cut in 1-inch squares
2 medium onions, cut in 1-inch wedges
3 medium tomatoes, cut in 1-inch wedges
1 teaspoon Lawry's Seasoned Salt

Combine Teriyaki Barbecue Marinade and cornstarch; pour over beef. Marinate 20 to 30 minutes, turning once to coat. Heat 2 tablepoons oil. Brown garlic and remove. Quickly sauté green pepper and onion over high heat until tender crisp; remove. Heat remaining 2 tablespoons oil. Sauté beef slices. Add green pepper, onion, tomatoes and Seasoned Salt. Heat thoroughly. Makes 6 servings.

Tijuana Torte

Tijuana Torte

A hearty combination of a perfectly seasoned, meaty sauce layered with tortillas and cheese.

1 pound ground beef
1 medium onion, chopped
1 can (1 lb.) stewed tomatoes
1 can (8 oz.) tomato sauce
1 can (4 oz.) diced green chiles
1 package (1 1/4 oz.) Lawry's Taco Seasoning Mix
12 corn tortillas
1 pound Cheddar cheese, grated

Brown ground beef and onion in skillet. Drain excess fat. Add stewed tomatoes, tomato sauce, green chiles and Taco Seasoning Mix. Combine thoroughly; bring to a boil, reduce heat and simmer, uncovered, 10 to 15 minutes. Place about 1/4 cup meat mixture in bottom of 13 x 9 x 2-inch baking dish. Place 2 tortillas side by side on meat mixture. Top each tortilla with some meat mixture and grated cheese. Repeat until each stack contains 6 tortillas layered with meat and cheese. Bake in 350°F. oven 20 to 25 minutes. To serve, cut each torte (stack) into quarters with a sharp knife before serving. Makes 4 to 6 servings.

Serving Suggestions:
Mexican Dinner Salad, Jicama Dessert.

Hints:
Make early in the day and bake just before serving. Or make ahead, bake and freeze and reheat, covered, in a 350°F. oven 35 to 40 minutes or until heated through. Freeze one "stack" for later use if only 2 servings are needed.

Prepare meat loaf mixture according to package directions on Lawry's Meat Loaf Seasoning Mix. Use a 9 x 5 x 3-inch loaf pan for all of the following recipes. Use all ground beef or a combination of beef, pork and lamb. Bake in 375°F. oven 1 to 1 1/4 hours. Drain excess liquid; let stand 10 minutes before slicing.

MUSHROOM: In 2 tablespoons butter, sauté 1 onion, chopped and 1/4 pound of sliced mushrooms. Combine with meat loaf mixture; add 1/2 cup grated Cheddar cheese; mix well.

CHEESE: Top meat loaf with slices of Cheddar OR Monterey Jack cheese 10 minutes before the end of the baking time.

ITALIAN: Serve sliced meat loaf with spaghetti sauce. Make sauce with 1 package Lawry's Extra Rich & Thick Spaghetti Sauce Mix OR 1 package Lawry's Spaghetti Sauce Mix with Imported Mushrooms and prepare according to package directions.

BACON: Top meat loaf with 1/4 cup ketchup OR chili sauce and 3 to 4 bacon slices before baking.

FRUIT: Top meat loaf with pineapple slices OR peach halves 20 minutes before the end of the baking time.

Layered Meat Loaf Delights

Serving Suggestions:
Baked potatoes (bake along with meat loaf), fresh vegetable or tossed salad.

Hints:
Meat loaves can be shaped and baked on a jelly-roll pan (a cookie sheet with sides) rather than a loaf pan.

1. Press 1/2 of the meat loaf mixture in the bottom of a 9 x 5 x 3-inch loaf pan.

2. Spread your choice of these filling combinations over meat:

   FRUIT: 1/3 cup currant jelly and 1 can (8 oz.) crushed pineapple, well drained

   ORIENTAL FILLING: 1 can (1 lb.) Oriental-style vegetables, well-drained and 2 tablespoons soy sauce

   CHEESE & CHILES: 4 to 6 slices Monterey Jack cheese and 1 can (4 oz.) diced green chiles, well-drained

3. Press remaining 1/2 of meat loaf mixture on top, pressing firmly and smoothing top. Bake in 375°F. oven 1 to 1 1/4 hours.

Fancy Easy Fish

This recipe works with most any fresh or frozen unbreaded fish.

1 package Lawry's Mexican Rice Seasoning Mix
1 can (1 lb.) tomatoes, cut up
1 teaspoon Lawry's Seasoned Salt
1 teaspoon Lawry's Seasoned Pepper
2 tablespoons chopped pimiento
2 pounds fish fillets OR steaks

Combine Mexican Rice Seasoning Mix, tomatoes, Seasoned Salt, Seasoned Pepper and pimiento. Place fillets in a 2-quart baking dish; pour sauce over fish. Cover and bake in 350°F. oven 30 to 35 minutes. Makes 8 servings.

Serving Suggestions:
Buttered rice, *Lemon Broccoletti*.

Hints:
Fillets are thinner than steaks. If fish is frozen it may be cooked frozen or thawed. Once thawed cook immediately. Fish is done when it flakes apart easily with a fork. Kinds of fish have very different flavors, so experiment with several varieties to find your favorite. Fillet of sole is usually readily available and does not have a strong flavor; it's a good fish to use with a sauce.

Spicy Taco Burgettes

These are good as snacks or for a luncheon or light supper dish.

1 pound ground beef
1/2 cup chopped celery
1/2 cup ketchup
1/2 cup water
1 package (1 1/4 oz.) Lawry's Taco Seasoning Mix
1 can (2 1/4 oz.) sliced ripe olives, drained
1 cup grated Cheddar cheese
2 packages (8 oz. each) refrigerator crescent rolls

Brown ground beef in skillet until crumbly; drain fat. Add celery, ketchup, water, Taco Seasoning Mix and olives. Bring to a boil, reduce heat and simmer, uncovered, 10 minutes, stirring occasionally. Cool slightly. Remove rolls from package and separate into 8 rectangles. (Do not separate into triangles.) Roll each rectangle into a square. Place equal amounts of cooled meat mixture and grated cheese in the center of each square. Fold up corners of the rolls, pinching them together on top. Place on an ungreased cookie sheet and bake in 450°F. oven 10 to 12 minutes or until golden brown. Makes 8 burgettes.

Hints:
For rolling dough, see directions for "Deep Dish Pizza." It is important to pinch the top of the dough together tightly. Moisten top edges with water if dough isn't sticking together. These freeze well.

Polynesian Pork Chops or Chicken

The bottled Sweet 'N Sour Barbecue Sauce eliminates the need to make the sauce from scratch.

4 loin pork chops, 3/4-inch thick OR 2 1/2 to 3 pounds chicken parts
1 green bell pepper, cut in 1-inch pieces
1 onion, thinly sliced
1 bottle Lawry's Sweet 'N Sour Barbecue Sauce
2 cups cooked rice

Arrange chops or chicken (skin side up) in 13 x 9 x 2-inch baking dish. Add pepper and onion. Pour Sweet 'N Sour Barbecue Sauce over meat and vegetables. Cover and bake in 350°F. oven 45 minutes. Remove cover and bake 15 minutes longer. Serve over rice. Makes 4 servings.

Serving Suggestions:
Cooked rice, *Oriental Vegetables*, almond cookies.

Hints:
Add 1/2 cup well-drained pineapple chunks if desired. To cook perfect rice, follow the package directions exactly. Use any leftover rice in a casserole with leftover meats, vegetables and cheese. It's a great way to be inventive with what you have on hand.

Frank and Saucy Casserole

Serving Suggestions:
Tossed green salad, fresh fruit.

Hints:
Curry powder gives a wonderfully distinctive flavor to this dish but if you don't care for curry, leave it out.

The meat and pasta (spaghetti) cook together right in the sauce.

6 bacon slices
1 1/2 cups chopped onion
1 green bell pepper, coarsely chopped
1 teaspoon curry powder, optional
1 package (1 1/2 oz.) Lawry's Spaghetti Sauce Mix with Imported Mushrooms
2 cups water
2 cups tomato juice
6 ounces spaghetti, broken in 2-inch pieces OR elbow macaroni
8 beef frankfurters OR smoked link sausages

In a large Dutch oven, fry bacon until crisp; drain on paper towels. Drain all but 2 tablespoons bacon fat and use to sauté onion and green pepper. Add curry powder, Spaghetti Sauce Mix with Imported Mushrooms, water and tomato juice; stir. Bring to a boil; add spaghetti and frankfurters or sausages. (Leave meat whole or cut in pieces.) Reduce heat and simmer, uncovered, until spaghetti is tender, about 10 to 12 minutes; stir frequently. Crumble bacon and sprinkle on top before serving. Makes 6 servings.

Glossary of Cooking Terms

Baste..brush or spoon liquid over food while cooking to keep food moist.

Blend..stir ingredients until mixed.

Boil..cook in rapidly bubbling liquid.

Broil..cook under direct heat in a broiler.

Brown..cook meat in fat over moderately high heat until surfaces brown.

Chop..cut food in small pieces.

Combine..mix two or more ingredients together.

Dash..one or two shakes or sprinklings of a seasoning.

Dice..cut in cubes. The cubes are 1/4-inches, unless otherwise specified.

Julienne..cut meat, vegetables and fruit in strips, about the size of wooden match sticks. Julienne size can vary depending upon the dish.

Marinate..let stand in a seasoned liquid, called a marinade, for a specified period of time to impart flavor and/or to tenderize.

Mince..chop very fine.

Pare..remove outer covering (apples, potatoes, carrots) with a knife or vegetable peeler.

Pinch..amount of dry seasoning you can pick up between your thumb and forefinger.

Roast..cooking by dry heat, uncovered, in an oven.

Sauté..fry quickly in small amount of hot fat until golden or lightly browned.

Shred..tear or cut in small strips.

Simmer..cook just below boiling point.

Stir..blend briskly with spoon or whisk.

Whip..beat rapidly with wire whisk, electric beaters or eggbeater to incorporate air and increase volume.

SNACKS AND LIGHT MEALS

Three squares a day is not the only way to eat. The varied lifestyles of today often dictate a different approach. We live in a changing world. Families are structured in many kinds of combinations. Women are working outside the home in increasing numbers. Children and men are becoming more actively involved in cooking. There is a shift in the ages of our population. All these factors affect the mealtime content and schedule. Traditional meal times arrive and often no one is home!

Individuals may find that they feel infinitely better eating several light meals a day rather than the usual three. Younger and older people often have different eating requirements. Many people are realizing that they don't require nearly as much food as they may have once thought and find that they feel better when eating lighter foods and less of them. Warmer weather also brings a change in eating habits with tendencies for lighter foods.

Protein sources, other than meat, are readily available and can be made into delicious entrees. Cheese and egg dishes are versatile and excellent for brunch, lunch, lighter suppers or dinner.

Snacks can be as simple and delicious as a piece of favorite cheese and fruit or fresh vegetables, chilled and ready for snacking. When a heartier snack is in order, sandwiches are always enjoyed. Teamed with soup, fruit, vegetable relishes or a salad, they constitute a meal. Sandwich making is incredibly creative, limited only by the imagination. Perhaps a throwback to childhood when our "comfort" food was peanut butter and jelly layered between thick slices of bread, sandwiches very often fill the bill when nothing else sounds appealing.

Though not included in this chapter, salads and some appetizers are also favorite choices for light meal eating. (See "Salads and More Salads" and "Party Starters.") The following pages are filled with a wide variety of recipes for sandwiches, hearty soups and egg and cheese dishes.

| Italian Cheeseburgers | Skyscraper Burgers |
| Gourmet Olé Burgers | Lawry's Chunky Taco Sauce |

Lawry's Seasoned Hamburgers

Perfect proportions of seasonings for tasty basic hamburgers.

1 pound ground beef
1 teaspoon Lawry's Seasoned Salt
1/2 teaspoon Lawry's Seasoned Pepper

Combine ingredients lightly. Shape in 4 patties. Broil or grill as desired. Makes 4 servings.

Italian Cheeseburgers

1 recipe Lawry's Seasoned Hamburgers, shaped in 4 patties
1/4 teaspoon leaf oregano, crushed
1/4 cup tomato sauce
4 slices Mozzarella cheese
4 toasted hamburger buns

Broil or grill patties for 3 to 4 minutes on each side. Combine oregano and tomato sauce. Top each patty with 1 tablespoon tomato mixture. Place slice of cheese on each patty. Return to broiler or grill until cheese melts. Serve on toasted buns. Makes 4 servings.

Skyscraper Burgers

Hints:
For a quick and easy sauce, canned cheese sauce or soup may be used.

Five story hamburgers topped with creamy hot cheese sauce.

1 recipe Lawry's Seasoned Hamburgers, shaped in 4 patties
4 bacon slices
4 Swiss cheese slices
4 toast slices
4 onion slices
4 tomato slices
2 cups hot cheese sauce

Wrap each patty with a bacon slice; secure with a toothpick. Broil or grill as desired. Place cheese slices on toast. Top with hamburgers. Add an onion and tomato slice to each patty. Top with hot cheese sauce. Makes 4 servings.

Gourmet Olé Burgers

Delicious hamburgers with a Mexican twist.

2 pounds lean ground beef
1 package (1 1/4 oz.) Lawry's Taco Seasoning Mix
1/2 cup white wine OR water
1 teaspoon Lawry's Seasoned Salt
1/2 teaspoon Lawry's Seasoned Pepper
1 can (4 oz.) diced green chiles
1 large tomato, coarsely chopped
4 green onions, chopped, including tops
1 cup grated Cheddar cheese
1/2 teaspoon Lawry's Seasoned Salt
Hamburger buns OR rolls
Shredded lettuce
Sliced ripe olives

Hints:
Make patties and freeze between layers of waxed paper or place patties on a cookie sheet and freeze, then wrap securely.

In a large bowl, mix together ground beef, Taco Seasoning Mix, white wine, Seasoned Salt, Seasoned Pepper and diced green chiles. Shape into 6 large patties; let stand at least 5 minutes before cooking. Broil patties to desired degree of doneness. Meanwhile, combine chopped tomato, green onion, Cheddar cheese and 1/2 teaspoon Seasoned Salt; toss lightly to combine. Spoon some tomato mixture over each patty and press lightly. Continue broiling until cheese melts. Serve on buns with shredded lettuce and ripe olives. Makes 6 servings.

Spicy Beef Boats

6 large French rolls
1 pound ground beef
1 cup water
1/2 cup orange juice
1 can (6 oz.) tomato paste
1 package Lawry's Sloppy Joes Seasoning Mix
1 can (8 1/4 oz.) refried beans, heated
1 can (4 oz.) diced green chiles
1 1/2 cups grated Monterey Jack cheese
6 tomato slices
1/2 cup sliced ripe olives, optional

Hints:
For crispier bread shells, heat hollowed rolls in a 400°F. oven for 10 minutes. Refried beans will spread more easily if heated.

Cut the top off each French roll; hollow out, leaving about 1/4-inch walls. Brown ground beef; drain fat. Add water, orange juice, tomato paste and Sloppy Joes Seasoning Mix. Bring to a boil, reduce heat and simmer, uncovered, 15 minutes. Spread the inside of each roll with beans; fill each with 1/2 cup Sloppy Joes mixture; sprinkle with chiles and top with cheese. Arrange on a cookie sheet and place under the broiler until cheese melts. Before serving, top with a tomato slice and sprinkle with sliced olives. Serve immediately. Makes 6 servings.

Soft Tacos con Pasas

Hints:
The raisins make this filling somewhat sweet. If you prefer a more traditional spicy flavor, substitute 1/2 cup chopped ripe olives.

Use fresh tortillas that are soft and flexible.

1 pound ground beef
1 package (1 1/4 oz.) Lawry's Taco Seasoning Mix
1/2 cup water
1 can (8 oz.) tomato sauce
1/2 cup raisins
8 corn tortillas
Melted butter OR margarine
1 cup grated Cheddar cheese
Lawry's Chunky Taco Sauce, optional

Brown beef until crumbly; drain fat. Add Taco Seasoning Mix, water, tomato sauce and raisins. Bring to a boil, reduce heat and simmer, uncovered, 20 minutes. Brush tortillas with butter and brown lightly in skillet. Spoon taco meat filling on tortillas. Sprinkle with Cheddar cheese. Fold to enclose. Serve with Chunky Taco Sauce, if desired. Makes 8 servings.

Bacon and Avocado Quesadillas

Quesadillas are a favorite Mexican snack.

2 avocados, peeled and coarsely mashed
1 3/4 cups grated Monterey Jack cheese
2 tablespoons Lawry's Bacon Onion Seasoning
3 tablespoons diced green chiles
4 (8-inch) flour tortillas
Melted butter

Combine avocados, cheese, Bacon Onion Seasoning and chiles. Divide mixture among 4 tortillas, spreading almost to edges; fold in half. Brush tortillas and skillet with butter. Fry over medium-low heat until golden brown on both sides and cheese melts. Makes 8 servings.

Sausage Pockets

Hints:
Use crumbled cooked Italian sausage in place of summer sausage if desired.

Pita or "pocket" bread is wonderfully versatile for all kinds of fillings.

1 pound summer sausage, cut in bite-size pieces
1 small onion, sliced in rings
1 green bell pepper, cut in 1-inch pieces
1 can (2 1/4 oz.) sliced ripe olives
8 large mushrooms, sliced
1 package (1 1/2 oz.) Lawry's Spaghetti Sauce Mix with Imported Mushrooms, prepared according to package directions
6 small rounds pita bread, sliced in half

In large skillet, brown sausage, onion and green pepper until vegetables are almost tender; drain fat. Add olives, mushrooms and Spaghetti Sauce. Bring to a boil, reduce heat and simmer, uncovered, 10 minutes. Fill each pita bread half with sausage-sauce mixture. Makes 6 servings.

Italian Sausage Sandwich _____

This is a "knife and fork" sandwich.

1 pound Italian sausage, cut in 1-inch pieces
2 green bell peppers, seeded and sliced
2 cans (8 oz. each) tomato sauce
1/4 cup dry red wine
1 package (1 1/2 oz.) Lawry's Spaghetti Sauce Mix with Imported
  Mushrooms
1 loaf unsliced French OR sourdough bread
Grated Parmesan cheese

Brown sausage; add peppers toward end of browning and sauté. Drain excess fat. Add tomato sauce, wine and Spaghetti Sauce Mix to sausage and green peppers. Bring to a boil, reduce heat, cover and simmer 30 minutes, stirring occasionally. To serve, slice bread 3/4-inch thick. Spoon meat mixture over bread and sprinkle with Parmesan cheese. Makes 8 servings.

Hints:
Use mild or hot Italian sausage.
Also good as a sauce over pasta.

138

Herb Sandwich Supreme

Hints:
To cut slices evenly, mark with toothpicks around the outside of loaf.

Use rye, sourdough, whole wheat or any favorite bread available in a round loaf.

1/2 cup softened butter
2 teaspoons Lawry's Pinch of Herbs
1/2 teaspoon Lawry's Seasoned Salt
1/4 teaspoon Lawry's Seasoned Pepper
1 large round loaf French bread, unsliced
2 tablespoons mayonnaise
6 to 8 slices cooked turkey
8 slices crisp bacon
2 cups grated Swiss cheese

Combine butter, Pinch of Herbs, Seasoned Salt and Seasoned Pepper. Slice loaf of bread crosswise into three sections. (Remove center section and use later for croutons or bread crumbs.) Spread cut surfaces of bread with seasoned butter mixture. Broil bottom half until golden brown. Spread mayonnaise on top half; arrange turkey on bottom half. Add bacon strips. Sprinkle with grated Swiss cheese. Place both sections under broiler until golden brown and cheese is melted. Put sandwich together and serve hot. Cut in wedge-shaped portions. Makes 6 to 8 servings.

The Mexican Hero

Hints:
When using raw onion in sandwiches, slice paper thin. A good sharp knife and a steady hand are essential.

Use taco-seasoned mayonnaise to flavor other favorite sandwiches.

1/2 cup mayonnaise
1 package (1 1/4 oz.) Lawry's Taco Seasoning Mix
1 long loaf sourdough French bread, split in half lengthwise
1 package (8 oz.) sliced salami
1 package (8 oz.) sliced bologna
1 package (8 oz.) sliced ham
2 large tomatoes, thinly sliced
1 onion, thinly sliced
1 1/2 cups grated Cheddar OR Monterey Jack cheese

Blend mayonnaise and Taco Seasoning Mix; spread half of the mixture on bread. Place a layer of salami, bologna and ham on bread; spread a little more taco-seasoned mayonnaise on ham. Add tomato and onion slices; top with grated cheese. Place under broiler until cheese melts. Makes 8 servings.

Tortilla Wrapped Sandwiches

Place about 1/2 cup of any of the following fillings in the centers of warmed 12-inch flour tortillas. Fold in sides and roll up like a burrito; secure with toothpick if necessary. Cut sandwiches in half if desired.

Tuna Fiesta

1 package Lawry's Italian Salad Dressing Mix
1/3 cup mayonnaise
1 can (6 1/2 oz.) chunk-style tuna, drained
3/4 cup chopped celery
3 to 6 tablespoons finely chopped onion
2 tablespoons chopped green bell pepper
1/4 cup diced green chiles
3 hard-cooked eggs, chopped
1 tablespoon chopped pimiento

Combine Italian Salad Dressing Mix and mayonnaise; blend well. Add remaining ingredients. Makes enough for 12 sandwiches.

Guacamole

2 avocados, peeled and coarsely mashed
3/4 teaspoon lemon juice
1/2 teaspoon Lawry's Bacon Onion Seasoning
1/2 teaspoon Lawry's Seasoned Salt
1/2 teaspoon Lawry's Garlic Salt
1/2 teaspoon Lawry's Lemon Pepper Seasoning
2 cups shredded lettuce
1 tomato, thinly sliced
1 cup grated Cheddar cheese

Blend together avocado, lemon juice and seasonings. Place 1/4 of this mixture in center of tortillas. Cover with 1/2 cup shredded lettuce, 2 slices tomato and 1/4 cup cheese. Makes 4 sandwiches.

Beef 'N Gazpacho

1 package (1 1/4 oz.) Lawry's Taco Seasoning Mix
1/4 cup water
3 medium tomatoes, peeled and chopped
1 cucumber, peeled and chopped
1 avocado, peeled and chopped
1 (2-pound) flank steak

Combine Taco Seasoning Mix and water; blend well. Add tomatoes, cucumber and avocado; toss and chill. Broil steak about 4 minutes on each side or according to taste. Slice thinly across grain; let cool. Add meat to tomato mixture. Place 1/2 cup of meat mixture in center of tortilla. Makes 12 sandwiches.

Hints:

To warm tortillas, wrap in foil and heat in oven, place on gas burner and turn once or heat in the microwave. All fillings, except guacamole, may be made ahead and refrigerated.

16 slices very thinly sliced ham
4 whole green chiles (fresh or canned), seeds removed
4 slices cucumber
4 slices Monterey Jack cheese

Tortilla Wrapped Sandwiches
Tuna Fiesta
Guacamole
Ramada
Beef 'n Gazpacho

Arrange 4 ham slices and 1 slice of each of the remaining ingredients in center of tortilla. Makes 4 sandwiches.

Minestrone

A meal-in-one soup for any occasion.

2 cans (10 1/2 oz. each) beef consomme
3 1/2 cups water
1/2 cup lentils
3 bacon slices, diced
1 can (8 oz.) tomato sauce
1 package (1 1/2 oz.) Lawry's Spaghetti Sauce Mix with Imported
   Mushrooms
2 cloves garlic
1/2 teaspoon Lawry's Seasoned Salt
1/2 teaspoon Lawry's Seasoned Pepper
1/2 cup coarsely shredded cabbage
1/2 cup smallest size uncooked elbow macaroni
1 package (10 oz.) frozen mixed vegetables OR 1 can (1 lb.) mixed
   vegetables, drained
2 tablespoons finely chopped parsley

Combine consomme, water, lentils and bacon in a large kettle. Bring to a boil, reduce heat, cover and simmer 1 hour. Add tomato sauce and Spaghetti Sauce Mix. Stir thoroughly. Insert toothpick into each garlic clove; add garlic cloves, Seasoned Salt, Seasoned Pepper and cabbage. Continue to simmer, covered, 25 minutes. Bring soup to a boil and add macaroni, vegetables and parsley. Cook, uncovered, until macaroni and vegetables are tender, about 10 minutes. Remove garlic cloves. Makes 6 to 8 servings.

Hints:
Beef broth may be used in place of consomme.

Hearty Potato Chowder

A soup you can make "from scratch" in just minutes.

6 bacon slices, cut in half
1 cup chopped onion
1 1/2 cups water
4 cups diced raw potatoes
1 1/2 cups milk
1 1/2 teaspoons Lawry's Seasoned Salt
1/2 teaspoon Lawry's Seasoned Pepper

In a 3-quart saucepan, cook bacon until crisp. Crumble and set aside. Remove all but 2 tablespoons of bacon drippings from saucepan. Sauté onion in drippings until tender. Add water and potatoes. Bring to a boil, reduce heat, cover and simmer 15 minutes or until potatoes are tender but not mushy. Add milk, Seasoned Salt, Seasoned Pepper and bacon. Heat thoroughly but do not boil. Makes 6 servings.

Hints:
For a thicker soup, cook 15 to 20 minutes longer before adding milk.

Minestrone
Corned Beef & Cabbage Soup
Sopa de Sonora

Corned Beef & Cabbage Soup

Two meals in one—serve a corned beef dinner and use the broth and leftover corned beef for this delicious soup.

Hints:
Soup freezes well.

3 cups corned beef liquid, strained from cooked corned beef
1 can (14 1/2 oz.) beef broth
1 can water
1 cup cooked cubed corned beef
1 cup shredded raw cabbage
1 cup peeled and diced raw potato
1/2 cup finely chopped onion
1/2 cup finely chopped celery
1/4 teaspoon Lawry's Garlic Powder with Parsley

Place corned beef liquid, beef broth and water in Dutch oven. Add remaining ingredients. Bring to a boil, reduce heat, cover and simmer 20 minutes. Makes 6 to 8 servings.

143

Sopa de Sonora

Condiments add flavor, glamour and color to this tasty soup.

1 pound boneless lean pork shoulder, trimmed and cut in 1-inch cubes
1 tablespoon salad oil
1 1/2 tablespoons Lawry's Minced Onion with Green Onion Flakes
1/4 teaspoon Lawry's Garlic Powder with Parsley
1 package Lawry's Chili Seasoning Mix
4 1/2 cups water
1 can (14 1/2 oz.) beef broth
1 cup dried pinto beans, rinsed
2 cups thinly sliced carrots
Lawry's Seasoned Salt, to taste

Condiments:
Cherry tomatoes, cut in fourths
Sliced green onions
Chopped cilantro
Lime wedges
Dairy sour cream
Lawry's Chunky Taco Sauce

In large Dutch oven, brown meat in hot oil. Add remaining ingredients, except carrots, Seasoned Salt and condiments. Bring to a boil, reduce heat, cover and simmer 1 1/2 hours. Add carrots, cover and simmer for about 30 minutes or until carrots are tender. Add Seasoned Salt to taste. Serve with condiments. Makes 6 to 8 servings.

Hints:
Use beef bouillon and water rather than beef broth; just follow package directions for bouillon proportions. May use 1 pound boneless beef chuck roast instead of pork.

Italian Sausage Soup

The aroma of simmering homemade soup can't be beat.

1 1/2 pounds mild Italian sausage, cut in 1/2-inch pieces
2 cloves garlic, minced or crushed
2 large onions, chopped
1 can (1 lb. 12 oz.) pear shaped tomatoes
2 packages (1 1/2 oz. each) Lawry's Spaghetti Sauce Mix with
    Imported Mushrooms OR 1 package (3 oz.) Lawry's Economy Size
    Spaghetti Sauce Mix with Imported Mushrooms
3 cans (14 1/2 oz. each) beef broth
1 1/2 cups dry red wine
1 large green bell pepper, chopped
2 medium zucchini, sliced 1/4-inch thick
2 cups water
3 cups uncooked elbow macaroni
Grated Parmesan cheese

Brown sausage; set aside. Sauté garlic and onion in sausage drippings; drain excess fat. In a large kettle, combine all ingredients except water, macaroni and cheese. Bring to boil, reduce heat, cover and simmer 2 hours, stirring occasionally. Add water and macaroni; simmer, uncovered, an additional 30 minutes. Top each serving with Parmesan cheese. Makes 8 servings.

Hints:
Sausage may be browned whole or in pieces in the oven at 350°F. If whole, prick sausages in several places to allow excess fat to drain. Regular whole tomatoes may be used instead of pear shaped if desired.

Chile Cheese Eggs

Created for those times when it appears there's nothing in the house to cook.

2 cans (8 oz. each) whole green chiles, rinsed and seeds removed
3/4 pound Monterey Jack cheese, grated
1/4 cup milk
8 eggs
1 package (1 1/4 oz.) Lawry's Taco Seasoning Mix

Line bottom of 8 x 8 x 2-inch baking dish with half of chiles. Arrange half of cheese on chiles. Add another layer of chiles. Combine milk, eggs, Taco Seasoning Mix and beat well; pour over chiles. Add remaining cheese. Bake, uncovered, in 350°F. oven 30 minutes or until the eggs are puffy and lightly browned. Makes 6 servings.

Avocado Omelette Olé

Omelettes are an excellent way to use leftover bits of meats and vegetables as fillings.

4 eggs
1 tablespoon water
1/4 teaspoon Lawry's Seasoned Salt
2 tablespoons butter OR margarine
1 small to medium avocado, peeled and sliced
2 tablespoons diced green chiles
2 tablespoons dairy sour cream

Beat eggs with water and Seasoned Salt. Melt butter in a 10-inch frying pan or omelette pan; add eggs. As eggs start to pull away from sides, allow the liquid eggs on top to run to the edges. When the eggs start to set, place avocado and one tablespoon chiles on one half. Fold the other half over; place sour cream on top and sprinkle with remaining chiles. Serve immediately. Makes 2 servings.

Puffed Eggs Monterey

A quick and easy souffle-like dish for brunch or a light supper.

6 eggs
1/2 cup milk
1 teaspoon Lawry's Seasoned Salt
1/2 teaspoon Lawry's Seasoned Pepper
2 tablespoons diced green chiles
3/4 cup grated Monterey Jack cheese
4 slices white bread
2 tablespoons butter

Combine eggs, milk, Seasoned Salt, Seasoned Pepper and chiles; beat lightly. Add cheese. Spread bread with butter; cut in half to make triangles. Arrange bread halves, buttered side out, around edge of 9-inch pie plate so points stand up. Place remaining bread, buttered side down, in bottom of pan. Pour in egg mixture. Bake in 350°F. oven 30 minutes. Cut in wedges to serve. Makes 6 servings.

Chili Cheese Jubilee

Chili Cheese Jubilee

1 medium onion, chopped
2 tablespoons butter
1 can (8 oz.) tomato sauce
1 package Lawry's Chili Seasoning Mix
1/2 cup water
2 eggs
1 cup light cream
1 package (6 oz.) corn chips
8 ounces Monterey Jack cheese, cubed
1 cup dairy sour cream
1/2 cup grated Cheddar cheese

Hints:
Coat casseroles with vegetable oil spray for easier serving and cleaning. Casserole may be frozen, without sour cream and Cheddar cheese topping.

Sauté onion in butter; add tomato sauce, Chili Seasoning Mix and water. Simmer, uncovered, five minutes. Beat eggs slightly, add cream and mix well. Remove tomato-chili mixture from heat. Add egg-cream mixture slowly, stirring constantly. Place 1/2 package of corn chips in bottom of 1 1/2-quart casserole. Add 1/2 of Monterey Jack cheese. Cover with 1/2 of sauce. Repeat layers once. Top with sour cream and sprinkle with grated Cheddar cheese. Bake, uncovered, in 325°F. oven 25 to 30 minutes. Makes 5 to 6 servings.

Quiche Mexicana

As served at Lawry's California Center.

Hints:

Flour tortillas, when baked or fried, make excellent pastry shells. Use tortilla cups, baked without filling, as containers for guacamole and other dips or chicken or tuna salad.

2 1/2 cups grated Monterey Jack cheese
6 eggs, well beaten
1/2 cup light cream
1/3 cup finely chopped onion
1 can (4 oz.) diced green chiles
1 jar (2 oz.) diced pimiento
1/4 teaspoon Lawry's Seasoned Salt
1/8 teaspoon Lawry's Garlic Powder with Parsley
Dash Lawry's Seasoned Pepper
4 (8-inch) flour tortillas
Salad oil

Combine all ingredients, except tortillas and oil, in a large bowl; mix thoroughly and set aside. Brush tortillas lightly with oil and place in small souffle or custard cups to form tortilla quiche-cups. Pour about 3/4 cup of egg mixture into each quiche-cup. Bake, uncovered, in 325°F. oven 20 to 30 minutes. Makes 4 individual quiches.

Bacon Cheese Souffle

Hints:

Eggs separate best when cold. Egg whites beat to greater volume when very fresh and at room temperature. To make collar for souffle dish, tape (using masking tape) a 2-inch piece of brown paper around the top of dish.

Souffles are not difficult—just follow directions, handle lightly and serve immediately.

1/4 cup butter
3 tablespoons flour
1 1/4 cups light cream
1/2 cup cooked, crumbled bacon
5 egg yolks, lightly beaten
1 tablespoon Lawry's Minced Onion with Green Onion Flakes
1/4 teaspoon Lawry's Seasoned Pepper
5 egg whites
1/4 teaspoon Lawry's Seasoned Salt
1/4 teaspoon cream of tartar
1 cup grated Cheddar cheese

In medium saucepan, melt butter, stir in flour and continue cooking until bubbly. Gradually add light cream, stirring constantly. Cook over low heat, stirring constantly until mixture thickens. Add bacon and beat in egg yolks; add Minced Onion with Green Onion Flakes and Seasoned Pepper. Pour mixture into large mixing bowl and set aside. Beat egg whites, Seasoned Salt and cream of tartar until very stiff but not dry. Fold in grated cheese. Fold egg whites/cheese mixture into yolk mixture. Spoon into **ungreased** 1 1/2-quart souffle dish with collar. Set souffle dish in glass dish filled 1-inch deep with hot water. Bake in 375°F. oven about 30 minutes or until souffle is puffy and golden brown. Serve immediately. Makes 6 servings.

Cheese Lasagna Casserole

A delicious meatless lasagna.

1 tablespoon salad oil
1 can (1 lb. 12 oz.) tomatoes
1 can (8 oz.) tomato sauce
1 package Lawry's Extra Rich & Thick Spaghetti Sauce Mix
1/2 teaspoon Lawry's Garlic Powder with Parsley
1 teaspoon Lawry's Seasoned Salt
1/2 teaspoon Lawry's Seasoned Pepper
1/2 pound lasagna (broad noodles)
3/4 pound Mozzarella cheese, sliced
3/4 pound ricotta cheese OR 3/4 pound well-drained cottage cheese
1/2 cup grated Parmesan cheese

Heat salad oil in large skillet. Add tomatoes, tomato sauce, Extra Rich & Thick Spaghetti Sauce Mix and seasonings; blend thoroughly. Bring to a boil, reduce heat and simmer, uncovered, 25 minutes; set aside. Boil lasagna in salted water until almost tender; drain and rinse. Pour 1/4 tomato mixture in bottom of 12 x 8 x 2-inch baking dish. Then layer 1/3 lasagna noodles and 1/3 each Mozzarella, ricotta and tomato sauce. Repeat layers 2 times, ending with tomato sauce. Sprinkle with Parmesan cheese. Bake, uncovered, in 350°F. oven 30 minutes. Let stand 10 minutes before cutting in squares. Makes 6 to 8 servings.

Hints:
Freeze freshly grated Parmesan cheese to have on hand for any dish that calls for it.

Cheese Strata

A marvelous brunch or light supper dish.

Butter OR margarine
6 slices bread, crusts removed
3 cups grated cheese
6 eggs
2 cups milk
1 tablespoon Lawry's Minced Onion with Green Onion Flakes
1 teaspoon Lawry's Seasoned Salt

Lightly butter 13 x 9 x 2-inch baking dish; arrange bread slices in bottom of dish. Sprinkle with **half** of cheese. In medium bowl, beat together eggs, milk and seasonings; pour over bread and cheese. Sprinkle with remaining cheese. Bake, uncovered, in 350°F. oven 35 minutes or until light golden brown. Let stand 5 minutes before serving. Makes 6 servings.

Hints:
Cheddar, Monterey Jack or Swiss cheese may be used. Add only one flavor or combine two or all three for a more interesting flavor.

Variations:

Mexican: Pour 1 bottle Lawry's Chunky Taco Sauce over the Strata 5 minutes before baking time is completed.

Herb: Mix 2 teaspoons Lawry's Pinch of Herbs into egg-milk mixture. Continue with basic directions.

Mushroom: Sauté 1/2 pound sliced mushrooms in 2 tablespoons butter; remove from heat and stir in 1 package Lawry's Mushroom Gravy Mix. Stir into egg mixture. Continue with basic directions.

Ham 'N Egg Special

Prepare the night before and bake for breakfast or brunch.

2 cups sliced fresh mushrooms
1 medium onion, finely chopped
1/4 cup butter
2 cups diced cooked ham
8 slices white bread, cubed
4 eggs
2 1/2 cups milk
1/2 pound Cheddar cheese, grated
1 tablespoon prepared mustard
1 teaspoon Lawry's Seasoned Salt
Dash Lawry's Seasoned Pepper

Sauté mushrooms and onion in butter; stir in ham. Place bread cubes in 13 x 9 x 2-inch pan; arrange ham mixture over bread. Combine remaining ingredients; beat well. Pour over bread cubes making sure all cubes are moistened. Cover; refrigerate overnight. Bake, uncovered, in 325°F. oven 55 to 60 minutes. Serve immediately. Makes 6 to 8 servings.

Mexican Corn Bread

Hints:
Batter will fill 18 muffin cups 2/3 full; bake 15 minutes. Make ahead and freeze or reheat just before serving.

Excellent for brunch.

1 cup butter
1 cup sugar
4 eggs
1 can (4 oz.) diced green chiles
1 can (1 lb.) cream-style golden corn
1/2 cup grated Monterey Jack cheese
1/2 cup grated Cheddar cheese
2 teaspoons Lawry's Bacon Onion Seasoning
1 cup sifted flour
1 cup sifted yellow corn meal
4 teaspoons baking powder

Cream butter and sugar; add eggs, one at a time, mixing well after each addition. Add chiles, corn, cheeses and Bacon Onion Seasoning; blend well. Sift together flour, corn meal and baking powder; add to corn mixture and blend well. Pour into a greased and floured 12 x 8 x 2-inch baking dish. Place in a preheated 350°F. oven and immediately reduce heat to 300°F. Bake for 1 hour. Cut in 12 squares.

JUST THE TWO OF YOU

Being a part of a twosome is one of life's joys except when it comes to cooking. The world of food focuses on families of four or more and the "twos" are confronted with leftovers and meal monotony.

There is hope! Lawry's recognized a need to find solutions to the special cooking problems of a small family. The solutions are right here in this chapter—recipes, hints and tips covering not just cooking but buying food and equipment, as well as dining suggestions.

The recipes in this chapter feature entrees which are usually the most difficult to "cut down" from larger recipes. These recipes were originally created to yield just two servings so the proportions are exactly right. Only occasionally will you end up with one-half a can of something and when you do, there is a suggestion for how to use it.

Cooking for just the two of you can be creative and fun, done with variety and imagination. Say goodbye to mealtime monotony!

Zucchini Mexicana

Here's the perfect way to turn a package of Lawry's Seasoning or Sauce Mix into several meals for two. Follow the directions for Taco Tempters, Meat Loaf Medley, Spaghetti Duo, Au Jus Favorites and Chili Specials and enjoy all these dishes prepared with products packaged in larger-than-two portions.

Taco Tempters

Prepare 1 package (1 1/4 oz.) Lawry's Taco Seasoning Mix according to package directions. Divide the meat in half; you will have about 2 cups total. Serve tacos at one meal and your choice of the following for another. Or, prepare 1 package (2 1/2 oz.) Economy Taco Seasoning Mix which makes about 4 cups. Meat freezes well.

Zucchini Mexicana

Hints:
Maintain a pantry of staple items suited to your individual taste.

1 very small zucchini, thinly sliced
1 cup Lawry's Taco Meat
1/2 cup grated Cheddar OR Monterey Jack cheese
1/4 cup Lawry's Chunky Taco Sauce

Line bottom and sides of a small casserole with sliced zucchini; top with Taco Meat, then cheese. Pour Chunky Taco Sauce over all. Cover and bake in 350°F. oven 20 to 30 minutes.

Bell Peppers Mexicana

Hints:
Learn to use substitutes instead of buying an item which won't be used up and may spoil. For example, ketchup works for tomato sauce; chocolate chips are good alternatives for squares and cocoa.

2 green bell peppers
1 cup Lawry's Taco Meat
1 can (8 oz.) whole kernel corn, drained
1/2 cup grated Cheddar cheese
Pimiento strips

Cut tops off green peppers (in zig-zagging pattern, if desired) and remove seeds. Parboil peppers until tender, yet colorful. In medium skillet, heat Taco Meat and corn thoroughly. Add cheese. Fill green peppers with meat mixture. Garnish with pimiento strips.

Meat Loaf Medley

Prepare 1 package Lawry's Meat Loaf Seasoning Mix according to package directions but do not cook. Divide meat mixture in fourths (about 1/2 pound each). Use 1/4 Meat Loaf Mixture in each recipe given on the next page. Also, prepare 1 package of Lawry's Spaghetti Sauce Mix with Imported Mushrooms or Lawry's Extra Rich & Thick Spaghetti Sauce Mix according to package directions, for use in these recipes. The following recipes may be frozen.

Green Pepper Special

2 medium green bell peppers, halved lengthwise, trimmed and cleaned
1/4 Meat Loaf Mixture
2 tablespoons chopped pimiento, optional
Grated Cheddar cheese
1 cup Lawry's Spaghetti Sauce, heated

Partially cook pepper halves in boiling water, about 2 minutes; drain. Combine Meat Loaf Mixture and pimiento; spoon into each pepper half. Arrange in shallow baking dish and top with cheese. Cover; bake in 350°F. oven 20 minutes. Serve with Spaghetti Sauce.

Hints:
Buy foods in the most versatile form. For example, a lemon provides juice, slices, wedges, twists and peel. A fresh apple can be eaten whole, used in a salad, sliced for apple Betty, cooked for apple sauce or baked.

Pizza Meat Loaf

1/4 Lawry's Meat Loaf Mixture
3 tablespoons ketchup
Pinch leaf oregano, crushed
1/4 cup grated Mozzarella cheese
2 tablespoons mushroom pieces, fresh or canned

Combine Meat Loaf Mixture, 2 tablespoons ketchup and oregano; blend well. Divide this mixture in half. Press 1/2 in bottom of 6 x 3 x 2-inch loaf pan. Place cheese and mushrooms in center, keeping away from edges. Cover with remaining Meat Loaf Mixture being sure to seal edges together. Spread 1 tablespoon ketchup over top and bake in 350°F. oven 45 minutes.

Hints:
Plan weekly menus with an eye to using one sauce or basic seasoning mix in two different ways for two separate meals.

Whenever possible, buy food items—meat, produce and breads—in one or two serving packages and portions.

Unstuffed Cabbage Rolls

1/2 cup chopped onion
1/3 cup uncooked long-grain rice
1/4 Lawry's Meat Loaf Mixture
3 tablespoons butter
1 can (2 oz.) mushroom pieces, drained
2 cups coarsely shredded cabbage
1 cup Lawry's Spaghetti Sauce

Sauté onion, rice and Meat Loaf Mixture in butter; mix together thoroughly. Add mushrooms and spread mixture in bottom of 8 1/2 or 9-inch pie plate. Top meat with cabbage and pour Spaghetti Sauce over. Cover and bake in 350°F. oven 30 to 35 minutes.

Hints:
Cabbage is a versatile vegetable and keeps well. Use in soups, for cabbage rolls and coleslaw. Serve cooked and buttered with caraway seeds for a change-of-pace side dish.

A partial can of tomato sauce or whole tomatoes adds flavor to a green vegetable such as zucchini or green beans.

Hamburger Patties with Sauce

Use 1/4 Meat Loaf Mixture and shape into 2 large hamburger patties. Broil or pan fry. Top with 1 cup prepared Spaghetti Sauce. Serve over buttered egg noodles.

Hints:
For faster thawing and cooking, freeze foods such as hamburger and chicken in single serving portions.

Spaghetti Duo

Prepare 1 package (1 1/2 oz.) Lawry's Spaghetti Sauce Mix with Imported Mushrooms according to package directions. Use in the following recipes. The sauce freezes well as does the Quick Basic Soup.

The Spaghetti Thing

Hints:
You may want to consider devoting a weekend day to cooking every so often. Here's how. Make up a list of menu items you enjoy. Be sure they freeze well. Shop for the ingredients, spend a day cooking and freeze each dish in small portions. Be sure to label and date all bundles going into the freezer and eat everything within six months. When the freezer's empty, cook for a day and fill it up again.

1/2 small green bell pepper, finely diced
1/2 cup cooked cubed ham, beef OR poultry
1 cup cooked spaghetti
3 tablespoons butter
3 eggs, beaten
2 tablespoons grated Parmesan cheese
1 cup Lawry's Spaghetti Sauce with Imported Mushrooms, heated

In a heavy skillet, lightly sauté green pepper, meat, spaghetti and 2 tablespoons butter, stirring occasionally. Add remaining butter and when melted pour eggs over mixture. Add 1/2 of cheese and cook, stirring gently until set, about 3 minutes. Pour Spaghetti Sauce over each serving and sprinkle with remaining cheese.

Quick Basic Soup with Variations

Hints:
Incorporate leftovers in standard recipes (salads, omelets, crepes) for interesting and versatile meals.

2 cups beef bouillon OR broth
1 cup Lawry's Spaghetti Sauce with Imported Mushrooms

Combine beef bouillon or broth and Spaghetti Sauce. Bring to a boil, reduce heat and simmer, uncovered, 10 minutes, stirring occasionally. Add one or a combination of the following garnishes: sour cream, chopped parsley or cilantro, avocado slices, chopped onion or grated cheese. Or, add one or a combination of the following ingredients to make a heartier soup: leftover meat or poultry, macaroni or other pasta, rice or vegetables.

AU JUS FAVORITES

Prime Rib

Hints:
Have rib cut from the small end of roast.

1 rib of a standing rib roast (2 1/2 to 3 1/2 lbs.)
Garlic, optional
Peanut OR salad oil
2 large baking potatoes, scrubbed
1 package Lawry's Au Jus Gravy Mix
Lawry's Seasoned Salt
Lawry's Seasoned Pepper

Rub the roast with garlic, if desired, and oil. Prop roast between the two potatoes, with the fat side up. Roast in 350°F. oven approximately 20 to 25 minutes per pound for rare or until a meat thermometer reaches 140°F. Let stand 5 minutes before slicing. While the roast is cooking prepare the Au Jus Gravy Mix according to package directions. Serve prime rib with au jus gravy, baked potatoes and your favorite vegetable. Have Seasoned Salt and Seasoned Pepper on the table for seasoning prime rib.

Shortcut Beef Hash

Use leftover beef and Au Jus Gravy for this recipe.

1 1/2 cups diced, cooked, trimmed roast beef
1/2 cup diced onion
1/2 cup diced, cooked potato
Butter
Dash Worcestershire sauce
Dash hot pepper sauce
Lawry's Seasoned Salt
Lawry's Seasoned Pepper
3/4 cup Lawry's Au Jus Gravy
2 eggs, poached OR fried

Brown beef, onion and potato in butter. Season to taste using Worcestershire sauce, hot pepper sauce, Seasoned Salt and Seasoned Pepper. Place in a 1-quart baking dish and pour 3/4 cup Au Jus over hash. Bake, uncovered, in 350°F. oven about 45 minutes or until the liquid is absorbed. After 20 minutes stir once; do not stir during the last 20 minutes. Remove from oven and pour off excess fat. To serve, top each portion with a poached or fried egg.

Hints:
Hash may be baked and refrigerated overnight and reheated the next day, or frozen.

Invest in a toaster oven. It can handle the majority of warming, baking and roasting done for one and two.

Stock up on seasoning blends. These eliminate the need for a shelf full of seldom used spices and they liven the taste of the most ordinary dish.

French Dip Sandwich

Split crusty French or Italian rolls in half lengthwise (or use slices of white bread), butter and toast. Place a portion of thinly sliced roast beef on rolls or bread. Spoon a generous amount of Lawry's Au Jus Gravy on each sandwich or serve with small individual bowls of hot Au Jus for dipping.

OR

Dip cut sides of toasted rolls in hot Au Jus before adding roast beef. Additional Au Jus may be served for dipping.

Hints:
Use salad dressing mixes in a variety of ways—to shake on vegetables, for dips, to season bread crumbs or to marinate meats and poultry.

Chili Specials

Prepare 1 package Lawry's Chili Seasoning Mix according to package directions. Serve bowls of steaming chili at one meal and/or try these dishes. Chili and Chili-Mac casserole may be frozen.

Chili-Mac Casserole

2 cups cooked small elbow macaroni
Lawry's Seasoned Salt
1 1/2 to 2 cups Lawry's Chili
1 cup grated Cheddar cheese
2 canned whole green chiles, cut in strips

In a greased 1-quart casserole, place 1/2 of macaroni; sprinkle with Seasoned Salt. Top with 1/2 of Chili and cheese. Arrange green chile strips over cheese. Add remaining macaroni, Chili and cheese. Bake, uncovered, in 350°F. oven 20 to 25 minutes or until heated and cheese is melted.

Hints:
Buy multipurpose equipment scaled to small quantity cooking. For instance, a 7-inch slope sided covered skillet doubles as an omelet pan, crepe pan, saucepan or sauté pan.

Chili Avocado Omelet

Hints:

A "souper" solution to leftovers: Freeze all leftovers, even the most miniscule amounts including meat, poultry, rice, vegetables and gravies. Prepare Lawry's Au Jus Gravy Mix according to package directions. Add an assortment of frozen leftovers directly to the Au Jus and simmer only until thawed and serve as hot soup.

4 eggs
1 tablespoon water
1/4 teaspoon Lawry's Seasoned Salt
Butter
1 cup Lawry's Chili
1/4 cup grated Cheddar cheese
1/2 avocado, peeled and sliced

In a small bowl, beat together eggs, water and Seasoned Salt. Pour mixture into well buttered 10-inch skillet. Cook omelet over medium heat, allowing liquid eggs to run to edges. When eggs are set, slide omelet onto serving plate. Place Chili, grated cheese and avocado slices on 1/2 of omelet; fold over other half. Serve immediately.

Chile Rellenos

Hints:

Casserole may be prepared and refrigerated overnight; do not add topping until after baking.

Cultivate a specialty such as Mexican, Italian, French or Chinese cuisine for entertaining purposes. Add the necessary condiments, equipment and dinnerware to your "basic" kitchen.

Butter
1 can (4 oz.) whole green chiles, rinsed and seeded
1/2 cup Lawry's Chunky Taco Sauce
1/4 pound sliced Cheddar cheese
1/4 pound sliced Monterey Jack cheese
2 eggs, well beaten
4 teaspoons flour
1 can (5.3 oz.) evaporated milk
1/2 cup Lawry's Chunky Taco Sauce

In bottom of lightly buttered 8 x 8 x 2-inch glass baking dish, arrange the chiles. Top with 1/2 cup Chunky Taco Sauce. Layer the cheese evenly on top of sauce. In small bowl, combine eggs, flour and milk; blend thoroughly. Pour over cheese and chiles. Bake in 325°F. oven 25 to 30 minutes. Remove from oven and spread 1/2 cup Chunky Taco Sauce over top. Bake 10 minutes longer. Let stand about 5 minutes before cutting.

Stuffed Baked Potatoes

Hints:

Use baked potatoes as a base for tasty entrees by topping with chili, meat stews or creamed turkey or chicken. For a quicker and different flavored baked potato, cut in half and rub cut sides with butter, Lawry's Seasoned Salt and Lawry's Seasoned Pepper. Bake in 350°F. oven 30 to 40 minutes.

For the best stuffed or unstuffed baked potatoes, follow the directions below.

To bake do not wrap in aluminum foil. Rub outside of scrubbed baking potato with oil or butter, pierce with fork to let steam escape during baking and bake in 350°F. oven 45 minutes to 1 hour, depending upon size. This method gives crispy, delicious skin.

To stuff, cut potatoes in half lengthwise and scoop out pulp, leaving just enough to retain shape. Whip potato pulp and add butter, milk or cream (or dairy sour cream), seasonings such as Lawry's Seasoned Salt, Seasoned Pepper, Garlic Salt, Bacon Onion Seasoning, Lemon Pepper Seasoning or Pinch of Herbs. Fill shells with whipped potato, top with grated Cheddar or Monterey Jack cheese and heat in 350°F. oven. Potatoes freeze beautifully and can be popped into the oven to heat without defrosting.

Savory Fish Fillets

Savory Fish Fillets

1 small zucchini, coarsely grated
1 small carrot, pared and coarsely grated
2 teaspoons lemon juice
1/4 teaspoon Lawry's Pinch of Herbs
Lawry's Seasoned Salt, to taste
Lawry's Seasoned Pepper, to taste
2 or 3 fresh fillets of sole OR turbot
1/2 cup chicken stock
1 1/4 cups Savory Sauce, heated

Combine zucchini and carrot, lemon juice and Pinch of Herbs; mix thoroughly. Add Seasoned Salt and Seasoned Pepper to taste. Spread generously on each fish fillet and roll. Place remaining zucchini-carrot mixture in bottom of small shallow baking dish. Arrange rolled fillets seam side down on mixture; add chicken stock. Bake, uncovered, in 350°F. oven 45 to 60 minutes. Serve with Savory Sauce.

Hints:
Use a blender or food processor for chopping, mixing, blending, crumbling and more. Saves time and cleanup.

Savory Sauce

1 package (1 1/2 oz.) Lawry's Spaghetti Sauce Mix with Imported
  Mushrooms
1 can (1 lb.) tomatoes, cut up
1 can (6 oz.) tomato juice cocktail

Combine all ingredients; blend well. Bring to a boil, reduce heat and simmer, uncovered, 15 minutes, stirring occasionally. Makes 2 1/2 cups sauce.

Hints:
Freeze leftover sauce.

156

Sesame Halibut Steaks

Hints:

Another good investment is an automatic meal sealing machine which bags leftovers, individual portions, sauces and other freezables into airtight pouches. These can be popped into boiling water for a meal in minutes. Or heat in the microwave after poking 3 to 4 holes in bag (use knife tip or fork tines) to allow steam to escape.

2 halibut steaks, 1 to 1 1/2-inches thick
1/3 cup melted butter
Dash Lawry's Garlic Salt
2 cups soft bread crumbs
1 teaspoon Lawry's Garlic Salt
1/8 teaspoon Lawry's Seasoned Pepper
2 tablespoons toasted sesame seeds

Brush the halibut with some of the melted butter and arrange in a shallow baking dish. Sprinkle with Garlic Salt. Combine the balance of melted butter and remaining ingredients; mound 1/2 of the mixture on each piece of halibut. Bake in 350°F. oven, uncovered, until fish flakes easily with a fork, approximately 25 to 30 minutes.

Buttered Rice with Pine Nuts

Hints:

Use slivered almonds in place of pine nuts if desired.

Collect individual baking dishes such as small souffles, custard cups or au gratins. These cut baking time and also help save clean up time.

1 cup water
1 tablespoon butter
1/2 cup uncooked long-grain rice
2 tablespoons pine nuts, toasted
1/2 teaspoon Lawry's Seasoned Salt

In small saucepan, combine water and butter. Bring to boil, add rice, reduce heat, cover and simmer 20 minutes or until rice is tender. When rice is cooked, add pine nuts and Seasoned Salt. Toss lightly.

Oriental Fried Rice

Hints:

May use julienne strips of cooked ham, turkey, chicken, pork or any combination of meats.

Buy a small scale for measuring noodles, chopped items, meat portions and other foods which don't fit into a cup. Measuring this way will be faster and more accurate.

Save frozen food foil pans, wide mouth jars and snap-lid plastic containers for use in freezing individual food servings.

2 tablespoons salad oil
1/4 cup sliced green onions
1/2 cup julienne strips cooked meat OR poultry
1 1/2 cups cooked rice
1/4 cup sliced water chestnuts
1 egg, slightly beaten
1 tablespoon soy sauce
1/4 teaspoon Lawry's Seasoned Salt
1/4 teaspoon Lawry's Seasoned Pepper
Minced parsley

In large skillet, heat oil and sauté onions and meat until lightly browned. Mix in rice and water chestnuts. Stir in remaining ingredients except parsley; cook until eggs are thoroughly mixed with rice mixture. Spoon mixture into bowl or mold, pressing it down firmly with the back of a spoon. Unmold onto heated platter. Sprinkle minced parsley over top. Serve with stir-fried vegetables.

Fran's Golden Crepes

4 eggs
1/2 cup milk
1/2 cup water
3 tablespoons salad oil OR melted butter
3/4 cup flour
1/2 teaspoon salt

Place all ingredients in blender jar. Blend 1 minute; stop and scrape down sides. Blend an additional 30 seconds or until smooth. Refrigerate batter 1 hour. Lightly oil a crepe pan and heat. Pour in about 3 tablespoons batter and swirl to cover bottom of pan evenly. Cook at medium heat until lightly browned, turning if desired. Repeat until all batter is used. Makes 16 to 18 crepes.

Hints:
Brush crepes with melted butter as they are cooked, then stack. Wrap stacks of 4 or any number in aluminum foil and freeze. A crepe pan is not essential but it does make the job easier. If one is not available, use an omelet pan or a regular skillet and simply control the size as you swirl the batter.

Cream Sauce for Crepes

2 tablespoons butter
2 tablespoons flour
1/2 cup chicken broth
2 tablespoons light cream
1 tablespoon dry sherry OR dry white wine
1 tablespoon grated Parmesan cheese
1/4 teaspoon Lawry's Seasoned Salt
1/8 teaspoon Lawry's Seasoned Pepper

In a small saucepan, melt butter over medium heat; stir in flour. Add chicken broth and cream. Cook and stir until thickened and smooth. Stir in wine, cheese, Seasoned Salt and Seasoned Pepper. Stir constantly, until cheese is melted. Makes enough sauce for 4 crepes.

Hints:
Find attractive dinnerware which will work in a variety of ways. For example, a one or two cup souffle can be a casserole for one or two, a soup bowl, a cereal bowl, salad bowl or dessert dish.

Chicken Crepes

1 recipe Cream Sauce for Crepes
Pinch rosemary
Pinch thyme
3/4 cup cooked shredded chicken
1/4 cup sliced almonds, sautéed
1 tablespoon chopped onion, sautéed
4 Golden Crepes
1/4 cup light cream
1 teaspoon dry sherry

Combine about 3 tablespoons Cream Sauce, rosemary, thyme, chicken, almonds and onion. Place approximately 1/4 cup filling on each crepe, roll and place seam side down on heat-proof platter. Add cream and sherry to remaining Cream Sauce; pour over crepes. Sprinkle with additional thyme, if desired. Bake, uncovered, in 350°F. oven 15 minutes. Makes 4 crepes.

Hints:
When preparing larger quantities of favorite recipes that require long cooking and/or contain numerous ingredients, divide into one or two serving portions and freeze.

Mushroom Crepes

1 recipe Cream Sauce for Crepes
1/8 teaspoon Lawry's Garlic Powder with Parsley
1 cup sliced mushrooms, sautéed
1 tablespoon chopped shallots OR green onion, sautéed
4 Golden Crepes
1/4 cup light cream
1 teaspoon dry sherry

Combine 3 tablespoons Cream Sauce, Garlic Powder with Parsley, mushrooms and shallots or green onion. Place approximately 1/4 cup filling on each crepe, roll and place seam side down on heat-proof platter. Add cream and sherry to remaining Cream Sauce; pour over crepes. Bake, uncovered in 350°F. oven 15 minutes. Makes 4 crepes.

White Gazpacho

1 large cucumber, peeled and diced
1/2 cup chicken broth
1 tablespoon white wine vinegar
1/8 teaspoon Lawry's Garlic Powder with Parsley
1/2 teaspoon Lawry's Seasoned Salt
1 cup dairy sour cream
Garnishes:

> chopped smoked almonds or toasted slivered almonds, chopped green onions, diced tomato

In food processor bowl or blender jar, place cucumber and chicken broth; process until pureed. Add remaining ingredients except garnishes and blend. Serve warm or cold with choice of garnishes.

Golden Glazed Cornish Game Hens

Hints:
May use glaze on chicken breasts or whole roasted chicken.

1 cup herb-seasoned stuffing mix
1/4 cup water
2 tablespoons butter, melted
2 Cornish game hens, about 1 pound each
1/2 cup apricot preserves
3/4 cup water
1 package Lawry's Brown Gravy Mix
Dash ground cloves

Combine stuffing mix, 1/4 cup water and butter; mix thoroughly. Stuff hens with dressing and truss. Place hens, breast side up, in 8-inch square baking dish; set aside. Combine remaining ingredients in small saucepan. Bring sauce to boil, stirring constantly; remove from heat. Spoon half the sauce over hens and use remainder for basting. Bake hens, uncovered, in 350°F. oven about 1 1/2 hours or until done. Baste occasionally during baking.

Tahitian Turkey

3/4 pound cooked turkey meat, (about 2 cups) cubed or cut in julienne
   strips
1/2 cup Lawry's Sweet 'N Sour Barbecue Sauce
1/4 cup diagonally sliced celery
1/4 green bell pepper, cut in 1-inch pieces
1/4 cucumber, sliced in 1/4-inch rounds
1/2 can (11 oz.) Mandarin orange segments, drained
Cooked rice OR chow mein noodles

Combine turkey with Sweet 'N Sour Barbecue Sauce in skillet or saucepan.
Bring to a boil, stirring often. Add celery, green pepper and cucumber;
continue cooking until vegetables are almost tender yet colorful. Add
Mandarin oranges and serve over hot cooked rice or chow mein noodles.

Hints:
Use cooked turkey wings, thighs
or breasts.

If a can of vegetables or fruit is
only partially used for a recipe,
plan an immediate use for the
leftover. For example a 1/2 can
of Mandarin orange segments
added to fresh spinach leaves,
slivered almonds and a sweet 'n
sour dressing makes a lovely
salad.

Tahitian Turkey

Salmon-Grapefruit Salad

Hints:

Add a coffee measure (2 table-spoons/1 ounce) to standard measuring equipment. Since it is half of a quarter cup, this measure works well when cutting recipes down.

Serve meals in style to avoid mealtime monotony. Find several unexpected places around the house to eat.

1 tablespoon Lawry's Tartar Sauce Mix
2 tablespoons water
1/3 cup mayonnaise OR salad dressing
1/3 cup dairy sour cream
1 tablespoon reserved grapefruit juice (see below)
1 can (7 3/4 oz.) salmon, drained
1/2 cup minced celery
Bibb lettuce
1 can (1 lb.) grapefruit segments, drained and juice reserved

In small bowl combine Tartar Sauce Mix and water. Stir in mayonnaise; blend thoroughly and let stand 30 minutes. Add sour cream and grapefruit juice. To 1/2 cup of sauce mixture, add salmon and celery; reserve remaining sauce. Line serving plate with lettuce. Arrange grapefruit segments alternately with salmon mixture on lettuce. Drizzle reserved sauce mixture over grapefruit. Serve as an entree.

Baked Pork Chops on Bacon Herb Stuffing

Hints:

Keep a supply of candles on hand at all times. Dining by candlelight makes you look and feel better and it makes the meal many times more appetizing.

Develop a collection of permanent centerpieces such as dried flowers, a bowl of shells or potted plants to coordinate with dinnerware and linens.

Learn a few fancy napkin folds to add interest to the dinner table. The 20-inch wash-and-use napkins are the most useful and versatile.

Stuffing

3 bacon slices
1/4 cup minced celery, including leaves
1 1/2 cups soft bread crumbs
3 tablespoons milk
2 teaspoons Lawry's Minced Onion with Green Onion Flakes
1/4 teaspoon Lawry's Pinch of Herbs
1/4 teaspoon Lawry's Seasoned Salt
Dash Lawry's Seasoned Pepper

Fry bacon until crisp; remove, drain on paper towels and crumble. Drain off half the bacon drippings and reserve for browning chops. In remaining drippings, sauté celery. Add bread crumbs, milk, seasonings and bacon. Spoon into 9-inch pie plate and set aside.

Pork Chops

2 loin pork chops, about 1-inch thick
1/2 teaspoon rosemary
1/4 teaspoon Lawry's Seasoned Salt
1/4 teaspoon Lawry's Seasoned Pepper
Minced parsley

Trim excess fat from chops. Crush rosemary and rub into each side of pork chops. Sprinkle with Seasoned Salt and Seasoned Pepper. Heat reserved bacon drippings in skillet and brown chops on both sides. Arrange chops over stuffing and sprinkle with parsley. Bake, covered, in 350°F. oven 45 to 60 minutes. Uncover during last 5 to 10 minutes.

Shrimp Sauté

2/3 to 3/4 pound fresh jumbo shrimp in the shell (8 to 12)
1/4 cup butter
1/4 teaspoon Lawry's Garlic Powder with Parsley
Juice of 1 lemon
Lawry's Seasoned Salt
Lawry's Seasoned Pepper
Minced parsley

Wash, shell (leaving tail attached), devein and butterfly shrimp. Heat butter and Garlic Powder with Parsley in 10 or 11-inch skillet over medium heat. Sauté shrimp quickly on both sides just until opaque and pink. Squeeze lemon juice over and season with Seasoned Salt and Seasoned Pepper. Turn the heat up to quickly boil down pan juices. Remove shrimp to hot serving plates; add juices and sprinkle with minced parsley. Serve immediately.

Hints:
Salad dressings keep well. Refer to the "Salads and More Salads" chapter for salad and dressing ideas. Salads are generally easy to cut down for two servings.

Veal Florentine

2 veal cutlets OR frozen veal patties
1 tablespoon butter OR margarine
1/2 cup beef bouillon
1 bay leaf
Lawry's Seasoned Salt, to taste
Lawry's Seasoned Pepper, to taste
1 package (10 oz.) frozen spinach, cooked and drained
1 cup Creamy Stroganoff Sauce
2 slices Cheddar cheese

If using veal cutlets pound until very thin. Brown veal quickly in butter. Add bouillon, bay leaf, Seasoned Salt and Seasoned Pepper. Bring to a boil, reduce heat and simmer, uncovered, 10 minutes. Arrange spinach in bottom of 8-inch pie pan or similar dish. Add Creamy Stroganoff Sauce to veal; mix well. Cover spinach with veal and sauce. Top with cheese; broil until cheese melts.

Hints:
Carrots are another versatile vegetable that keep well. Serve cooked or raw, grated for salads or as an ingredient in a vegetable stuffing for fish.

Partially used packages of nuts should be sealed and refrigerated or frozen.

Creamy Stroganoff Sauce

1 package Lawry's Stroganoff Sauce Mix
1 1/2 cups water
1/2 cup dairy sour cream

Combine Stroganoff Sauce Mix and water in a saucepan; stir thoroughly. Bring to a boil, reduce heat, cover and simmer 10 minutes. Blend in sour cream and heat. Makes 2 cups.

Hints:
Use leftover sauce for creamed chicken or turkey.

Celestial Chicken

1 large chicken breast, halved and boned
1 tablespoon butter OR margarine
1/3 cup apricot preserves
1 1/2 tablespoons lemon juice
1 teaspoon Lawry's Lemon Pepper Seasoning
Slivered almonds OR toasted sesame seeds

Arrange chicken in shallow pan and dot with butter. In a saucepan, combine apricot preserves, lemon juice and Lemon Pepper Seasoning; blend well. Heat until preserves melt and the mixture is thoroughly blended. Pour apricot sauce over chicken and sprinkle almonds on top. Bake in 350°F. oven, uncovered, 35 minutes or until done, basting occasionally. If necessary, cover with foil to prevent excessive browning.

Hints:
Try one-dish meals where the vegetable and/or starch item is cooked right along with the meat, fish or poultry.

Saucy Herbed Pasta 'N Vegetables

8 to 10 ounces uncooked spaghetti
1 teaspoon Lawry's Pinch of Herbs
1 teaspoon Lawry's Garlic Powder with Parsley
1/2 cup sliced fresh mushrooms
2 cups thinly sliced zucchini
1 package Lawry's Extra Rich & Thick Spaghetti Sauce Mix, prepared
   according to package directions

Cook spaghetti according to package directions; add Pinch of Herbs and Garlic Powder with Parsley to water. Add mushrooms and zucchini to spaghetti during last 5 minutes of cooking and cook until vegetables are tender, about 5 minutes. Drain and serve with heated Extra Rich & Thick Spaghetti Sauce over top.

Hints:
Make your own "T.V." dinners from leftovers.

Foil packaged seasoning mixes are good additions because they have a long life and can be used to cook several different dishes which can then be frozen.

Mexican Meat Loaf

1 package (1 1/4 oz.) Lawry's Taco Seasoning Mix
1 tablespoon water
1/2 pound lean ground beef
1 egg, beaten
1/2 cup soft bread crumbs
1/2 cup canned tomatoes, cut up
1 or 2 slices green bell pepper

In a bowl, combine Lawry's Taco Seasoning Mix and water. Blend in beef, egg, bread crumbs and 1/4 cup tomatoes. Shape into loaf or lightly press into 5 3/4 x 3 1/4-inch loaf pan. Arrange green bell pepper and remaining 1/4 cup tomatoes on top. Bake, uncovered, in 350°F. oven 35 to 45 minutes.

Hints:
Don't assume that the smallest size container is always the best buy. With careful planning a large size may save money if it is used in the preparation of several dishes.

Hints:

Choose snack items carefully as most are packaged in larger sized containers. It may be a good time to re-evaluate snacking habits and begin to use more versatile foods, such as raw vegetables, cheeses and bases such as tortillas which freeze well.

4 slices uncooked turkey breast (about 3/4 pound)
2 tablespoons flour
1/4 teaspoon Lawry's Seasoned Salt
1/8 teaspoon Lawry's Seasoned Pepper
2 tablespoons butter

Sauce

1 cup chicken broth
1/4 cup dry white wine OR Vermouth
1 teaspoon lemon juice
3/4 teaspoon Worcestershire sauce
1/4 teaspoon marjoram
1/4 teaspoon Lawry's Garlic Powder with Parsley

Flatten each turkey slice between wax paper, using a meat mallet or rolling pin. Combine flour, Seasoned Salt and Seasoned Pepper; lightly coat each slice. In medium skillet, heat butter and quickly sauté turkey slices on each side. Remove to warm platter; keep warm. Add sauce ingredients to skillet; bring to boil. Over high heat, reduce liquid to about 3/4 cup. Pour over turkey slices just before serving.

The following recipes are very easy to cut in half. Some may make slightly more than two servings if the recipe is for 6 to 8 servings originally.

Marinated Family Steak (see page 111)
Halibut Kabobs (see page 112)
Stuffed Grilled Hamburgers (see page 114)
Sally's Shrimp in Curried Mayonnaise (see page 31) \
Emilie's Mexican Chicken Kiev (see page 32)
Lemon Lettuce Steak (see page 31)
Chicken Jerusalem (see page 33)
Peach 'n Chicken Teriyaki (see page 36)
Pork Chops Olivette (see page 35)
Fettuccine (see page 36)
Eileen's Rice Pilaf (see page 37)
Cassata (see page 39)
Dessert Fruit Tacos (see page 40)
Flaming Peaches (see page 41)
Sausage and Eggplant Creole (see page 43)
Pizza Pork Chops (see page 47)
Steak au Poivre (see page 45)
Chicken Breasts in Wine (see page 128)
Chicken Marengo (see page 48)
Parmesan Fried Chicken (see page 50)
Lemon Lamb Lawry's (see page 52)
Most salad and vegetable recipes (see "Salads and More Salads" and "California's Vegetable Bounty")

PREPARE AHEAD DISHES

Busy schedules demand an organized, plan-ahead approach. There are many obvious benefits—many foods actually taste better when cooked the day before they are served, and on those days when there is no time to cook, you can still serve attractive, delicious meals to your family and entertaining need not be relegated only to weekends.

Planning and preparing foods ahead also saves time and money. Shopping and food preparation can be organized to take advantage of special buys and to utilize every morsel of food (a whole chicken, simmered with water and seasonings for chicken soup or stew with part of the cooked chicken shredded for another dish such as chicken salad, burritos, etc.).

If freezer space is available, so much the better. Cook ahead, wrap, label and freeze a number of dishes for later use. The dishes in this chapter, as well as many others throughout the book, are all freezable. They also yield four or more servings so that portions can be frozen for later use. If your family is small, refer to the "Just the Two of You" chapter for other ideas such as preparing several dishes from one basic ingredient and/or Lawry's product.

Here are some specific hints:

● Take paper and pencil in hand and get your food shopping organized.

● Prepare a special menu plan calendar. Use foods you have in the house and add what you need to buy for specific recipes. Make your grocery list from the plan and stick to it. You'll be amazed at how this system will curb impulse buying, a real money-wasting habit.

● Shop once a week with this very defined grocery list—always on a full stomach. Last minute shopping trips before dinner tend to lead to expensive snack foods and other extras which simply put you over-budget.

● Shop on Friday nights after the dinner hour. Stores are generally stocked for Saturday selling and there are fewer customers shopping, so your trip is faster and hassle-free.

● Plan a Cook-a-Thon, a day or two a month spent cooking and freezing dishes for later use.

● Invest in a meal sealing machine. It's great for bagging foods which can then be labeled and frozen. These then pop right out of the freezer and into boiling water or the microwave for an instant meal.

● When practical, always buy food in whole form. This includes everything—chicken, turkey, cheese, lunch meat and vegetables. It's cheaper to do the cutting and shredding yourself.

● Substitute less expensive cuts of meat when possible, such as blade chops for center cut chops, round steak for flank steak. Get to know cuts other than tender steaks, roasts and ground round. Consider beef ribs, liver, kidneys, blade chuck roasts and shanks.

● Buy foods in the most versatile form. For example, a lemon provides juice, slices, wedges, twists and peel. A fresh apple can be eaten whole, used in a salad, sliced for apple Betty, cooked for applesauce or baked.

● Keep a container in the freezer and fill it with leftovers from each meal—a spoonful of gravy, an ounce of chicken or beef, spaghetti or chili, vegetables, rice or mashed potatoes. When you have enough for a meal, if it needs extra liquid, add Spaghetti Sauce Mix or Au Jus Gravy Mix and enough water to give a soup-like consistency. The result is delicious.

● Review freezing procedures and foods that may be frozen successfully. You may be surprised at just how many foods are freezable.

Make your "prepare ahead day" a real event, and before you know it, you'll have the whole family involved and all the help you need. Ready?

Osso Bucco Milanese

Osso Bucco Milanese

An Italian favorite.

1/3 cup flour
1 1/2 teaspoons Lawry's Seasoned Salt
1 teaspoon Lawry's Seasoned Pepper
4 veal shanks
Salad oil
1 large onion, chopped
2 carrots, diced
2 stalks celery, diced
1 package Lawry's Brown Gravy Mix
1/2 cup dry white wine
1 can (1 lb.) tomatoes, cut up
1/4 teaspoon Lawry's Garlic Powder with Parsley
1 bay leaf
1/2 teaspoon leaf basil, crushed
Minced parsley
Grated lemon peel

Combine flour, Seasoned Salt and Seasoned Pepper. Dredge veal shanks in seasoned flour and brown on all sides in hot oil. Remove shanks and sauté onion, carrots and celery until onion is transparent. Add Brown Gravy Mix, wine, tomatoes, Garlic Powder with Parsley, bay leaf and basil; blend thoroughly. Return shanks to pan. Bake, covered, in 350° F. oven 1 1/2 to 2 hours or until tender. Garnish each serving with minced parsley and grated lemon peel. Makes 4 servings.

Serving Suggestions:
Buttered egg noodles, *Garbeano Salad.*

Hints:
If unable to find pre-packaged shanks, ask your meat cutter for assistance. If veal is unavailable, use lamb shanks and have them cut in pieces or part way through the bone for easier eating.

The Day Before Brisket

Serve this delicious brisket to guests as well as family.

1 tablespoon liquid smoke
Lawry's Seasoned Salt
Lawry's Garlic Powder with Parsley
6 to 7 pound brisket of beef, unseasoned
1 large onion, finely chopped
1 cup ketchup
1/4 cup water
3 tablespoons butter
1 1/2 tablespoons brown sugar
1 tablespoon Worcestershire sauce
2 teaspoons liquid smoke
1 1/2 teaspoons dry mustard
1 teaspoon celery seed

Rub liquid smoke, Seasoned Salt and Garlic Powder with Parsley on both sides of meat. Place in baking dish, cover tightly with aluminum foil and refrigerate for at least 8 hours. Add onion, re-cover and bake in 325°F. oven 2 hours. Cool and slice in 1/4-inch thick slices. Combine remaining ingredients and heat. Pour sauce over meat slices and re-cover. Refrigerate 4 hours or overnight. Bake in 325°F. oven 1 hour to heat through. Makes 8 to 10 servings.

Serving Suggestions:
Cooked new potatoes, *Cathy's Coleslaw Relish Mold.*

Hints:
Freeze after slicing meat and adding sauce.

Picadillo

This colorful dish is adapted from an Ernest Hemingway favorite.

1 pound lean ground beef
1/4 teaspoon Lawry's Garlic Powder with Parsley
1/4 cup Lawry's Minced Onion with Green Onion Flakes
1 package Lawry's Mexican Rice Seasoning Mix
Pinch of leaf oregano, crushed
Lawry's Seasoned Salt, to taste
Lawry's Seasoned Pepper, to taste
1 cup red wine
1 cup raisins, plumped in water
1 small green bell pepper, chopped

Brown ground beef; drain fat. Add remaining ingredients except green pepper; blend thoroughly. Bring to a boil, reduce heat and simmer, uncovered, 20 minutes, stirring occasionally. Add green pepper during the last 5 minutes; cook just until heated. Makes 6 servings.

Serving Suggestions:
Fluffy rice, fruit salad, warm corn tortillas.

Hints:
Recipe may easily be doubled or tripled for a large group.

Basque Stew

A hearty lamb stew with olives added for flavor and color.

2 pounds lamb stew meat, cut in 2-inch cubes
1/4 cup flour
2 teaspoons Lawry's Seasoned Salt
1/4 teaspoon Lawry's Seasoned Pepper
1/4 cup salad OR olive oil
2 cups water
1 package Lawry's Brown Gravy Mix
1 green bell pepper, coarsely chopped
1/2 teaspoon marjoram
3 cloves garlic, crushed
2 medium potatoes, peeled and sliced 1/4-inch thick
2 medium onions, sliced
1 cup chopped celery
2 tomatoes, cut in wedges
1 jar (3 oz.) pimiento-stuffed green olives, drained

Dredge meat in mixture of flour, Seasoned Salt and Seasoned Pepper. Brown meat in salad oil; drain fat and add water. Bring to a boil, reduce heat, cover and simmer 1 1/2 hours. Measure pan juices and add water, if necessary, to make 2 cups. Blend in Brown Gravy Mix and pour over meat. Add remaining ingredients, except tomatoes and olives. Bring to a boil, reduce heat, cover and simmer 25 minutes. Place tomato wedges and olives on top of mixture. Cover and simmer 5 minutes. Makes 8 servings.

Serving Suggestions:
Warm sourdough bread, *Peach Pudding Cake.*

Hints:
Beef may be used in place of lamb. To freeze, do not add tomatoes and olives.

Pot Roast Favorites

Pot roasts are wonderful do-aheads. Here are three very different versions.

Spicy Summer Pot Roast

Serving Suggestions:
Boiled new potatoes or mashed potatoes, *Orange and Red Onion Salad*.

1 package Lawry's Pot Roast Seasoning Mix
1 1/2 cups water
1/4 cup cider vinegar
2 tablespoons pickling spice
3 1/2 to 4 pound 7-bone beef pot roast

In a 5-quart Dutch oven, combine Pot Roast Seasoning Mix, water, cider vinegar and pickling spice; blend well. Place meat in liquid and spoon some over meat. Bring to a boil, reduce heat, cover and simmer 2 1/2 to 3 hours or until meat is tender. Slice meat thinly and serve with gravy. Makes 6 to 8 servings.

Pot Roast Orientale

Serving Suggestions:
Fluffy rice, *Tangy Bean Sprout Toss*, almond cookies.

1 package Lawry's Pot Roast Seasoning Mix
1 1/2 cups water
3 1/2 to 4 pound 7-bone beef pot roast
1 can (1 lb.) Chinese-style vegetables, drained
1 jar (2 1/2 oz.) sliced mushrooms, drained
2 to 4 tablespoons soy sauce

In a 5-quart Dutch oven, combine Pot Roast Seasoning Mix and water; blend well. Place meat in liquid and spoon some over meat. Bring to a boil, reduce heat, cover and simmer 2 1/2 to 3 hours or until tender. Add remaining ingredients and heat. Makes 6 to 8 servings.

Note: Pre-packaged fresh and frozen Chinese vegetables are also available and may be substituted for canned.

Orange Pot Roast

Serving Suggestions:
Buttered egg noodles, *Zesty Green Beans*.

Hints:
Buy either a blade-in or a boneless pot roast. Trim any excess fat before cooking.

1 package Lawry's Pot Roast Seasoning Mix
1 1/2 cups water
3 1/2 to 4 pound 7-bone beef pot roast
2 oranges, thinly sliced
1 large onion, cut in wedges

In a 5-quart Dutch oven, combine Pot Roast Seasoning Mix and water; blend well. Place meat in liquid and spoon some over meat. Add orange slices and onion. Bring to a boil, reduce heat, cover and simmer 2 1/2 to 3 hours or until meat is tender. Remove orange slices and onion before serving. Garnish with additional orange slices or wedges and parsley, if desired. Makes 6 to 8 servings.

Chicken Costa

Chicken and vegetables are simmered in savory spaghetti sauce.

2 1/2 to 3 pounds chicken parts
1 1/2 teaspoons Lawry's Seasoned Salt
1/3 cup salad oil
1 medium onion, finely chopped
1/2 cup chopped celery
1/2 teaspoon Lawry's Seasoned Pepper
1/2 teaspoon basil, crushed
1 package (1 1/2 oz.) Lawry's Spaghetti Sauce Mix with Imported
  Mushrooms
1/2 cup dry white wine
1 1/2 cups water
4 large carrots, cut in 1/2-inch pieces
4 medium potatoes, peeled and quartered
1/2 teaspoon Lawry's Seasoned Salt

Serving Suggestions:
Homemade biscuits, *Zucchini Vinaigrette.*

Hints:
If desired, buy a whole chicken and cut up for this dish.

Rub chicken with 1 1/2 teaspoons Seasoned Salt. Heat salad oil in Dutch oven. Fry chicken until golden brown, removing pieces as they brown. Add onion, celery, seasonings, Spaghetti Sauce Mix with Imported Mushrooms, dry white wine and water; blend thoroughly. Add chicken and remaining ingredients. Bring to a boil, reduce heat, cover and simmer 45 minutes or until tender. Makes 4 to 6 servings.

Chicken Costa

Chicken Stew Mexicana

Serving Suggestions:
Hot cooked rice, *Nopalitos Salad,
Yolanda's Capirotada.*

Hints:
Kitchen scissors are a handy way to cut up whole canned tomatoes. Drain juice and cut tomatoes right in the can.

Corn and olives are frequently used ingredients in Mexican-inspired dishes.

1/4 cup flour
1/2 teaspoon Lawry's Seasoned Salt
1 package Lawry's Chicken Taco Seasoning Mix
1 1/2 to 2 pounds chicken thighs, skinned
3/4 cup water
1 can (1 lb.) tomatoes, cut up
1 can (17 oz.) whole kernel corn, drained
1 can (3 1/2 oz.) pitted black olives, drained and halved
2 tablespoons diced green chiles

Combine flour, Seasoned Salt and Chicken Taco Seasoning Mix in a large plastic bag. Place chicken thighs in bag and shake to coat; set aside. In a 3-quart casserole, add remaining ingredients, chicken and remaining seasoned flour; blend well. Bake, uncovered, in 350°F. oven about 1 hour 20 minutes. Makes 4 to 6 servings.

Pork Chops with Saucy Caraway Kraut

Serving Suggestions:
Boiled or mashed potatoes, fresh fruit.

Hints:
Make ahead just to point of baking and refrigerate overnight (up to 24 hours). Add 15 minutes to baking time if refrigerated.

Apples, onions, caraway and sauerkraut are great flavors with pork.

6 pork chops
1/2 medium onion, sliced in rings
2 tablespoons salad oil
1 can (1 lb.) sauerkraut
1 package Lawry's Mushroom Gravy Mix, prepared according to package directions
1 apple, chopped
1 teaspoon caraway seed
Apple rings and cinnamon to garnish

Brown pork chops and onion in salad oil. Drain sauerkraut and rinse well; squeeze out excess moisture. Combine 1/2 cup gravy with sauerkraut, apple and caraway; place in bottom of 13 x 9 x 2-inch baking dish. Arrange pork chops and onions on sauerkraut and spoon remaining gravy over chops. Cover and bake in 350°F. oven 1 hour. Garnish with apple rings sprinkled with cinnamon. Makes 6 servings.

Spicy Pork

A good dish to have on hand in the freezer for lunch or dinner.

1 pound boneless pork OR beef, cut in 1-inch cubes
1 tablespoon salad oil
1 medium onion, chopped
1 package (1 1/4 oz.) Lawry's Taco Seasoning Mix
1/4 teaspoon Lawry's Garlic Powder with Parsley
1 can (1 lb.) tomatoes, cut up
1/4 teaspoon oregano
1 bay leaf
1 can (3 1/4 oz.) pitted ripe olives, drained

In Dutch oven, brown pork in oil. Add onion and cook until tender and lightly browned; drain fat. Blend in Taco Seasoning Mix and remaining ingredients. Bring to a boil, reduce heat, cover and simmer 1 1/2 hours, stirring occasionally. Uncover last 15 minutes if there is too much liquid. Makes 4 servings.

Serving Suggestions:
Cooked rice, or as a filling for corn or flour tortillas.

Hints:
For a spicier flavor, add 1 can (4 oz.) diced green chiles.

Chilaquiles

As served at Lawry's California Center.

1 medium onion, chopped
2 tablespoons salad OR olive oil
1 can (1 lb. 12 oz.) tomatoes
1 package Lawry's Mexican Rice Seasoning Mix
1/2 teaspoon Lawry's Seasoned Salt
1 can (4 oz.) diced green chiles
1 package (6 1/4 oz.) tortilla chips
1 pound Monterey Jack cheese, grated
1 cup dairy sour cream
1/2 cup grated Cheddar cheese

To make sauce, sauté onion in salad or olive oil. Add tomatoes, Mexican Rice Seasoning Mix, Seasoned Salt and green chiles. Bring to a boil, reduce heat and simmer, uncovered, 10 to 15 minutes. In buttered, shallow, 2-quart casserole, arrange 1/2 each of the following in layers: tortilla chips, sauce and Monterey Jack cheese. Repeat layers; top with sour cream. Bake, uncovered, in 325°F. oven 30 minutes. Sprinkle with Cheddar cheese and bake 10 minutes longer. Let stand 15 minutes before cutting into squares. Makes 6 to 8 servings.

Serving Suggestions:
Gazpacho, Open Face Pattypan Squash.

Hints:
For a different flavor, Lawry's Enchilada Sauce Mix or Taco Seasoning Mix may be substituted for the Mexican Rice Seasoning Mix. Reduce amount of diced green chiles to 2 tablespoons if using Taco Seasoning Mix. Casserole may be frozen before baking; just don't add the sour cream layer until ready to bake. Be sure to use a shallow casserole; if the layers are too deep it just doesn't come out as well.

Pozole

Serving Suggestions:
Mexican Dinner Salad, warm corn tortillas.

Hints:
Freeze without the garnishes.

Also called Fire Soup, this traditional Mexican dish can be mild, as is this version, or "fired up" by adding hot chile peppers.

1 package Lawry's Beef Stew Seasoning Mix
4 cups water
1 1/2 pounds boneless beef chuck, cut in 1/2-inch cubes
1/2 cup chopped onion
1 1/2 teaspoons Lawry's Seasoned Salt
2 cans (15 oz. each) white hominy, drained
1 can (1 lb.) tomatoes, cut up
1/4 cup diced green chiles
1/4 cup flour
1/2 cup water
Garnishes: shredded cabbage, sliced radishes, chopped green onion

In a 3-quart saucepan, combine Beef Stew Seasoning Mix and water; blend well. Add beef, onion and Seasoned Salt. Bring to a boil, reduce heat, cover and simmer 1 1/2 hours. Add hominy, tomatoes and green chiles; cover and continue simmering 30 minutes. Combine flour and water; add to meat mixture. Continue simmering, uncovered, and stir until thickened. Garnish each serving with cabbage, radishes and green onions. Makes 6 to 8 servings.

Meatball Skillet Stew

Serving Suggestions:
Mashed potatoes, *Coleslaw with Peanuts.*

Hints:
May freeze entire dish or meatballs only. Frozen meatballs are good to have on hand for a variety of dishes. Freeze meatballs on a cookie sheet, then place in a plastic bag. That way you may just use a few as needed.

1 pound ground beef
1/3 cup dry bread crumbs
1 teaspoon Lawry's Seasoned Salt
1/4 teaspoon Lawry's Seasoned Pepper
1/3 cup milk
1 egg, beaten
1 tablespoon salad oil
1 package Lawry's Brown Gravy Mix
1 1/2 cups water
4 medium carrots, cut in 1-inch pieces
1 medium onion, quartered
1/2 cup coarsely chopped green bell pepper

Lightly combine ground beef, bread crumbs, Seasoned Salt, Seasoned Pepper, milk and egg. Shape into 12 meatballs. Heat oil in skillet and brown meatballs on all sides; drain fat. Add Brown Gravy Mix and water; mix well. Add vegetables. Bring to a boil, reduce heat, cover and simmer 30 to 40 minutes. Makes 4 to 6 servings.

Lasagna Roll-Ups

A different way to prepare lasagna.

Lasagna Roll-Ups

1 pound ground beef
2 cloves garlic, crushed
2 teaspoons Lawry's Seasoned Salt
1/2 teaspoon Lawry's Seasoned Pepper
1 can (1 lb. 12 oz.) tomatoes, cut up
1 can (6 oz.) tomato paste
1 package (1 1/2 oz.) Lawry's Spaghetti Sauce Mix with Imported
   Mushrooms
8 lasagna noodles, cooked and drained
8 ounces ricotta cheese
8 ounces Mozzarella cheese, grated
1/2 cup grated Parmesan cheese

Serving Suggestions:

Capri Salad, Lawry's Garlic or
Herb Bread.

Hints:

Cottage cheese may be substituted for ricotta; however, drain thoroughly.

Brown ground beef in Dutch oven; drain fat. Add garlic, Seasoned Salt, Seasoned Pepper, tomatoes, tomato paste and Spaghetti Sauce Mix with Imported Mushrooms; stir thoroughly. Bring to a boil, reduce heat, cover. Simmer 30 minutes, stirring occasionally. On wax paper, lay two noodles side by side. Spread with 1/4 of ricotta. Then spread with 1/2 cup of meat mixture and 1/4 of Mozzarella and Parmesan cheeses. Roll up noodles. Place, seam side down, in 12 x 8 x 2-inch baking dish. Prepare remaining 3 roll-ups. Top roll-ups with remaining meat sauce. Bake, uncovered, in 350°F. oven 20 to 30 minutes or until heated. Makes 4 servings.

Lou's Sausage Supper

Serving Suggestions:
Apple Valley Salad, ice cream.

Hints:
If link sausage is used, add a pinch of anise to give Italian flavor. Mild or hot Italian sausage may be used, depending upon your preference.

The flavor of this dish improves when cooked the day before.

16 to 24 ounces sausage (Italian OR link), cut up
1 medium onion, chopped
2 large green bell peppers, chopped
3 celery stalks, chopped
1 1/2 tablespoons Lawry's Pinch of Herbs
1 teaspoon Lawry's Seasoned Salt
1/4 teaspoon Lawry's Garlic Powder with Parsley
1 can (6 oz.) tomato paste
2 1/2 cups water
1 cup uncooked long-grain rice
1 can (2.3 oz.) sliced ripe olives, drained
Grated Cheddar cheese
Dairy sour cream

Brown sausage in Dutch oven; add onion, green pepper and celery and sauté. Drain excess fat. Add remaining ingredients except olives, cheese and sour cream. Bring to a boil, reduce heat, cover and simmer 25 to 30 minutes or until liquid is absorbed. Stir in olives and top with cheese; cover until cheese melts. Serve topped with sour cream. Makes 8 servings.

Rolled Beef in Beer Gravy

Serving Suggestions:
Potatoes Au Gratin, Minted Peas.

Hints:
Pound round steak with a metal or wooden meat mallet or use the edge of a saucer. The steak may also be run through a mechanical meat tenderizer at the meat market.

Beer adds a delightful flavor to this rich, brown gravy.

1 cup chopped onion
3 tablespoons butter OR margarine
1/2 teaspoon Lawry's Pinch of Herbs
1 1/2 cups dry or toasted bread cubes
1 1/2 pounds round steak, 1/4 to 1/2-inch thick
2 tablespoons salad oil
1 package Lawry's Brown Gravy Mix
1 can (16 oz.) beer

Sauté onions in butter. Add Pinch of Herbs and bread cubes; mix well. Pound round steak to flatten; spread bread mixture over steak. Roll up and secure with wooden picks or tie with string. Brown steak roll in hot oil. Remove meat and drain fat. Add Brown Gravy Mix and beer. Bring to a boil, stirring constantly. Return meat to pan, reduce heat, cover and simmer two hours or until tender. During cooking turn meat several times. Add more beer or water if the gravy becomes too thick. To serve, slice diagonally and spoon gravy over. Makes 4 to 6 servings.

Lamb Cassoulet

Cassoulets, hearty French country dishes, are great party fare.

1/4 pound bacon, diced
2 pounds boneless lean lamb shoulder, cut in 1-inch cubes
1 large onion, chopped
1/4 pound salami, cut in 1-inch pieces
2 cans (1 lb. each) white beans
2 cans (1 lb. each) stewed tomatoes
1 1/2 teaspoons Lawry's Seasoned Salt
1/2 teaspoon Lawry's Seasoned Pepper
1 bay leaf

In Dutch oven, cook bacon until crisp. Remove and set aside. Brown lamb in bacon drippings; remove cubes as browned. Sauté onion in drippings; add salami when onions are almost finished and quickly sauté. Drain fat. Return bacon and lamb to Dutch oven; add remaining ingredients. Cover and bake in 400°F. oven 40 minutes. Remove cover and bake an additional 30 to 40 minutes or until lamb is tender. Makes 8 to 10 servings.

Serving Suggestions:
Fresh, warmed sourdough bread and sweet butter, red wine, fruit and cheese.

Hints:
May be baked and frozen.

Brunswick Stew

This traditional, hearty chicken stew is colorful and flavorful for any occasion.

2 1/2 to 3 pounds chicken parts
Lawry's Seasoned Salt
Lawry's Seasoned Pepper
1/4 cup butter
2 medium onions, halved and sliced
1 can (1 lb. 12 oz.) tomatoes, cut up
1 package (1 1/2 oz.) Lawry's Spaghetti Sauce Mix with Imported Mushrooms
2 cups water
1 cup chopped celery, including leaves
1 package (10 oz.) frozen lima beans
1 package (10 oz.) frozen whole kernel corn
2 tablespoons flour
1/4 cup water

Sprinkle chicken parts liberally with Seasoned Salt and Seasoned Pepper. In Dutch oven, sauté seasoned chicken in butter until lightly browned; remove chicken and keep warm. Sauté onions in Dutch oven until tender. Add tomatoes, Spaghetti Sauce Mix with Imported Mushrooms, water and celery. Bring to a boil, reduce heat, add chicken, cover and simmer for 45 minutes. Add beans and corn; cover and simmer 15 minutes. In small bowl, blend flour and water. Add to chicken mixture and stir until thickened. Makes 6 servings.

Serving Suggestions:
Serve with biscuits or dumplings.

Hints:
Chicken may be boned after cooking (before adding vegetables) if desired.

California Fruited Pork Stew

Serving Suggestions:
Cooked rice, sourdough bread.

Hints:
Mixed dried fruit is colorful and interesting but one flavor of dried fruit may be used.

A wonderful spicy flavor plus fruit makes this stew distinctive.

1/4 cup flour
1 teaspoon Lawry's Seasoned Salt
1/2 teaspoon Lawry's Seasoned Pepper
1/2 teaspoon ground ginger
1/4 teaspoon ground cinnamon
1 pound boneless lean pork shoulder, cut in 1-inch cubes
2 tablespoons salad oil
3 1/2 cups water
1 package Lawry's Beef Stew Seasoning Mix
2 1/2 tablespoons Lawry's Minced Onion with Green Onion Flakes
1 package (8 oz.) mixed dried fruit, pitted
1 apple, cored and chopped
1 orange, peeled and divided in segments

Combine flour, Seasoned Salt, Seasoned Pepper, ginger and cinnamon. Dredge pork in seasoned flour. In Dutch oven, sear meat in hot oil. Add water, Beef Stew Seasoning Mix and Minced Onion with Green Onion Flakes. Bring to a boil, reduce heat, cover and simmer 45 minutes. Add mixed fruit and simmer 20 minutes. Add apple and orange; simmer 10 minutes longer. Makes 4 servings.

California Fruited Pork Stew

Italian-Style Lamb Shanks

Lamb shanks, when available, are good choices for make-ahead dishes.

6 lamb shanks (about 3/4 pound each)
1 to 2 tablespoons salad oil
1 package (3 oz.) Lawry's Spaghetti Sauce Mix with Imported Mushrooms
2 cans (8 oz.) tomato sauce
3 cups water
1/4 cup salad oil
2 medium onions, sliced in 1/4-inch thick rings

Rub lamb shanks with oil and arrange in a heavy roasting pan. Brown, uncovered, in a 450°F. oven 30 minutes, turning the shanks for even browning. Meanwhile, prepare Spaghetti Sauce Mix with Imported Mushrooms according to package directions using tomato sauce, water and 1/4 cup salad oil. After shanks are browned, remove from oven; top with onions and prepared spaghetti sauce. Return to oven and reduce heat to 375°F.; continue cooking, covered, 1 hour or until tender. Baste occasionally. Makes 6 servings.

Serving Suggestions:
Buttered egg noodles, *Lila's Creamy Spaghetti Squash.*

Hints:
Trim lamb shanks of any excess fat before browning.

Curried Beef

This mildly flavored curry is a marvelous company dish.

1 1/2 pounds boneless round steak, cut in narrow 1 1/2-inch strips
1 package Lawry's Tenderizing Beef Marinade, prepared according to package directions
2 tablespoons butter
2 teaspoons curry powder
1/2 teaspoon Lawry's Seasoned Salt
1/4 teaspoon Lawry's Seasoned Pepper
1 1/4 cups water
1 large onion, sliced
1 tart apple, cored and chopped
1/3 cup raisins
Hot cooked rice

Serving Suggestions:
Fresh fruit or ginger ice cream and an assortment of hot teas.

Condiments:
Chopped peanuts
Flaked coconut
Chutney
Cooked, crumbled bacon
Chopped hard-cooked eggs

Marinate steak according to package directions for 10 to 15 minutes **only**. Brown meat in butter on high heat in large skillet. Mix in curry, Seasoned Salt, Seasoned Pepper and water. Add onion, apple and raisins. Bring to a boil, reduce heat, cover and simmer 45 minutes. Serve over rice with condiments in side dishes. Makes 4 to 6 servings.

Stuffed Lamb Breast

Serving Suggestions:
Eileen's Rice Pilaf, Artichokes Vinaigrette.

Hints:
Slice and top with gravy prior to freezing. The stuffing may also be used with flank or round steak, though these cuts should be simmered rather than roasted.

1/4 cup chopped onion
1/4 cup chopped celery
1/4 cup chopped parsley
1/4 cup butter
1 teaspoon Lawry's Pinch of Herbs
1/2 teaspoon Lawry's Seasoned Salt
1/4 teaspoon Lawry's Seasoned Pepper
1 cup soft bread crumbs
1 1/4 pounds boned breast of lamb
1/4 cup mint jelly
1 package Lawry's Brown Gravy Mix, prepared according to package directions

Sauté onion, celery and parsley in butter until just tender. Add seasonings and bread crumbs; mix well. Trim lamb of any excess fat. Place stuffing on lamb and roll up; tie securely with string. Place on rack in roasting pan; cover. Bake in 325°F. oven 1 1/2 hours. Add mint jelly to prepared brown gravy, stirring until jelly melts. Slice lamb and serve with gravy. Makes 4 to 6 servings.

Festive Turkey Casserole

Serving Suggestions:
Cranberry relish, Zesty Green Beans.

Hints:
Freeze leftover turkey or chicken in package sizes suitable for casseroles such as this.

A delicious use for leftover turkey or chicken.

1 package (6 oz.) long-grain white and wild rice
1/2 pound fresh mushrooms, sliced
1 small green bell pepper, chopped
3 tablespoons butter
2 1/2 tablespoons Lawry's Minced Onion with Green Onion Flakes
2 teaspoons Lawry's Seasoned Salt
1/4 teaspoon Lawry's Seasoned Pepper
3 cups cooked, cubed turkey OR chicken
1/2 cup sliced almonds, toasted
1 jar (2 oz.) diced pimiento
3/4 cup turkey OR chicken broth
1/2 cup whipping cream
3 tablespoons grated Parmesan cheese
3 tablespoons butter

Cook rice according to package directions but **do not** add packet of seasonings. In greased 13 x 9 x 2-inch baking dish or 3-quart casserole dish, combine all ingredients except Parmesan cheese and butter. Cover; bake in 350°F. oven 30 minutes. Remove cover; sprinkle with Parmesan cheese and dot with butter. Increase heat to 450°F. and bake 5 minutes longer. Makes 6 to 8 servings.

EATING TO FEEL GREAT AND LOOK GOOD

Feeling great and looking good are goals well worth reaching. The food we eat is only one of the many factors which contributes to that goal, but it is one of the most significant. The specific food requirements of individuals vary but there are some basics which apply to nearly everyone.

Meal planning for healthy eating should take into account the need for nutrients in adequate amounts. Perhaps the best way to discuss healthy eating would be to talk about each of the basic groups separately.

Protein, the basic building unit of the body, is composed of sub-units called amino acids. The variety of amino acids comprising the protein found in a food is what makes one protein better or more complete than another. Animal sources have the most complete proteins and are best for those who find they need to limit calories. Vegetable proteins generally are packaged by nature with more carbohydrates, which add to calories, than some people handle well or need. A nutritionally complete meal is difficult to provide from vegetable sources alone. Foods which are the most complete sources of proteins are eggs, fish, poultry, meats (especially organ meats), dairy products and, to a lesser degree, some vegetable sources like beans (especially soybeans), nuts and seeds. Due to their less complete make-up in amino acids, a variety of vegetable proteins should be served in a meal if they are the primary protein source.

Cost of protein is a concern in meal planning. A more expensive cut of beef, such as filet mignon, is not superior to less expensive round steak or lean ground beef in terms of protein provided. The desirability of filet mignon is really only related to your preference for the flavor and texture of filet as opposed to round steak.

The main source of energy (calories) in most meals comes from carbohydrates, a general term for the sugars and starches in foods. The capacity for effectively turning carbohydrate to energy varies greatly from person to person. Your body is your best indicator. It sends signals that communicate what nutrients you need. The best sources of carbohydrates are complex starches, such as baked potatoes.

Perhaps the most controversial and least understood of the food groups are fats. The amount of fat which can be considered healthy for most people is unlikely to be exceeded in a meal which is well planned in terms of all the other nutrients. Remember that some specific fats, mostly from vegetable oils, are necessary for good bodiy functioning and will be supplied adequately in a salad dressing containing oil.

An extremely important factor in keeping the body healthy is fiber, which comes from cellulose contained in vegetables, fruits and the outer covering of seeds and grains. Non-digestible fibers provide bulk and aid the intestinal tract by keeping waste traveling properly through its system.

There are other important factors necessary for the digestion and utilization of these nutrients. Serving meals in a pleasant, attractive atmosphere contributes to a sense of well-being and relaxes the body and mind so that food is more easily digested and utilized. Preparing foods with care preserves the nutrients contained in those foods.

Our physical appearance is enhanced when good eating habits are adopted. There is a clearness to the complexion, a glow and sheen to hair and skin and a generally healthy look.

Just eating right isn't the total picture; exercise is an important factor as well. Just as the body's capacity to handle some of the nutrients is an individual matter, so is exercise. What is right for you isn't necessarily right for another. Your lifestyle, interests and location are important factors which determine whether or not an exercise program works for you. Californians have great opportunities for a variety of outdoor exercise—from jogging to roller skating—year 'round. A mild climate certainly does help! But climate isn't all that critical. Walking, one of the easiest and best exercises, can be done anywhere at any time. Whatever you choose, enjoy it!

Before making any major changes in either your eating or exercise habits, discuss the program with your doctor and get some professional advice.

Start now and stick to it. The rewards are yours!

Healthy Reminders

- Eat leisurely, never on the run.
- Chew food slowly and thoroughly. The digestive process begins in the mouth.
- Learn to really savor the flavor of food. Think about what you're eating and enjoy it.
- Discuss pleasant, light topics at the table. It's more relaxing than discussing the family budget!
- Broil or roast meats, fish and poultry to help cut calories and reduce fat intake.
- Learn to enjoy steamed or stir-fried vegetables. These cooking methods help retain valuable nutrients.
- Use fresh vegetables and fruits as soon as possible after purchase.
- Avoid excesses in any food or food group. Balance and moderation are the keys.

A WINNING COMBINATION...LAWRY'S PRODUCTS AND YOUR MICROWAVE

If you lead an active life, the microwave oven is a boon. Learning to use your microwave does, however, take time and practice to achieve satisfactory results. Experiment with your microwave and discover what it can do for you and how it best fits into your cooking style.

You may find that your microwave best suits your needs when used in combination with your conventional oven. Parts of a recipe might be done most efficiently in a microwave and the finishing cooking completed in the oven, range top or on the grill. Or, you may prefer to do the majority of your cooking in the microwave.

Whatever your choice, study your manufacturer's manual in order to understand your particular brand of oven and what it can do. Attend cooking classes and see, first-hand, how the experts do it. And above all, keep practicing. You will soon discover that there isn't anything mysterious about this remarkable appliance.

Lawry's products can be prepared quickly and easily, either conventionally or in a microwave oven. In addition, the following products contribute color as well as flavor to meats, fish and poultry prepared in the microwave: Spaghetti Sauce Mix, Brown Gravy Mix, Sweet 'N Sour Barbecue Sauce, Teriyaki Barbecue Marinade and Tenderizing Beef Marinade. Seasoned Salt is excellent on ground beef and turkey patties.

Spaghetti Sauce Mix with Imported Mushrooms

(1 1/2 oz. package)

Combine ingredients following package directions. Microwave at HIGH power 15 minutes, stirring after 10 minutes.

Extra Rich & Thick Spaghetti Sauce Mix

Combine ingredients following package directions, cover with wax paper. Microwave at HIGH power 15 minutes, stirring every 4 minutes.

Meat Loaf Seasoning Mix

Combine ingredients following package directions. Cover dish with plastic wrap, venting 2 corners. Microwave at 70% power 25 to 30 minutes, turning dish after 15 minutes. Let stand 10 minutes before slicing.

Beef Stew Seasoning Mix

Cut meat into 3/4-inch cubes, coat with flour. Omit browning and reduce water to 2 1/2 cups. Add MIX, cover and microwave at HIGH power 10 minutes. Stir in vegetables (cut in small cubes) and 1 teaspoon LAWRY'S SEASONED SALT; microwave at HIGH power 10 minutes. Microwave at 50% power 45 minutes or until tender, stir after 30 minutes; add peas during last 5 minutes.

Brown Gravy Mix

Combine MIX with 1 1/4 cups water in 4-cup container; blend well. Microwave at HIGH power 3 minutes; stir occasionally. Microwave an additional 3 to 5 minutes.

Tenderizing Beef Marinade _____

In large plastic bag, prepare marinade according to package directions. With fork, deeply pierce 2 1/2 to 3 lbs. of meat in several places. Marinate meat 15 minutes, turning several times; remove meat from bag. Place meat on rack in baking dish.

Note:
For best results, use rolled roasts or cuts of meat at least 2 1/2-inches thick.

BY TIME
Microwave at HIGH power 10 minutes. Reduce power to 50%, microwave 13 to 15 minutes per pound, turning roast over after half of total cooking time.

BY TEMPERATURE
Microwave at HIGH power 10 minutes. Insert temperature probe. Microwave at 50% power to 100°F, turn roast over. Microwave at 50% power to 140°F. Let stand 10 minutes before carving.

Taco Seasoning Mix _____

(1 1/4 oz. package)

Microwave meat at HIGH power 5 to 6 minutes; drain fat. Combine MIX and 1/2 cup hot water; cover. Microwave at HIGH power 6 minutes, stirring after 4 minutes.

Taco Joe Seasoning Mix _____

Microwave meat at HIGH power 5 to 6 minutes; drain fat. Combine MIX, tomato paste and 1 1/2 cups hot water. Microwave at HIGH power 15 minutes, stirring after 8 minutes.

Sloppy Joes Seasoning Mix _____

Microwave meat at HIGH power 5 to 6 minutes; drain fat. Combine MIX, tomato paste and 1 cup hot water. Microwave at HIGH power 8 minutes, stirring after 4 minutes.

Chili Seasoning Mix _____

Microwave meat at HIGH power 5 to 6 minutes; drain fat. Combine ingredients following package directions. Microwave at HIGH power 10 minutes, stirring after 6 minutes.

Enchilada Sauce Mix

Combine ingredients following package directions. Microwave sauce at HIGH power 10 minutes, stirring after 5 minutes. Assemble enchiladas following package directions. Microwave at HIGH power 15 minutes, turning dish after 8 minutes.

Super Size Taco Shells

Arrange 5 shells at a time in an upright position on microwave roasting rack. Microwave at HIGH power 2 1/2 to 3 minutes, turning rack every minute. Watch carefully to avoid scorching.

Regular Taco Shells

Arrange 5 to 7 shells at a time in an upright position on microwave roasting rack. Microwave at HIGH power for 2 1/2 to 3 minutes, turning rack every minute. Watch carefully to avoid scorching.

Pot Roast Seasoning Mix

Combine MIX and 1 cup water. Pierce meat with fork in several places. Place roast in 13 x 9 x 2-inch glass baking dish; add liquid. Cover with plastic wrap, venting 1 corner (or use oven cooking bag). Microwave at 50% power 25 to 30 minutes per pound. After 15 minutes of cooking, add 4 POTATOES and 2 ONIONS, quartered; and 4 CARROTS cut in 1/2-inch pieces. Cover and vent. Continue cooking remaining time or until vegetables are tender.

Chicken Taco Seasoning Mix

Combine chicken, MIX and 3/4 cup water in glass baking dish; cover with wax paper. Microwave at HIGH power 6 minutes, stirring after 4 minutes.

Burrito Seasoning Mix

Microwave meat at HIGH power 5 to 6 minutes; drain fat. Combine MIX and 1 1/4 cups hot water; cover. Microwave at HIGH power 6 minutes, stirring after 4 minutes.

Appetizers

Antipasto on a Skewer 11
Bacon and Avocado
    Quesadillas 137
Bagna Cauda 11
Boursin Cheese Spreads 25
California Marinated
    Mushrooms 20
California Olive Dip 15
Cheese 'n Bean Dip 15
Chili Apple Dip 11
Clam Dip 15
Cool as a Cucumber Dip 17
Crispy Potato Skins 23
Delectable Eggplant Dip 16
Easy Mini-Pizzas 126
Guacamole con Cilantro 9
Herb Cheese Spread 24
Herbed Mushroom
    Appetizers 18
Hot Crabmeat Appetizers 20
Jiffy Pâté 12
Karen's Roquefort Appetizer
    Bread 9
K.T.'s Hot Pepper Cocktail
    Jelly 16
Lemon Pepper Dip 15
Lettuce Roll-Ups 21
Mabel's Curried Almonds 23
Marg's Square Meatball
    Appetizers 20
Mexican Blintzes 9
Mexican Cheese Ball 10
Mexican Fondue 17
Mexican Meatballs 23
Nachos con Guacamole 22
Pastacies 10
Picante Taco Dip 13
Pollo Pâté 12
Sally's Shrimp in Curried
    Mayonnaise 31
Stuffed Mushrooms 19
Taco Crescents 21
Tallegio 22
Tortellini 25
Tuna Tartar Pâté 12
Zucchini Fingers 13

Barbecue

Barbecued Fish 115
Barbecue Sauce for Poultry and
    Pork 121
Butterfly Leg of Lamb 113
California Poultry
    Marinade 120
California Vegetable Kabobs 118
Fiesta Kabobs 113
Grilled Lemon Potatoes 115
Halibut Kabobs 112
Lawry's Herb Bread and
    Variations 117
Lawry's Garlic Bread and
    Variations 116
Lawry's Seasoned
    Hamburgers 135
Lemon Lamb Shish Kabobs 111
Marinated Family Steak 111
Mini Beef Rolls Madrid 114

Pineapple on a Spit 118
Roasted Corn on the Cob 119
Savory Fruit Basting Sauce 120
Steamed Mushrooms 118
Stuffed Grilled
    Hamburgers 114
Quick and Easy Barbecue
    Ideas 121

Beverages

Cappuccino 40
Eric's Orange Sunrise Special 27
Glistening Champagne
    Punch 26
Julie's Sangria 27
Margaritas 65
Mexican Coffee 65
Sober Sangria 27
Yeteve's Summer Swizzle 27

Bread

Eardley's Spoon Bread 37
Mexican Corn Bread 149
Lawry's Garlic Bread and
    Variations 116
Lawry's Herb Bread and
    Variations 117

Casseroles

Cheese Lasagna
    Casserole 148
Cheese Strata 148
Chicken Avocado
    Enchiladas 74
Chicken Tortilla Stack 58
Chilaquiles 172
Chile Cheese Eggs 145
Chile Rellenos 155
Chili Cheese Jubilee 146
Chili-Mac Casserole 154
Enchiladas Suisse 72
Festive Turkey Casserole 179
Frank and Saucy
    Casserole 133
Green Chile Enchiladas 51
Ham 'N Egg Special 149
Lamb Cassoulet 176
Lasagna 44
Lasagna Roll-Ups 174
Lou's Sausage Supper 175
Mexican Lasagna 69
Pork 'N Raisin Enchiladas 64
Puffed Eggs Monterey 145
Sour Cream Tortilla
    Casserole 53
Tamale Casserole 70
Tijuana Torte 130
Zucchini Sausage Lasagna 30

Casseroles, Meatless

Cheese Lasagna Casserole 148
Chilaquiles 172
Chili Cheese Jubilee 146
Eggplant Cheese
    Casserole 101
Green Chile Enchiladas 51
Sally's Baked Potato
    Casserole 102
Sour Cream Tortilla
    Casserole 53

Crepes

Cream Sauce for Crepes 158
Chicken Crepes 158
Fran's Golden Crepes 158
Mushroom Crepes 159

Desserts

Avocado Lime Pie 41
Baltic Babushka 39
Cappuccino Creme 40
Carrot Cake 55
Cassata 39
Dessert Fruit Tacos 40
Flaming Peaches 41
Jicama Custard Dessert 71
Mexican Fudge Sauce 64
Mixed Fruit 68
Peach Pudding Cake 55
Pineapple on a Spit 118
Sherry Trifle 54
Tortilla Flats 64
Yolanda's Capirotada 66

Eggs and Cheese

Avocado Omelette Olé 145
Bacon Cheese Souffle 147
Cheese Strata 148
Chile Cheese Eggs 145
Chile Rellenos 155
Chili Avocado Omelet 155
Ham 'N Egg Special 149
Machaca de Huevos 74
Puffed Eggs Monterey 145
Quiche Mexicana 147

Fish

Barbecued Fish 115
Cioppino 29
Elvira's Aji de Salmon 57
Fancy Easy Fish 132
Halibut Kabobs 112
Paella Valenciana 35
Red Snapper Veracruz 73
Sally's Shrimp in Curried
    Mayonnaise 31
Savory Fish Fillets 156
Sesame Halibut Steaks 157
Shrimp Sauté 162
Stuffed Baked Fish 34

Marinades

California Poultry
    Marinade 120
Lemon Marinade for
    Lamb 111
Steak Bora Bora
    Marinade 120

Meats

Beef

Beef Ragout 30
Beef Tomato 129
California Pot Roast 44
Curried Beef 178
Fiesta Kabobs 113
Lemon Lettuce Steak 31
Marinated Family Steak 111
Orange Pot Roast 169
Pot Roast Orientale 169
Prime Rib 153
Richard N. Frank's Famous
    Leftover Hash 43

Rolled Beef in Beer
  Gravy   175
  Shortcut Beef Hash   154
  Spicy Summer Pot Roast   169
  Steak Au Poivre   45
  Steak Picado   69
  The Day Before Brisket   167

Meats
Frankfurters
  Chili Cheese Dogs   129
  Frank and Saucy
    Casserole   133

Meats
Ground
  Bell Peppers Mexicana   151
  Burritos   123
  Chili-Mac Casserole   154
  Gourmet Olé Burgers   136
  Green Pepper Special   152
  Hamburger Patties With
    Sauce   152
  Italian Cheeseburgers   135
  Lasagna   44
  Lasagna Roll-Ups   174
  Lawry's Seasoned
    Hamburgers   135
  Meatball Skillet Stew   173
  Meat Loaf Delights   131
  Mini Beef Rolls Madrid   114
  Picadillo   168
  Pizza Meat Loaf   152
  Unstuffed Cabbage Rolls   152
  San Fernando Mish
    Mash   46
  Skyscraper Burgers   135
  Soft Tacos con Pasas   137
  Spicy Taco Burgettes   132
  Stuffed Grilled
    Hamburgers   114
  Supper Nachos   67
  Taco Joe   123
  Taco Pizza   126
  Tacos   123
  Tamale Casserole   70
  Tijuana Torte   130
  Torta Mexican-Style   72
  The Spaghetti Thing   153
  Tostadas   123
  Zucchini Mexicana   151

Meats
Lamb
  Basque Stew   168
  Butterfly Leg of Lamb   113
  Italian-Style Lamb Shanks   178
  Lamb Cassoulet   176
  Lemon Lamb Lawry's   52
  Lemon Lamb Shish
    Kabobs   111
  Osso Bucco Milanese   167
  Stuffed Lamb Breast   179

Meats
Pork
  Arista Fettina Marinato   31
  Baked Pork Chops on Bacon
    Herb Stuffing   161
  California Fruited Pork Stew   177
  Chile Verde   57

Fruit Stuffed Pork Roast   29
Lou's Sausage Supper   175
Pizza Pork Chops   47
Polynesian Pork Chops or
  Chicken   132
Pork Chops Olivette   35
Pork Chops with Saucy
  Caraway Kraut   171
Pork 'N Raisin
  Enchiladas   64
Sausage and Eggplant
  Creole   43
Spicy Pork   172
The Spaghetti Thing   153
Zucchini Sausage
  Lasagna   30

Meats
Veal
  Osso Bucco Milanese   167
  Veal Florentine   162

Mexican
Arroz con Pollo   66
Bacon and Avocado
  Quesadillas   137
Bell Peppers Mexicana   151
Burritos   123
Chicken Avocado
  Enchiladas   74
Chicken Flautas   58
Chicken or Turkey Molé   68
Chicken Stew Mexicana   171
Chicken Tortilla Stack   58
Chilaquiles   172
Chile Cheese Eggs   145
Chile Rellenos   155
Chile Verde   57
Chili Albondigas   59
Chimichangas   71
Creamy Chayote Soup   59
Creamy Mexican Dressing con
  Cilantro   50
Dessert Fruit Tacos   40
Elvira's Aji de Salmon   57
Emilie's Mexican Chicken
  Kiev   32
Enchiladas Suisse   72
Ensalada Esmeralda   81
Ensalada de Noche Buena   61
Ensalada Tropical   61
Eric's Orange Sunrise Special   27
Fiesta Rice   124
Gazpacho   60
Gourmet Olé Burgers   136
Green Chile Enchiladas   51
Guacamole con Cilantro   9
Jellied Gazpacho Salad   128
Jicama Custard Dessert   71
Jicama Salad   82
Julie's Sangria   27
Luncheon Tostada Salad   63
Machaca de Huevos   74
Margaritas   65
Mariachi Chicken   126
Mexican Blintzes   9
Mexican Caesar Dressing   49
Mexican Cheese Ball   10
Mexican Coffee   65

Mexican Corn Bread   149
Mexican Dinner Salad   61
Mexican Dressing   63
Mexican Fondue   16
Mexican Fudge Sauce   64
Mexican Lasagna   69
Mexican Meatballs   23
Mexican Meat Loaf   164
Nachos con Guacamole   22
Nopalitos Salad   63
Orange and Red Onion
  Salad   80
Picadillo   168
Picante Taco Dip   13
Poached Chicken in Chunky
  Taco Sauce   71
Pork 'N Raisin Enchiladas   64
Pozole   173
Red Snapper Veracruz   73
Sober Sangria   27
Soft Tacos con Pasas   137
Sopa de Sonora   144
Sour Cream Tortilla
  Casserole   53
Spicy Pork   172
Spicy Refried Beans   123
Spicy Taco Burgettes   132
Steak Picado   69
Supper Nachos   67
Taco Crescents   21
Taco Joe   123
Taco Pizza   126
Tacos   123
Tamale Casserole   70
The Cartwheel Salad   49
The Mexican Hero   139
Tijuana Torte   130
Torta Mexican-Style   72
Tortilla Flats   64
Tortilla Soup   60
Tortilla Wrapped
  Sandwiches   140
Tostadas   123
White Gazpacho   159
Yolanda's Capirotada   66
Zucchini Mexicana   151

Pasta
Fettuccine   36
Pasta Verdura   32
Saucy Herbed Pasta 'N
  Vegetables   164
The Spaghetti Thing   153

Pizza
Easy Mini-Pizzas   126
Deep Dish Pizza   127
Taco Pizza   126

Poultry
Arroz con Pollo   66
Brunswick Stew   176
Celestial Chicken   164
Chicken Avocado
  Enchiladas   74
Chicken Breasts in Wine   128
Chicken Costa   170
Chicken Flautas   58
Chicken Jerusalem   33
Chicken Marengo   48

Chicken or Turkey Molé   68
Chicken Stew Mexicana   171
Chicken Tortilla Stack   58
Chimichangas   71
Emilie's Mexican Chicken
  Kiev   32
Enchiladas Suisse   72
Festive Turkey Casserole   179
Golden Glazed Cornish Game
  Hens   159
Holiday Roast Turkey with
  Herbed Corn Bread
  Dressing   48
Mariachi Chicken   126
Parmesan Fried Chicken   50
Peach 'n Chicken Teriyaki   36
Poached Chicken in Chunky
  Taco Sauce   71
Polynesian Pork Chops or
  Chicken   132
Sherried Chicken   47
Tacos   123
Tahitian Turkey   160
Tender Turkey Sauté   165
The Spaghetti Thing   153
Tostadas   123

Rice
Buttered Rice with Pine Nuts   157
Eileen's Rice Pilaf   37
Fiesta Rice   124
Oriental Fried Rice   157
White Rice with Artichokes   38

Salad Dressings
Avocado Dressing Deluxe   94
Claudia's Creamy Pepper
  Dressing   97
Confetti Dressing   49
Country Style Dressing   95
Creamy Caesar Dressing   97
Creamy Green Goddess
  Dressing   50
Creamy Lemon Lime   94
Creamy Mexican Dressing con
  Cilantro   50
French Vinaigrette
  Dressing   94
Fresh Mint Dressing   96
Homemade Bacon
  Dressing   97
Honey Lime Fruit Dressing   96
Lemon Garlic Dressing   93
Mary Alice's Salad
  Dressing   97
Mexican Caesar Dressing   49
Mexican Dressing   63
Onion Sour Cream
  Dressing   96
Peanut Dressing   93
Roquefort Romaine
  Dressing   93
Tangy Hawaiian Dressing   96

Salads
Apple Valley Salad   77
Artichokes Vinaigrette   79
Basque Salad   89
Bohemian Potato Salad   87
Caesar Salad   84

Capri Salad   77
Cathy's Coleslaw Relish
  Mold   92
Chef's Salad Pacifica   125
Chicken Piquant Salad   90
Cobb Salad   85
Coleslaw with Peanuts   53
Crab-Cado   90
Crunchy Turkey Salad   90
Cucumber Sour Cream
  Mousse   92
Eggplant Relish Salad   78
Ensalada de Noche Buena   61
Ensalada Esmeralda   81
Ensalada Tropical   61
Eva's Pea-Nut Salad   83
Garbeano Salad   82
Gazpacho   60
Jellied Gazpacho Salad   128
Jicama Salad   82
Karen's Spaghetti Squash
  Salad   91
Lima-Mushroom
  Vinaigrette   81
Limelight Salad Marcus   80
Luncheon Tostada Salad   63
Marinated Summer Salad   77
Marinated Vegetables Italia   78
Mary Alice's Macaroni
  Salad   87
Mashed Potato Salad a la
  Mold   86
Mexican Dinner Salad   61
Nopalitos Salad   63
Orange and Red Onion
  Salad   80
Oriental Tuna Salad   92
Pasta Salad   86
Picnic Potato Salad   87
Salad Bowl a la Lawry's   46
Salad Niçoise   84
Salmon-Grapefruit Salad   161
Spring Asparagus Salad   82
Summer Beef Salad   89
Tabbouleh   83
Tangy Bean Sprout Toss   77
The Cartwheel Salad   49
Tomato and Mushroom Salad   84
Turkey Salad Supreme   89
Vegetable Medley   79
White Gazpacho   159
Wilted Spinach Salad   78
Zucchini Vinaigrette   79

Sandwiches
French Dip Sandwich   154
Herb Sandwich Supreme   139
Italian Sausage Sandwich   138
Sausage Pockets   137
Spicy Beef Boats   136
The Mexican Hero   139
Tortilla Wrapped Sandwiches   140

Sauces
Barbecue Sauce for Poultry and
  Pork   121
Cream Sauce for Crepes   158
Creamy Stroganoff Sauce   162
Gourmet Tomato Sauce   34

Mexican Fudge Sauce   64
Savory Fruit Basting Sauce   120
Savory Sauce   156

Soups
Beef & Vegetable Soup   124
Cream of Romaine Soup   109
Cream of Spinach Soup   107
Creamy Chayote Soup   59
Creamy Peanut Soup   109
Chili Albondigas   59
Corned Beef & Cabbage Soup   143
French Onion Soup   45
Gazpacho   60
Ginger Avocado Soup   108
Hearty Potato Chowder   142
Italian Sausage Soup   144
Minestrone   142
Napa Valley Corn Chowder   106
Pozole   173
Quick Basic Soup with Variations   153
Sopa de Sonora   144
Spiked Tomato-Beef
  Consomme   107
Tortilla Soup   60
White Gazpacho   159

Stews
Basque Stew   168
Beef Ragout   30
Brunswick Stew   176
California Fruited Pork Stew   177
Chicken Stew Mexicana   171
Cioppino   29
Meatball Skillet Stew   173

Vegetables
California Vegetable Kabobs   118
Deviled Cauliflower   100
Eggplant Cheese
  Casserole   101
Festive Brandied Yams   104
Grilled Lemon Potatoes   115
Gingered Carrots   100
Hattie's Five Bean Bake   99
Lawry's Creamed Spinach   51
Lemon Broccoletti   100
Lila's Creamy Spaghetti
  Squash   103
Minted Peas   106
Open Face Pattypan
  Squash   104
Oriental Vegetables   105
Potatoes au Gratin   103
Ratatouille   106
Roasted Corn on the
  Cob   119
Roasted Onions   102
Sally's Baked Potato
  Casserole   102
Spicy Refried Beans   123
Steamed Mushrooms   118
Stuffed Artichokes   99
Stuffed Baked Potatoes   155
Stuffed Mushrooms on a
  Skewer   103
Zesty Green Beans   102
Zucchini Custard   104
Zucchini Mexicana   151

GREETINGS!

This handy page is designed for you to:

1. Order additional copies of **The Great California Lifestyle COOKBOOK.** Should you wish to send the book as a gift, list the recipient's name(s) and address(es) on a separate sheet and attach to order form. We will enclose a gift card so fill in **your** name as indicated on the order form.

2. Be placed on our mailing list to receive our informative, quarterly newsletter, "The Center Fold."

3. Request the Lawry's Products Mail Order Form and price list. (Note: We encourage you to ask your supermarket manager to stock these items, too.)

Send To: Lawry's Foods, Inc.
P.O. Box 30101
Dept. GCLC
Los Angeles, Ca. 90051

- -

☐ Please add me to your mailing list to receive "The Center Fold"

☐ Please send me the Lawry's Products Mail Order Form

☐ Please send me_____copies of **The Great California Lifestyle COOKBOOK** at $9.95 each* plus $2.00 per book for shipping and handling. For California delivery add $.60 sales tax per book.

Enclosed is my check made payable to Lawry's Foods, Inc. in the amount of $_____

*Price subject to change with future printings.

name_____

street_____

city_____ state_____ zip_____

daytime phone number (area code)____ (phone)_____
(To be used should we need to contact you regarding your order)

_____
Your name as you would like it signed on gift card

- -

☐ Please add me to your mailing list to receive "The Center Fold"

☐ Please send me the Lawry's Products Mail Order Form

☐ Please send me_____copies of **The Great California Lifestyle COOKBOOK** at $9.95 each* plus $2.00 per book for shipping and handling. For California delivery add $.60 sales tax per book.

Enclosed is my check made payable to Lawry's Foods, Inc. in the amount of $_____

*Price subject to change with future printings.

name_____

street_____

city_____ state_____ zip_____

daytime phone number (area code)____ (phone)_____
(To be used should we need to contact you regarding your order)

_____
Your name as you would like it signed on gift card

- -

☐ Please add me to your mailing list to receive "The Center Fold"

☐ Please send me the Lawry's Products Mail Order Form

☐ Please send me_____copies of **The Great California Lifestyle COOKBOOK** at $9.95 each* plus $2.00 per book for shipping and handling. For California delivery add $.60 sales tax per book.

Enclosed is my check made payable to Lawry's Foods, Inc. in the amount of $_____

*Price subject to change with future printings.

name_____

street_____

city_____ state_____ zip_____

daytime phone number (area code)____ (phone)_____
(To be used should we need to contact you regarding your order)

_____
Your name as you would like it signed on gift card